What they're saying

—*The Washington Post*

So how does one find a mortgage seller? Among other options, Lorelei Stevens, president of Wall Street Brokers, Inc., a Seattle firm that buys private mortgages, recommends looking in classified ads for buyers of notes.

—*The Wall Street Journal*

Mortgage-note buyer Lorelei Stevens of Wall Street Brokers in Seattle thinks the following skills would help: marketing, making public presentations, negotiation, business math, real estate finance and knowledge of the relevant law.

—*Newsweek*

As an attorney with long experience handling note transactions, I can truly say that I have never encountered anyone with a better grasp of the subject than Lorelei Stevens, and that includes the legal aspects as well as the business and personal issues.

—Harold B. Coe, Senior Partner
The Coe Law Group, PLLC

It was my pleasure to present Lorelei Stevens with our Industry Achievement Award at the NoteWorthy Convention in 1999. It was an honor well deserved. Her book is a "must read."

—Hank Harenberg, CEO
Capital Concepts, Inc.

Actual cases from one of the few real pros in the note business.
—Bill Broadbent, co-author, *Owner Will Carry: How to Take Back a Note or Mortgage Without Being Taken*

Fast Cash is absolutely the best book a hopeful note buyer—or any ambitious member of the human race—will find any time soon. It takes the reader on a fascinating journey into the dreams and frustrations of the note buying business, narrated by an extraordinary woman who virtually personifies the field. If you don't read another business book this year, read *Fast Cash*.

—Jerry W. James, attorney and note buyer

FAST CASH

FAST CASH

How I Made
A Fortune
Buying Notes

Lorelei Stevens

MERRIL PRESS
Bellevue, Washington

FAST CASH

First Edition
Published by Merril Press

Typeset in Times New Roman by Merril Press, a division of Merril
Mail Marketing, PO Box 1682, Bellevue, Washington 98009. Additional copies of this book may be ordered from Merril Press,
$19.95. Telephone 425-454-7009. Fax 425-451-3959. E-mail
address: books@merrilpress.com. Website www.merrilpress.com.
Cover design by Northwoods Studio.

LIBRARY OF CONGRESS CATALOGING-IN-PUBLICATION DATA

Stevens, Lorelei 1950-
  Fast Cash : how I made a fortune buying notes / Lorelei
Stevens.
    p.   cm.
  Includes bibliographical references and index.
  ISBN 0-936783-39-7 (pbk.)
  1. Real estate investment. 2. Mortgages. 3. Promissory
notes. 4. Business enterprises--Finance. I. Title.

HD1382.5.S735.2004
332.63'244--dc22
                                    2004048291

PRINTED IN THE UNITED STATES OF AMERICA

Contents

To my father,
Larry L. Stevens

Introduction

The note industry has needed a book like this for years. *Fast Cash* is an easy read about a hard business—a hard business to explain, and Lorelei Stevens has done a remarkable job of making it not only understandable, but also fascinating.

I say that not just because Lorelei Stevens happens to be my daughter, but because it's true. All you have to do is read some of the note industry journals to see how loaded with jargon and business slang they are. That's fine for us in the industry, but it's not so fine for others who might be interested in making a fortune.

Fast Cash takes us inside the note buying business through the eyes of a veteran note buyer. What we see is a business that involves a great deal of money and the problems that go with a great deal of money. It's how people face those problems that makes the industry so absorbing to those of us who work in it every day. It's how Lorelei Stevens shows us those people that makes this a truly extraordinary book.

For the first time, I can recommend something to both the interested layman and the professional note buyer, and be confident both will enjoy it.

Lorelei wasn't always a veteran note buyer, of course, but she's the third generation of our family to be in the business. She paid her dues by starting out as my secretary. She studied hard and got her real estate license, then her broker's license, and went on to handling note closings.

During Lorelei's mid-twenties, I guided her through the details as she became first a note broker and then a note buyer. From the beginning she possessed a real talent for the business. Within a few years she could separate the good deals from the bad with the eye of an expert. I was very proud of her progress.

It has been one of life's great pleasures to watch Lorelei develop into a leading figure in the note buying industry.

Larry L. Stevens, Founder
Wall Street Brokers, Inc.
Seattle, Washington

Author's Preface

I wrote *Fast Cash* because there aren't many books in circulation devoted exclusively to *buying* notes—in particular, seller-financed real estate notes. It's true that conferences and seminars have been teaching eager learners how to *broker* "cash flows," "commercial paper," and other financial products that most Americans have never heard of—yet most instructors only cover note *buying* as an incidental topic along with more glamorous opportunities. But note buying all by itself has eluded the popular surge of interest in making a fortune.

In fact, note buying is an important, if small, industry that serves the economic heart of America: the home owner and the small business owner. It supplies capital to a wide variety of deserving people struggling with a need for fast cash. These are the people who have sold their home or business and financed the sale themselves with a note secured by the real estate or the business assets.

Without seller-financing, home buyers and hopeful entrepreneurs who can't find conventional loans would be left out of the American dream of home ownership or being their own boss.

And without note buyers, these do-it-yourself financiers would be unable to convert their valuable notes into fast cash when circumstances demand. Note buyers make a market for thousands of solid citizens that help drive the economy—and could be your next-door neighbor.

The problem is, you don't know because nobody's told you about them.

So, I decided to correct the omission. And I decided to do it in a completely new way: I'm going to tell you what it's *really* like—from more than thirty years of personal experience. No hype. No hoopla. Just real life stories of what I've done buying notes.

The only departure from real life in *Fast Cash* was changing names and, in a few instances, details, to protect the privacy of my clients.

Nobody writes a book alone, even though only one name appears on the cover. So many people have helped me for so many years that it would be impossible to thank them all, but it would be ungrateful of me not to try.

I am deeply indebted to attorneys Harold B. Coe and Robert H. Stevenson for their many hours of counsel in the intricate law of note buying. I also learned a great deal about the law and practical side of note buying during conversations with the late, distinguished George Coats, a true pioneer of our industry. And without the encouragement of Steve Francks, Executive Vice President of the Washington Association of Realtors, I would never have become a licensed instructor in seller financing and note buying.

It was Dennis M. Eagan of the *Washington State Bar News* who prompted my 1985 debut article that led to more than a hundred more in the newsletters, *NoteWorthy Newsletter* and *The Paper Source Journal*. Jonathan Richards and George Rosenberg, publishers of *NoteWorthy Newsletter*, have faithfully devoted space for my monthly column for many years. The couple who are the principals of the *The Paper Source Journal*, publisher Alison B. Mencarow, and president and editor W. J. Mencarow, have requested many articles from me and also publish a monthly column written just for their publication. I am grateful to *NoteWorthy Newsletter* for selecting me as their 1999 Industry Achievement Award winner, and to Hank Harenberg for presenting the award with his characteristic enthusiasm.

I dedicated this book to my father, Larry L. Stevens, not only because he's my father and taught me the note business, but also because he's been a pillar of strength through the ups and downs and a great mentor at all times.

Gloria Check has been our executive assistant for more than twenty years, and time and again has proven to be more executive than assistant. I don't know how many deserving notes she's rescued or how many bad notes she's thwarted.

Robert A. Richards, CPA, our accountant, has kept our books in shipshape order for more than thirty years and taught me the importance of good records how details can make the difference between making a fortune and losing one.

So many people have helped me along the way, that I cannot give them all the credit they are due. But some helped so much I have to mention them: particularly attorney Jerry W. James, who is amazingly smart about notes; bankruptcy lawyers David A. Kubat and A. Stevens Quigley, who helped me tremendously in the bankruptcy arena; Bernice Funk, our first in-house lawyer, who worked diligently for many years; note buyer and instructor John Behle, who encouraged me to accept my first note seminar speaking engagement; note buyer Tom Brophy of Cascade Funding, who spends generous amounts of time on the phone with me just talking about the industry; and retired Texas lawyer John Merchant, who big-heartedly gave his time to help with legal research.

A big thank-you to Joanne Biederman, general manager of Trust Accounting Center in Anacortes, Washington, for excellent servicing of many of our notes. My gratitude to Brent Mallett, senior title officer, Ticor Title Company, who kept our title records straight for years. And I can't thank attorney Joseph M. Vincent enough for helping me with numerous intricate legal issues.

My thanks to Alan M. Gottlieb of Merril Press, who accepted my manuscript for publication, and to Ron Arnold, editor-in-chief of Merril Press, for guiding me through the mysteries of the book publishing world. And my heartfelt thanks to my husband Manfred E. Schärig, who put up with my long hours at the keyboard writing this book.

Last, the virtual army of note payors and sellers, business associates, lawyers and real estate agents who have touched my life and made it better. You know who you are and you have my gratitude.

Whatever merit this book may have belongs to these fine people. Any errors of fact or judgment are mine alone.

Lorelei Stevens
Wall Street Brokers, Inc.
Seattle, Washington

PART ONE

Basics

FAST CASH

Chapter 1

Beginnings

"This evening we have Lorelei Stevens, president of Wall Street Brokers" said Emily Cunningham, chairman of the local civic group I'd been invited to. "She's going to tell us all about Wall Street Brokers and the note buying business."

Polite applause from the audience of about thirty—a mixed group of active people at their monthly meeting.

"I'm a note buyer."

My opening line met with blank stares. As usual.

"That means I buy notes at a discount and collect the full balance, which gives me a handsome profit."

Ears perked up and eyes sharpened at those last two words, "handsome profit." As usual.

"When I buy a note, the seller wants fast cash. So that's the motto of Wall Street Brokers, *Fast Cash*."

More ears perked up and more eyes sharpened at those last two words, "fast cash." As usual.

Now I had their attention.

1

"I know that some of you may not know what a note is, so let's lay down some basics so we can get right to that 'handsome profit' and 'fast cash' part."

That drew a few chuckles and more relaxed body language.

"Let's start with what it is that I buy—notes. Let's keep this informal. What's a note? Anyone?"

Nobody stirred for a moment, then a hand went up about four rows back. A dark-haired man leaned out and peered at me, but I couldn't see his name tag. I nodded for him to speak.

"Hi, I'm Tod Ledbetter. What's a note? It's like a big IOU. For example, I signed a note on my car. You know, I made a down payment and pay the rest in monthly installments. Everybody buys things that way. You sign a note for what you owe and they keep the title to the car as security. So I'd say a note's just a promise that you'll pay. Written down, of course."

"Good!" I said. "**A note is a written promise to pay**. Now what good is a promise to pay? What makes a note so valuable that I could make a living as a note buyer?"

A middle-aged woman in the front row spoke up.

"Ms. Stevens, my name is Linda Everett, and I'm a loan officer down at Principal Commercial Bank. I deal with notes all the time. It's my guess that you deal with real estate notes, am I right?"

"That's right," I replied with a smile. "And why would you guess that?"

"Well, the security for a real estate note is real estate, of course, and if you ever had to foreclose on the note for lack of payment, you'd still come out alright because real estate keeps its value. You wouldn't have as much luck dealing with automobile notes or furniture notes or some other personal property."

"You're right on target," I said. "Did everybody follow that? One of the things that makes a note valuable is the security behind it. **Security is something of value pledged to insure payment of an obligation.** And real estate notes have land and buildings as security—usually the building is a home. So that's the kind of note I buy, real estate notes."

A balding man whose name tag read "Randall" looked puzzled and said, "You mean that you buy the note but not the property?"

"Right," I said, waiting to hear his point.

"Okay, I understand about security, and all that. But you're saying that the owner can just sell a note to anyone he wants. I don't understand. I thought the bank owned the mortgage."

"Good point. I don't buy bank mortgages. I work a different way. It's like this: let's say you sell your home, you get a down payment from your buyer and then take a note for the balance owing. The buyer sends you monthly payments until the note is paid off. There's no bank involved. You financed the purchase yourself. That's called seller financing."

"Seller financing. Hmm," pondered Randall. "Not everybody could afford to do that."

"That's true, but enough people do it that there's a substantial market in seller financed notes. That's the kind of notes I buy."

Emily Cunningham piped up: "Do you ever buy notes that are second mortgages?"

"Yes, Emily, that's very common in seller financing, even though I call them second liens. Liens go by different names: they might be called mortgages, or deeds of trust, or trust deeds. But they're all liens.

"A lien is a claim against property for payment of some debt. Let's say a bank has a *first lien* on a property. And let's say I buy a note on the same property. I have a second lien. The bank has a first lien. If my second lien note has to be foreclosed, I would just get what was left over after the first lien was paid, and that might be nothing."

"So you'd discount the note more because of the greater risk," said an impeccably dressed African-American man from the doorway.

Glancing over to the meeting room's double doors, I said, "Mel Curtis, don't just stand there, come on in. People, this is the sales manager where I got my car. After we got to know each other, he sold me a note, too."

"She knows her business," Curtis said, ushering in a shorter man clad in jeans and a World War II-style bomber jacket. "This is my friend Art Morales."

Emily got up and found seats for the two latecomers.

"Now, where were we?" I said.

"You were going to give a deeper discount to a second lien note because of the greater risk," said Curtis.

"Right. Yes, I would pay less for the note. A lot less, most likely. Not like the good first lien note you sold me, Mel. Note buyers want first lien notes whenever they can get them. This gets into that 'handsome profit' part. Remember, you make a handsome profit by paying a discounted price but collecting the full balance owing, plus interest. You're much more likely to collect the full balance with a first lien note."

"Give us an example," suggested Emily.

"Okay," I said. "Here's a first lien note example. Let's take a hypothetical family that sells its house for $100,000. Let's say they receive a $20,000 down payment from the buyer and finance the $80,000 balance in the form of a note. There's nothing owing to a bank so it's a first lien note. At a later time, when the balance owing is down to $60,000, they decide to sell the note for fast cash. They contact me and I calculate the value and offer them $54,000. That's a discount of $6,000. They sell me the note for $54,000 cash and I collect the monthly payments until the entire $60,000 is paid off, plus interest. That's my handsome profit."

"Okay," said Randall. "What if it's a second lien note?"

"Now we're beyond routine calculation. There's no such thing as a normal price to pay. When I'm offered a second lien note, I know the bank comes first if there's any problem, so I look for all kinds of things that might knock its value down and make the discount deeper."

"Like what?" asked Tod Ledbetter.

"Simple things like the credit rating of the person who's paying the note—the payor. If the payor is on time and up to date, I'll offer more than if he's frequently late or behind.

"What else might push your discount deeper?" asked Randall.

"More complex matters like the condition of the property, such as whether it's well maintained or run-down, or if the previous owner promised to repair the roof and failed to do it. So many kinds of problems can crop up in second lien notes that you need keen judgment, and that's something you only get with experience. Second lien notes are not for first-time note buyers."

"Okay," said a slim woman that looked a thirty-something, "I'm Sara Winslow, and let's say that I'm a first time note buyer. What *is* for the first-timer? Tell me how you do it."

"That's really two questions, Sara," I replied. "The first one we won't go into much, and that's how do you find notes in the first place. A lot of people just put an ad in the classified section of their newspaper saying they buy notes. There's more to it, but it adds up to letting people know you're there and that you buy notes.

"In my case, I'm well-established, my company is well-known, and note owners contact me with notes for sale. Your real question is what do I do next.

"So this is what happens: someone calls me with a note they want to sell. The first thing I do is ask them for the money figures. What was the sales price of the real estate? What is the current balance owing, the monthly payment and the interest rate?

"And then I ask about the security—what kind of property is it, location, condition, things like that.

"Then I want to know if the payment record is good—
by that I mean, has the payor been paying on time and not
missed any payments? Are the payments up to date? Has anything happened that might make the payor unable to pay? Ill-
ness, job layoff. That sort of thing.

"Based on this and a few other things, I'll take out my
calculator and come up with a preliminary offering price, with
the understanding that it can change if I find anything unexpected.

"If the note seller says they'll take my offer, we sign a
preliminary sale agreement and I have them send me all the
required documents so I can investigate the note thoroughly.

"That investigation is called 'due diligence' and that's
where I go through my checklist of technicalities."

"Technicalities?" interrupted Randall. "This sounds
pretty technical to me already."

"Yes, I guess it does," I admitted. "But my due diligence gets into more detail, very important detail. Bear with
me while I explain, okay?"

Randall nodded, seeming a little grumpy.

"Okay, first, I check to make sure the note seller has
the original note, because a copy won't do.

"Then I get copies of the payment record and documents showing the down payment.

"Then I run a credit check on the payor to make sure
they're creditworthy.

"Now I can check with the payor to make sure they
agree on the balance owing and the terms.

"At some point I get an appraisal on the property to
make sure the security is really secure.

"I get a title report, to make sure there is no cloud on
the title.

"I check out all the documents surrounding the note,
things like the original purchase and sale agreement for the
property, the closing statement and the deed to the property.

Those documents can have mistakes in them that make a note undesirable or even worthless.

"And last, I check to make sure there's fire and hazard insurance on the property—you'd be surprised to see how many homes don't have it."

"Is that the whole checklist?" asked Emily.

"Pretty much," I answered. "There could be a few more things. But if everything checks out, we close the deal. I sign the final papers and place the cash in escrow. The note seller signs the formal papers and delivers the original note to escrow after endorsing it to me. The assignment of the lien is recorded in the county recorder's office. Now the note is officially mine and released to me by escrow, and the cash is the note seller's.

"But it's not over. I've spent a lot of money buying the note with fast cash. Now I have to get it back, plus interest and my 'handsome profit.' So here's how that works.

"Escrow sends instructions to the note payor to begin making payments to me.

"The payor keeps on sending the payments to me until I receive the final payment and have completed a lucrative transaction.

"Last, I return the original note to the payor marked "Paid In Full" along with other release documents. Then we're done."

A man who had remained silent the whole time said, "It's definitely not a get rich quick scheme."

Everyone laughed. Mel Curtis said in his booming voice, "It's a get rich *slowly* scheme."

Everyone laughed more, including me.

"Well," I said, "That concludes my talk for this evening. You can find more information on my website at www.wallstreetbrokers.com. If you have any questions right now, I'll be happy to answer them during refreshment time. And thanks for inviting me."

Emily Cunningham stood and spoke over the light applause, the clatter of chairs and shuffling of feet, "Thank you, Ms. Stevens, for your interesting talk. We certainly have a lot to think about. And next month we have home remodeling with Bob Hale."

As I drifted with the group toward the refreshment table, Mel Curtis brought his friend to my side. "Ms. Stevens, this is Art Morales. He's a longshoreman at the marine terminal. He helps me every now and then when I have trouble with a shipload of imported cars."

"Glad to meet you, Art," I said, extending my hand.

Shaking my hand earnestly, Art said, "Ms. Stevens, could I come to your office and talk to you about buying notes? I'm really interested."

"Well," I stalled, not quite knowing what to say. It sounded like I was being asked to give private lessons in note buying. I glanced at Mel for a signal of some sort. He just watched to see what I would do.

I finally just blurted, "What about lunch?"

Art's eyes lit up. "Okay, let me take you to lunch. I have Thursdays off. Name the time and place and I'll be there."

Chapter 2
The Original Note

The building where my business is located has a nice restaurant on the ground floor, the Wall Street Grill. The next Thursday at noon, I sat at one of its tables across from Arturo Miguel Morales, the son of migrant farmworkers from Mexico.

The waiter brought my salad and Art's French dip sandwich. Art slipped off his denim jacket and rolled up the sleeves of his blue work shirt. He leaned toward me in preparation for serious conversation.

"I was born and raised in Yakima. When I was 12, things got real bad and my parents sent me to live with an uncle in the Bay Area. He treated me like a son, made sure I went to school, helped me when I got in trouble. When the time came, he helped me get into his line of work, longshoring. That must have taken some doing because it's hard to get into the union. Then about ten years ago, I moved up here to be closer to my folks.

"Anyway, since then I've been saving money. I'm looking for something to do with it, and Mel said that buying notes might be the best thing."

I was taken aback by Art's intention.

"Art," I said carefully, "buying notes takes cash. A lot of cash. An ordinary note could take twenty or thirty thousand dollars."

Art looked me in the eye. "Thirty thousand?" he said softly. "I've got more than twice that."

I raised an eyebrow and whistled under my breath. "Okay," I said, "What do you want from me?"

"Tell me about note buying. If you could tell me just the three most important things about note buying, what would they be?"

This guy's sharp, I said to myself.

Aloud, I said, "Nobody's ever asked me that, Art. I'd have to think a little for the top three. Of course, the handsome profit is the whole reason for buying notes, but that's not what you're asking. I'd say what you're getting at is this: the single most important thing *you* need to know is having the original note and not a copy."

"You mentioned that Tuesday at the meeting," said Art. "Why is that so important?"

"Well, how do I explain this? Let me just tell you a story."

"Okay, shoot," said Art.

"Alright, then. This was about two years ago. Our firm had been negotiating for several days by telephone with a man named John Blake. He had a note secured by a good property in Oregon and all the financial details looked outstanding. It was the kind of note we prefer to buy—a perfect payment record, all the documents in order, and a good appraisal of the property's value.

"John Blake was being as cautious and methodical as we were, which we consider a good sign.

"In fact, Mr. Blake told us in advance that he would

not mail the note to us at closing, but would hand it to us in person—when his check was ready. He had a business trip to our city coming up, and he would close the deal then, face to face.

"With a note seller that careful, I was tempted to skip my usual lecture on the importance of the original note."

Art interjected—through bites of his French dip—"But you didn't, right?"

"Right. My business sense prevailed so I repeated what I had already said to him several times: 'Are you sure you have the original note?'

"And he said, 'Yes, I do.'

"I didn't want to sound insulting, but I pressed the issue. I told him that many note sellers actually have a photocopy, and not the original.

"Then I said to him, 'You can only sell the original note. So will you please do a few tests for us?'

"Well, of course, Blake was a little annoyed, but he agreed.

"I told him, 'I'll hang on the phone and you hold the note up to the light to make sure it's not altered and is the original.'

"He did.

"'Okay,' I said to him, 'now, run your fingers over the back of the note so you can feel the indent of the signature.'

"He did.

"'It's the original note,' he said.

"That sounded good enough to me. As far as I was concerned, we had that settled.

"The big day arrived and Blake came in for his check. He gave me the note, and I examined it carefully.

"Well, it didn't look like the original note to me."

Art dabbed his mouth with his napkin and squinted at me curiously. "How could you tell?"

"Easy. I got out my magnifying glass and studied the note in detail.

"Then I said, 'This is a photocopy, Mr. Blake.

"He was dumbfounded.

"I went on: 'A very good photocopy. But it's not the original note.'

"He just said, 'You're kidding.'

"I told him, 'No, I'm not kidding at all. The average person might think it was the original, but not me, with my magnifying glass. Here, take a look.'

"I had him go over the whole note, point by point, showing him it was a very sharp photocopy.

"When he looked through the magnifying glass, he could see.

"I told him, 'I'm sorry, Mr. Blake, but we can't pay you.'"

Art looked sympathetic. "Man, that must have been a letdown."

"It was. He just stood there looking gloomy for a moment, then lit up like a light bulb. He started talking fast, like this (I mimicked Blake's machine-gun delivery as best I could): 'Look, I know an attorney in town. Let me go talk to him and we can get this straightened out in a hurry. Don't go away. This won't take long.'

"There was no harm in trying, I thought, so I agreed to wait."

Art asked, "Did he ever come back?"

"Oh, yes. About an hour later he came trotting back into my office with an Affidavit of Lost Note.

"He was very proud of himself. 'Here,' he said. 'All fixed.'

"I suppressed my chuckle because this transaction was so important to him. But his affidavit was as worthless as his photocopy of the note.

Art asked, "Why?"

"Like I explained to Mr. Blake, such affidavits are sometimes used to *release* a lien on property. But they're not for selling an original note.

"He argued with me. He said, 'But my attorney told me this is what I need.'

"I just told him, 'I know you got this from an attorney. Let me explain this graphically, okay? I can show you what I mean easier than I can tell you. Will you wait a minute?'

"He said, 'Sure.'

"Then I went and made copy of the check I was to give him.

"Then I wrote out an Affidavit of Lost Check.

"I came back in and gave him both the copy of my check and the affidavit.

"I said, 'Since you're giving me a copy of the lost note and an Affidavit of Lost Note, I'm giving you a copy of my lost check and an Affidavit of Lost Check.'

"He got it instantly.

"He smiled and said, 'Nobody's going to cash this copy of your check, are they?'

"I smiled back and said, 'I don't think so.'

"He looked grim and said, 'Nobody will cash out my copy of the note, either, I see. Well, let me go talk to that attorney once more.'

Art said, "Persistent, anyway."

"Oh, yes. As it turned out, Blake's attorney looked up the law, and was very embarrassed. He apologized and told John the lost note had to be found.

"Back in my office, he asked what he could do.

"I gave him my list of places to look for the lost note. 'This is something I've built up over the years,' I told him. 'It's probably in one of the places listed.'

"Blake went back home and called me about a week later. Sure enough, he found the lost original note—and in the most ordinary of places: a box of stuff in the back of his garage.

"After all this adventure, John Blake didn't want to make another special trip, so he mailed the original note to me, and I mailed the original check to him."

"Now, Art," I said looking him in the eye. "Do *you* get it?"

"I get it!" Art giggled like a kid. Then he laughed out loud. "That's great!" he said. "But, hey, I gotta run. Can we do this again next Thursday?"

"Okay," I said. "Same time, same place."

We got the same table at the Grill and both ordered the same lunch as the week before. I'd been thinking about those top three most important things about note buying. I thought I had Number 2 and Number 3 picked out, but I felt like I really needed to emphasize Number 1, only buying the original note.

"Art, I'm going to tell you about a couple more deals where the original note was in question."

"But I got the idea last week," he complained.

"Yes, you got the idea, but not the importance. Or the consequences."

"Oh."

"You just have to put up with it, Art. I want you to understand this."

"Okay, I'll be patient. Tell me the story."

"Alright, this one is about a note seller named Don Harder. He's an interesting guy. He contacted me some time ago with a note for sale. Now I have to explain about Don: he's one of the city real estate industry's more colorful elder statesmen, which is a polite way of saying he's a lively old codger. He's one of my favorite people.

"Now, Don co-owned the note with his daughter Ellie, who lives in Montana. She's also a real estate broker. With two such knowledgeable people selling such a good real estate note I felt there would be no problem.

"As it turned out, while we were doing our preliminary investigation of the note, ol' Don came into our Seattle office for a visit. He'd known my father—who founded Wall Street Brokers—for more than forty years, but they hadn't seen each other for at least twenty.

"'Larry Stevens! You have white hair,' he said in mock astonishment.

"'So do you!" my father shot back at him.

"As you'd expect, they spent a few minutes chuckling and going over the old days back when they both had dark hair, and then we got down to business.

"Don Harder has always had a reputation for going to the edge, risking everything, and at the last minute coming out on top. But now, I found, his cliff-hanger days were over. He told me that he wasn't as sharp as he once was, and had put his daughter Ellie in charge of the note he wanted to sell. He had a copy of the note, which he gave me, but he didn't know where the original was.

"That was the first danger sign. The deal still looked good to me, but I called Ellie on the phone just to make sure she had the original note.

"Well, she assured me it was in her possession. But then I told her I was worried that her father might not be up to taking care of the details on this deal. She agreed that we needed to follow things very closely.

"When our attorney completed the paperwork and we were ready to close, I called Ellie again and asked her to send me the original note.

"She was embarrassed to say that what she had thought was the original turned out to be only a copy. She didn't have the original note!

"This happens so often that I have a routine procedure to locate missing originals. Art, you remember last week I told you about giving John Blake a list of places to look for a lost note?"

"Sure. And it was right in one of the easiest places."

"Good memory. But, like everything, there's more to it. Something I've learned is that whoever closed the real estate sale often has the original note. So, the first thing I did was to talk to the title insurance company that handled the sale of the real estate and ask them to search their files and see if they had the note.

"The title insurance company reported back saying the sale file was so old they couldn't find it. The note really was lost."

"Wow," said Art, leaning over his sandwich with a troubled expression. "Really lost! What can you do about *that*?"

"The next best alternative is to ask the payor to sign a replacement note."

"A replacement note," repeated Art. "What if the payor won't sign it?"

"You're in real trouble. Note payors don't have any obligation to sign a replacement note. Don and Ellie Harder were fortunate to have a cooperative payor, a very proper lady named Doris Cooper. She did everything they asked.

"So, now we had the replacement note signed by the payor. Then, just one day later, the title insurance company called saying they had found the missing file, and the original note was in it.

"Here's where it gets complicated. When they forwarded it to me, I saw that the original note didn't look anything like the copy of the note I was buying. It had different payment terms, different amounts, different everything!"

Art gasped. "That's nuts! How can that be?"

"Don't panic," I grinned. "Let the story tell itself. Now, I suspected something had gone wrong back at the original property sale. So, I asked the title insurance company to check some more. As I thought, one note had been signed only to be rejected and replaced with another. I had the original of the first note that had been rejected. Here's where it got really crazy: The original of the valid note was still missing!"

Art moaned and rolled his eyes. "You have to have nerves of steel to be in this business," he said.

"That's true," I said, "but get this: On the day scheduled for closing, Don Harder with the snow white hair came in – and he had the correct original note! He found it in another file. It seems that he had borrowed against the note at one time, and when he repaid the loan, the lender returned his note. He filed the note in his loan file, not in his property file. He had forgotten about it until the last minute. Old Mister Cliff-hanger was still doing cliff-hangers!

"But look where that left me. Now I had four notes: my working copy, the discarded early note, the valid replacement note, and – finally – the real original note.

"That was all we needed. We cancelled the replacement note and returned it to the payor. We bought the real original note and everything turned out well. So you see how involved things can get about the original note?"

"Yes, I do see," said Art. "And I apologize for thinking I was so smart. I really appreciate you taking all this time with me. Thank you."

"You're welcome, Art. I'm enjoying this myself because it makes me think about how to explain a subject that can get complicated in a hurry."

"I see that it does," nodded Art.

"There's one more I want you to hear about buying only the original note. I always think of this one as our 'problem child' example. You'll see why.

"It's about a guy named Zack Martin. He had seller-financed a tavern building two years before, and now wanted to sell the note. He said it was secured by both the real estate and the business assets. The balance owing was over $50,000, but the value of the security was well over $150,000. It sounded interesting, so I asked him a few questions, first about the sale of the property.

"Zack said that he and his ex-wife Willa had sold the tavern property prior to their divorce and that the note had been awarded to him in their divorce settlement.

"Okay, Art, let me tell you something about divorces: you can practically bet on it that important details have been overlooked. So I asked Zack if his former wife had endorsed the original note and delivered it to him.

"Zack told me that his lawyer had taken care of it. That sounded good to me. So I told him we'd be interested in buying it and to come in with the original note and several supporting documents.

"A few days later, he brought everything into our office. I verified that it was the original note and not a copy. Then I looked at the back of the note and saw that his ex-wife had indeed endorsed it.

"That was a big relief. I had visualized the pain of getting his ex-spouse to sign papers—you want to avoid that because it's always messy.

"Well, I offered Zack Martin a cash price that he accepted—something in the high forty-thousands—so we signed a preliminary agreement.

"This guy seemed friendly and charming and we just visited with him for awhile. He traded war stories with my father Larry. They were about the same age, and had both served in the Marines during the Korean conflict. It all went very well, I thought.

"As soon as he left, I gave the file to Katy Durant, our in-house attorney, and she began our due diligence.

"She ordered a copy of the divorce decree and settlement papers. She wanted to verify that the divorce was final and that the court actually awarded the note to Zack Martin.

"Well, Katy found that the divorce was legitimate, alright, but the decree said nothing about who got the note. That was suspicious. So Katy compared the ex-wife's signature on the tavern sale papers to the endorsement signature on the back of the note. They didn't match.

"Katy came into my office and said, 'Lorelei, we have a forged signature here.'

"Are you sure?" I asked her.

"'It could be genuine, but I don't think so,' Katy replied.

"I decided to check this out myself. Willa Martin lived only a few miles from my office, so I took the unusual step of calling her to arrange an in-person visit.

She lived in an aging neighborhood in a well-kept older home. I rang the doorbell and watched the front door slowly open to the width of the chain-lock. Willa Martin's haunted face peered through and asked what I wanted.

"'I'm Lorelei Stevens,' I told her. 'I called you about the note your ex-husband wants to sell my firm. This is it here.' I raised it so she could see what I held. 'Will you look at the back of it, please, and tell me if that's your signature?"

A wobbly hand reached out and took the note. Willa Martin looked carefully and then shook her head sadly.

"'Sorry,' she said. 'I didn't sign that.'

"'I see,' I said. I explained to her that Zack wanted to sell the note for fast cash, but it needed her real signature. I asked if she would endorse the note and whether she expected any money from the sale. Poor woman, she was so timid.

"She thought about it and finally said she'd endorse the note if she got some of the cash.

"I told her to talk it over with her lawyer and let me know how much she wanted from the sale of the note.

"Well, she called the next day and said she'd endorse the note if she got $5,000. I relayed that to Zack. I heard that he went to Willa several times during the next week, and after each visit she called me and said she'd accept less, first $4,000, then $3,000, then $2,000. Finally she said she'd allow him to have all the money.

"I remember that last call very clearly. Willa Martin told me, "I just want Zack out of my life. I don't care about the money. I just want him gone.'

"That was hard for me to deal with. I asked if she was certain she wanted to allow this. She assured me, with her voice trembling, that it was. It was so sad.

"Well, anyway, I cleared it with Willa's lawyer, and we sent a courier to get her genuine signature on the papers.

"Now we could close the note sale. Katy got the final papers ready and Zack Martin came in to sign them.

"He was a different man this time. He was not friendly. He was not charming. We told him that if he wanted to be paid, he must first sign a statement on the back of the note, admitting that he had forged the signature of Willa Martin without her knowledge or authority. He resentfully signed the statement and the final transaction papers.

"Katy now had possession of the original note, properly endorsed, so she gave Zack his money and wished him well.

"As he went out the door, I heard Katy scurrying around muttering, 'Where's the note? Where's the note? It was here just a second ago!'

"At first I thought she was joking, because it's an office rule to always get the original note. But it was no joke. The note was missing!

"Then I saw Katy rush out the door and down the hallway. I quickly followed and saw her grab Zack by the hand. There was the note, crumpled up in his fist like a piece of garbage. He had walked out with it!

"Katy snatched the note from Zack's hand and he dashed off.

"She brought the note back to the office. There, we uncrumpled the note, ironed it flat, and put it in our file.

"That was the last of Zack Martin and the last of our troubles with this note. The payor hasn't missed a payment since."

Art sat there dazed. "Son of a bitch," he finally said, then caught himself. "Oh, sorry, Ms. Stevens. I forgot myself. But that was a hell of a story. You sure see a lot of human nature buying notes. I had no idea."

"Still want to buy notes?" I asked, eyeing him skeptically.

"Oh, yeah," he said. "I've known guys like Zack all

my life. I know how to deal with them just fine. You bet I want to buy notes."

"Well, come back next week and we'll get to the second and third most important things. But I can't keep this up forever. A couple more lunches and you'll be on your own."

"That should be plenty. I'll be here."

FAST CASH

Chapter 3
Security

"Thanks for coming early," I said to Art Morales, who appeared in our reception room wearing a dressy button-down shirt and slacks. "I wanted you to see our offices and watch the end of a real note transaction."

"Hey, great," Art beamed. "You know how much I appreciate this, Ms. Stevens. I'm going to make good on all this time you're giving me."

"Don't worry about that," I said. "You've been buying lunch and I've got something in mind when the time comes. For now, just come on into my office and have a seat. This won't take long."

Art took the visitor's chair as I sat behind my desk and moved a stack of papers front and center. "This," I said, "is the file of a deal we've been working on for nearly a year. The reason I wanted you to see this one is because it's an example of the second most important thing about note buying. Can you guess what it is?"

"No way. I was doing good enough to get all that stuff about only buying the original note. There's a lot to this note buying I didn't realize."

"Well, don't feel bad. It took me two weeks to narrow it down to the top three, and I've been in the business more than thirty years. So here it is: Number Two on the list is the security."

"The property?" mused Art, cocking his head in a thoughtful pose. "Okay, I can sort of see that. If the property's not worth anything, the note isn't either. It's your only backup."

He sat up straight and nodded his head. "Okay, let's see the papers."

"Alright," I said, pushing one sheet forward, "this is the only thing I wanted you to see. It's the closing statement for a house in Seabeck, Oregon, right on the coast. We just sold it to a nurse who works at the little community hospital nearby. She made a respectable down payment and we're seller-financing it with a note she signed for the balance due."

I sat back to watch the effect.

"Wait a minute," sputtered Art. "You're not buying a note here. You're selling a house."

"You're pretty sharp today, Art. And the reason we're selling a house is that it was the security for a note we had to foreclose. That's the real story I want to tell you about security. Come on, let's go down to the Grill and I'll fill you in."

Art laughed as he got up, "You're full of tricks today."

"The business is full of tricks," I said as we made our way out to the elevator. "And this was one of the scariest."

Art pushed the "down" button for us and I began: "Some years ago we bought a note secured by this small house in a nice little town. We looked it over and found it was an attractive home in a cute neighborhood."

"Cute neighborhood," Art mocked as the elevator doors opened and we stepped in. "Never saw one of those."

"Take my word for it. Anyway, we felt the transaction was very secure. We bought the note and got our payments on time for more than a year, when suddenly the money stopped. No explanation."

"Jeez," said Art as we rode to the ground floor. "That's scary already."

"We thought so. We repeatedly tried to contact the couple paying the note—Arnie and Pepper Black were their names. Nothing."

We stepped into the lobby and went to the Grill.

"So here we were ninety days later and still no payments. It was time to have the property inspected, just in case we had to foreclose. I sent our staff lawyer Katy down to do the inspection. She could only examine the exterior, since we had no right to enter the premises. She came back with photos that really shook us up. The place was trashed."

The Grill's hostess seated us at our customary table and the waiter just asked, "The usual?"

We both nodded and I went on: "Katy had interviewed the neighbors and got horror stories about a bunch of unsavory characters coming and going at all hours of the day and night."

"Note buying is getting a little rough for me," said Art, only half teasing.

"It gets worse—and better. But Katy's final report was worse. We probably faced an expensive foreclosure *and* a nasty eviction. We had to do something and do it soon. We needed an attorney licensed to practice law in Oregon, and by a stroke of luck, I had met one while I was teaching a note course for a real estate association.

"His name was David Taroday and his offices were near ours. I told him we wanted to file a foreclosure against the Black property right away. He advised us to do a nonjudicial foreclosure rather than going to court because it would cost less money and take less time, so I told him to go ahead.

"Well, I called Taroday a week later and he told me the foreclosure was going just fine. But the week after that I still hadn't received any documents. My phone calls with him began to sound like a bad movie script: 'Oh, I forgot. I'll get right on it.' 'Oh, it's right here on my desk. I'll send it right over.' 'Oh, I just got a new secretary and she misplaced the file.' Then he stopped returning my calls altogether."

Art just shook his head.

"Yeah," I acknowledged, "it was getting pretty bad. I called the title insurance company and asked if any foreclosure had been filed on the property. They examined the public record and said there was no evidence of any foreclosure at all.

"Now I had two problems: the property and the attorney. So I found another lawyer, a guy named Roger Law."

"Hah," said Art. "Good name for a lawyer."

"True. But first I had to deal with David Taroday through the bar association. It came out that he had serious personal difficulties that affected his work. He sent me an apology and refunded my money. I think the bar association called him up for a disciplinary hearing."

Our food arrived and we began lunch.

I continued, "Anyway, while I was getting my money back from Taroday, Roger Law was getting the kind of results I had wanted to begin with. He sent me all the documents and didn't need to tell me the foreclosure was going just fine. I could see it happening. The only problem now was I had lost six valuable months in the confusion.

"With the foreclosure under way, it was time to go check on the property again. I first called the neighbors that had complained about the unsavory characters and found that nobody had been around lately and the house seemed abandoned. Then I sent Katy back to the house to change the locks.

"While the locksmith was working, a neighbor came over and told Katy that the police had come just a few days earlier and took Arnie and Pepper Black away. Katy checked with the local sheriff and found that the Blacks would be gone for a very long time. We never learned what their offense was, but the legal system had saved us from having to evict them."

"Sounds like a drug deal," said Art through a bite of his French dip sandwich.

"That's what we thought. Whatever it was, we got a totally wrecked home back. Now we had a decision to make. Was it worth trying to repair? Well, we got an estimate for putting the house back in tip-top condition, and—lucky us—found it was well worth the cost.

"When we did the arithmetic, we saw that we had enough equity in the property to cover all the repairs, all the lawyers' fees, the original cost of the note, and—get this—still yield a profit. The security saved us. So we fixed it up and sold it to the nurse."

I let Art digest that. He said, "So your nightmare in Seabeck turned into a dream after all."

"Good way to put it," I said. "Now I want to tell you about a note that was a real dream in more ways than one."

"I'm ready for a good one."

"**A**lright. This was about four years ago. A woman named Jan Townsley called with a question: her father Michael lived in Mexico and needed to sell a substantial note. Could we give an immediate price quote?"

Art broke in: "Mexico? Where in Mexico?"

"I don't remember its name. It was a little village near Oaxaca. All I remember is they make Indian rugs there."

"Oaxaca? Indian rugs?" husked Art, eyes wide. "That's gotta be Ixtapa."

"You know the place?" I asked.

"Of course I know the place. That's where my folks came from. I've got relatives there."

"That's incredible! Well, what a super coincidence."

"Go on, I want to hear this."

"Okay, where were we? Oh yes, I asked Jan for a few details.

"First, what was the security for the note? She said it

was a first lien on a newer 4,000 square foot house on 20 acres. That was good.

"Then, where was the property located? Well, it was practically right here, in a rural area not too far from Seattle. That was even better.

"Then, what was the current value of the property? It was worth four times what the payor owed.

"'Wow,' I thought, 'this sounds like a good one!'

"I gave Jan our quote and she said she'd check with her dad.

"We spoke back and forth for the next two months, covering various questions. Finally, she called to say her dad wanted to sell his note and said he'd be in our office in a week. You'll like this part:

"The reason he was in Mexico was to work with poor but talented children who wanted an education so they could have a decent life. His dream was to build a school in this little village, and he was almost finished when he ran out of money. All the school needed was a roof. He was selling his note to put a roof on a school for village kids.

"It touched me to the heart. This generous man was donating his own time and money to help these kids, and in a very solid way. This was not just another note transaction. I was proud to be part of it."

"You should be. I know about that school. It made waves in that town. You see, all the rug makers in Ixtapa live in brick houses, they've been well-off since their rugs became popular in the 1980s, they sell all over the world. But the families that don't make rugs are still poor, they live in adobe houses out on the fringe. That school is for their kids. But I didn't know about the man who built it. Who is this guy?"

"Michael Townsley is his name. He came to our office, sat right where you did in front of my desk. When he arrived, he told us frankly that another note buyer had offered him more money, but had requested amendments to the documents that showed him they didn't understand the complexities. We did, and that's why we got the note."

The Grill's server took our plates and brought coffee.

"Mr. Townsley emphasized that we were working against a deadline: the building needed its roof before the school year began. We finished the preliminary agreement and Mr. Townsley departed for the airport, on his way back to Mexico.

"Our first task was to locate the original note—sound familiar?"

"Oh, yes," said Art.

"A servicing agent had handled the money payments, but told us they didn't have the original note. So we called Mr. Townsley in Mexico. He had what he thought might be the original. It appeared to him that the signatures on the note were signed with a pen that had started running out of ink – he didn't think it was a copy. He express mailed it to us and it turned out to be only a copy."

Art said, "So much for that."

"Right. Then he sent us a copy of a five-year-old letter, showing that the original note actually had been sent to the servicing agent. We called them, hoping they hadn't lost it. They checked again and, sure enough, they'd had it all along. It was a simple mixup and the note hadn't been missing in the first place!"

"That's too easy," said Art.

"Don't get cynical," I said. "Now the last thing in our due diligence was to inspect the security—*that* was too easy. It's barely thirty miles from here. We drove out toward Fall City and along the way saw these big gated estates, huge parcels of land and brand-new 4,000-square-foot homes, barns, and stables along a scenic riverside. Horses everywhere. People certainly live the good life out there.

"Then we saw the property that secured Mr. Townsley's note. It was dazzling! A beautiful home in a perfect setting—meadows, forests and a mountain backdrop. The value of the security was so great there was no need to ever worry about the safety of this note!"

Art said, "So the security was really secure. I get it. Now, what about the school? How did it get finished?"

"Well, we sent the final documents to Mr. Townsley to have them signed and notarized. Because of title insurance requirements, the only acceptable notary in Mexico was a United States Consular Services official, so he had to go into Oaxaca.

"We closed the deal a day before the deadline. The money got to Mr. Townsley in time and the roof was built. The school opened on schedule and the note's paid regularly since then—everybody's happy."

"Great story," said Art.

I told Art there were a couple more he needed to hear, but lunch was over and I had to take a couple of deposits to the bank.

"You going to walk?" Art asked.

"Yes," I said.

"I've got time today. I'll go with you and you'll talk."

I said, "Fine," and here's what I told him:

One day as I sat at my desk working through the usual stack of papers, I thought I heard my executive assistant Gloria in the next room say something strange.

"They live in a barn?" I asked loudly. "Did you say the payors on a new note *live in a barn*?"

"That's what I said," the answer came back as I stepped into the adjoining office.

Gloria grinned at me. "The payors are two cousins. And they live in a barn."

"Is this a joke?"

No, it was real. A few years back, the note sellers—an aging couple named Gene and Avis Turn—had purchased 24 acres of young second-growth timber in an isolated rural area of Washington State. And in a clearing they assembled an 1,800 square foot pre-engineered metal building of the kind you see on farms all over the country.

The photo they e-mailed showed what I'd have called a utility building—one of those long metal-ribbed structures on a concrete slab with two big truck doors on one end—but the Turns called it "The Barn," so we did, too.

Gene Turn, an electrician by trade, had himself sheet-rocked, insulated and hand-wired the dwelling half of The Barn—he left the truck-door end of the building as a garage and storage area. In the living area, Gene had installed a free-standing pellet stove and a large capacity water heater. A nice kitchen and bathroom. Carpeting. All the comforts of home.

The Turns lived in The Barn comfortably for six years. Then Avis Turn developed a chronic heart condition and the couple was forced to sell in order to live close to medical help.

They'd sold to a pair of cousins, Jenny and Megan Riefschneider. The Riefschneider cousins, unlike most, had been close since childhood. They were country girls, both born in neighboring towns not far from their new property. They had moved their collection of dogs, cats, chickens and horses onto the timbered acreage, and felt right at home living in The Barn.

Jenny was a rock-steady worker, held a good job with the county and had built up stellar credit. Megan, a computer nerd type, was just the opposite: still trying to find her purpose in life, wandering from job to job, and skipping out on some of her financial obligations.

The Turns had sold the property for $100,000, and Jenny had paid $25,000 cash down. The value of the timber was of secondary importance to the cousins—it was a well-spaced stand of 20-foot-tall Douglas fir that wouldn't become commercial for a decade or more. And besides, it was the charm of the trees, the land and The Barn the cousins wanted.

Because Jennifer had great credit and had paid 25% cash down, we turned a blind eye to Megan's employment and financial woes. Jennifer's perfect payment history showed us she alone could handle the financial obligations of the property, so we offered $65,000 for the note.

Though it was unusual, we knew there was value backing the note due, both in Jennifer's responsible lifestyle and the fair market price of the property itself. We decided to buy the note, even though some of my staff objected.

For several hours I listened to comments like, "I know that notes are scarce in this economy, but aren't we lowering our standards buying a note secured by a barn?"

In the end, my decision to buy was firm.

Now for the sellers: the Turns needed fast money to pay for medical expenses—they told me they had no medical insurance.

We began our due diligence and immediately ran into a stumbling block. The Riefschneider cousins had no fire/hazard insurance covering The Barn! The Turns had lived there for six years with no insurance as well!

This was a violation of the terms of the note and also a risk we didn't want to take. We didn't want to lose money if part of the security was destroyed.

We explained the situation to Jennifer Riefschneider, who thought her cousin Megan had obtained the insurance. She was surprised—and not so surprised—that Megan had failed to follow up. Jennifer assured us she'd get insurance in the next few days, and apologized for any problems this had caused the Turns in getting their money.

But Jennifer soon discovered that fire/hazard insurance was not easy to get for a pre-engineered metal building. One agent told her they *might* insure it if she installed electric baseboard heaters and removed the pellet stove. Jennifer could find no insurance coverage quickly, but promised to continue looking.

This delay forced us to make a decision. We weighed the pros and cons. We wanted to buy the note because we felt the cousins would pay. Also, we wanted to help the Turns get some much-needed fast cash.

But we didn't want to risk The Barn accidentally burning down and losing the security. The Turns assured us that it was little or no risk—they'd never insured it and never had a problem.

Be that as it may, we knew this much: if The Barn was destroyed, the acreage would remain intact. We knew the land was worth more than 60% of the price the cousins paid for the property. So our risk of loss was limited to the value of The Barn - the value of the timber was negligible even if it was destroyed too.

We finally compromised with the Turns. We would give them $45,000 in immediate cash and hold the remaining $20,000 in escrow until the cousins got the insurance or paid off the note, whichever came first. If The Barn was destroyed before then, the money would be released to us.

We bought the note.

Several months later there was still no insurance. Avis Turn responded well to medical treatment. The cousins enjoyed a quiet country life. The $20,000 remained in escrow. And The Barn still stood.

"And you left it at that?" asked Art.

"Not really. After six more months the cousins finally got insurance and escrow released the $20,000 to the Turns."

I figured I'd cap off my security stories to Art with another nightmare note. Here's how it went:

If anyone asked what was the most bizarre note our firm ever saw, among the top contenders would be one that a man named Gene Smythe wanted to sell us several years ago.

Mr. Smythe's call began unremarkably. His mother had

recently passed away, and before her death assigned a note she owned to her five grown sons.

When I asked how long his mother had held the note before assigning it, Mr. Smythe replied, "Nine years."

That's a well-seasoned note—a good indicator of a desirable transaction. However, that was the last good thing he told us.

Mr. Smythe then began reciting a long list of problems.

First, he told me the note's payor, Bruce Dart, had been diagnosed with heart disease and might die. The medical expenses were so high his note payments were six months late.

And, oh yes, the house on the property had burned down a year and a half earlier. And, oh no! It wasn't covered by fire insurance.

I stopped Gene Smythe right there. This note sounded hopeless. I was going to reject it out of hand.

But it was so bad—it sounded like a soap opera—I got curious. I told Mr. Smythe I'd check into it and call him back.

The first thing I found was that the taxes were a year and a half delinquent and Mr. Dart hadn't notified the tax department about the house burning down. That should have been another bad thing, but I realized that the majority of the taxes went for the house, not the land. However, the assessed value of the land only, without the house, was double the amount owing on the note. So even though there was no house left, there was still plenty of security.

Bruce Dart, then living in a trailer home on the property, proved to be highly cooperative. He explained that after thousands of dollars worth of tests and scans, his heart disease turned out to be diabetes, which was now under control with diet and exercise.

Mr. Dart emphasized that he had paid on time for 9

years, except for the six months when he was undergoing the endless tests and needed to pay his medical bills. He proudly said that he had no bills and no credit card debt—and in fact owed no one except on this property. He'd also received a "quit claim" deed from his ex-wife—it wasn't recorded, but it legally put the property in his hands alone.

I told him that it was important to have the proper forms submitted to the tax assessor so he wouldn't be assessed for the non-existent house. Also, his ex-wife's deed should be recorded to prove the property was in his name only.

Okay, this note began to sound interesting. I talked once more with Gene Smythe and asked about the fact that his mother had assigned the note to her five sons. I would have to get all five to sign the transaction. However, one son, Pete Smythe, had died from a drug overdose a year earlier. Worse, his widow Sandy was also a drug abuser. It would be hard to find her and harder to talk her into signing the papers.

Despite that obstacle, I decided to go ahead and buy the note.

Closing it was horrendous. The first title insurance company we went to refused to insure us, but we got it from another. We went to the four living sons and got them and their wives to sign the papers. After an extensive search, we finally located Pete's widow and then spent hours convincing her to sign the papers so their children would have some trust money. Almost done.

Now the final step. We went to see Bruce Dart and helped him fill out all the real estate tax papers to get his property re-assessed for land only. Also, we agreed to record his ex-wife's deed for him. That meant we had to have the original deed. Mr. Dart smiled and took a scorched metal box from a shelf and opened it for me. There, covered with ashes and water stains, lay the deed. The box and its contents had survived the house fire—sort of.

Dart and I drove together to the county recorder's

office. The clerk looked at the charred edges and raised an eyebrow. Mr. Dart and I both cringed, fearing she wouldn't take it.

"See if you can clean up the worst burnt edges," she said, "and we'll record this for you."

Just about done. My final step was making arrangements for Mr. Dart to begin paying into a reserve account to cover his back payments and 1/12th of his taxes each month.

We made it! The transaction finally closed. And it has paid well.

Lesson? What looked like worthless junk turned out to be a gem—if you examined it only in the exacting light of the security.

I stood with Art at the entrance to my office building. "Next week is your last visit," I warned him.

"I know."

"See if you can figure out what the third most important thing is. You've had plenty of clues today."

He nodded and walked away.

I went back to work.

Chapter 4
The Payor

"It's the person that pays," said Art Morales. "No doubt about it."

He stood in my office doorway wearing the same jeans and bomber jacket as the evening we met.

"I'm impressed," I said. "How did you guess?"

"It wasn't a guess, really. You said I had plenty of clues from the stories last time. It was all about making sure you got the money. Well, who pays the money?"

"You've learned a lot," I said. "But you seem a little subdued today. Anything wrong?"

"No, I'm fine. Let's go to lunch. And tell me about the person that pays."

He still looked subdued to me, but I chalked it up to the fact this was to be our last "lunch date" to talk about note buying.

So, I told him a couple of stories about the payor as we went through lunch:

An attorney named Conrad Burke contacted my firm some time ago trying to help an elderly client named Maude Cooper sell a note.

The property that secured Mrs. Cooper's note was in the poor section of a nearby city, and a drive-by inspection revealed that it was one of those "cosmetically challenged" residences. In plain language, it was a dump.

Which is not to say the home had no value—it certainly did. It was structurally sound and in reasonable repair. It just didn't look nice.

The note had two payors, a mother and daughter named McLean. Their credit report looked as bad as their home. But their payment record was exemplary. They had lived in the house for six years and had kept up their payments on the note all that time. They had a decent equity in the house, based upon the $60,000 they'd paid for it six years earlier.

So, even though it wasn't a wonderful situation, I thought there was adequate value to secure the note. I called the attorney and told him the cash price I was willing to pay.

It seems that Mr. Burke had also shopped Mrs. Cooper's note to a client of his who had recently entered the note buying business. The other note buyer, Michael Martin, had offered a higher price—unrealistically high, I thought— so I was the backup offer.

I had a gut feeling that Martin's high-priced offer would fall through and the note would end up in my hands. I followed my hunch and did some due diligence. I knew a real estate lady, Estelle Greer, who had been in the area for 30 years and asked her what the property was worth. Estelle estimated it at about $60,000 – the property had held its value over the years.

I ordered a title report. To my surprise, I found that about a year earlier a foreclosure had been started. That didn't make any sense because the note payment record was perfect. When I examined the foreclosure notice, it turned out that the

McLeans were behind on their real estate taxes. Burke had started the foreclosure to protect Mrs. Cooper.

But I noticed that the delinquent taxes had been paid, so I assumed everything was taken care of. But I was curious.

I called the payor to see just who she was. Katie McLean was a 45-year-old woman with two younger children, ages 9 and 12, and a 25 year old daughter, Elizabeth, who was developmentally disabled. Elizabeth had a pair of 7-year-old twins and a toddler, but she had moved out some months earlier—with a new infant—leaving three of her children with her mother. So Katie was taking care of five kids! The state was paying her a supplement every month to support the grandchildren.

If I had thought Gene Smythe's complicated note was a soap opera, this Cooper note sounded like the grand opera of soaps.

The mother/grandmother was living there with all these kids—and her boyfriend, who had stuck with her to help raise the five children.

Katie told me it was hard for her, but she always paid her house payment. When I asked, she said yes, she hadn't paid her taxes.

"When I found out about those taxes," she said, "I was scared to death I was going to lose my home and not have any place for my kids and my girl's kids. And we'd lose everything we'd put into it over the years.

"I didn't know where I was going to get all that money for the taxes. Then my friend Irma told me about this TV show called *The Helping Hand*. Irma said they find people in trouble and have them tell their story on TV.

"I was afraid to do it at first, but I wasn't going to let them take my home away. So I called them and went on television. I told them about my mortgage payments and how hard it was to keep up with them and then to have all those taxes on top of everything."

Katie must have been convincing, because viewers sent in $9,000 to help her. It paid the taxes, the attorney fees and foreclosure costs, and even allowed her to pay some mortgage payments in advance.

Katie's determination really impressed me. I could hear the certainty in her voice when she said that she wasn't going to lose that house. This was one strong woman.

As the days turned into weeks, I wasn't sure I'd end up with that note. I kept in touch with Mr. Burke, who cordially chatted with me, and kept me abreast of developments. At first the elderly Mrs. Cooper couldn't find the original note, which held up the sale. Then she finally dug it out of some files in her basement and Mr. Burke sold it to Michael Martin.

A month later Mr. Burke called, and I thought he just wanted to chat some more. He told me all about receiving an appraisal on the property for a lot more than my real estate lady Estelle said—$75,000. Even the tax assessor's valuation was $72,000, and it was insured against fire for $89,000.

I told Mr. Burke it was a better note than I'd thought, and that Mr. Martin was very lucky.

"Well," said Mr. Burke, "That's the real reason I'm calling. Mr. Martin hasn't paid anything yet. I'm tired of waiting around for the money. Would you be interested in buying the note—immediately?"

My hunch was right. I told him we'd buy it, but with special arrangements. It didn't fit our company's guidelines: the payor's credit was not good, and the property was messy, among other things. So I bought the note personally with my own money.

For a while I considered trying to turn the note over, to sell it for a quick profit. I asked another institutional buyer, thinking it might fit their guidelines. They were interested at first, but when they saw the credit report and the pictures of the property, they rejected it. It was clear that I was going to keep this note, warts and all.

I talked it over with my father Larry, and as founder of the company he recommended that we transfer the note into a family partnership—he didn't mind sharing some of the personal risk. So, there the note remains, with regular mortgage payments coming in and a very determined woman making sure the taxes are paid.

Sometimes that gut feel and the strength of the payor are what really counts in note buying.

Art just nodded at the story, chewing on his customary French dip sandwich. He seemed preoccupied, but I went on to the next example of the payor's importance.

A note broker named Ruth Carson called me with a problem. She had submitted a note to a bank, which had specifically committed to purchase it for an attractive price if the payment record was perfect for the past year.

The payment record was not only perfect, but payments had also been paid a few days early for the past year. In addition, the property appraisal was excellent. However, neither of the two payors, David Lancaster and Anthony Powell, was creditworthy. Public records indicated they had a string of bankruptcies, collections, and other unpaid debts. The bank refused to honor its original commitment.

Ruth told me that the note seller, Herbert Shaw, was threatening to sue her and turn her into the authorities because the bank rejected the transaction. She didn't understand why the bank turned it down after assuring her that creditworthiness of the payor didn't matter, so long as the payment record was good for at least a year. She was very concerned and needed a fast closing.

Ruth asked if I would buy the note. I looked it over, seeing the security was a one-bedroom home in Idaho. I compared the perfect payment record with the detrimental public records against David and Anthony, and it made no sense to me. Yet a perfect payment record was strong evidence of a good transaction. I offered the note broker a lower price for the note, but still enough for her to make half of what she would have realized with the bank's original offer.

But now I had some investigation to do. I contacted David and Anthony by telephone and an intriguing story unfolded.

David was a young man who had indeed declared bankruptcy twice. He told me it was because of overwhelming medical bills that had triggered a long string of bad debts. He had been born with severe asthma and required hospital treatment once a month. When he entered the workplace as a young adult, his medical bills mounted and soon swamped his meager income, which was further reduced by frequent medical absences.

The financial information I had been provided showed that he had paid nearly 15 percent down on the house. How was that possible with these circumstances? David explained that his grandmother Harriet had loaned him the down payment, but he had since paid it back.

Okay, but how was it possible to maintain an absolutely perfect payment record paid early every month for the past year?

David explained his situation. He was now receiving disability income from the Social Security Administration, which in itself was not enough to make the payments and pay for other living expenses. However, he shares the home with Anthony, who is also receiving disability income.

Anthony had been in an automobile accident several years earlier that fractured a vertebra in his neck, leaving him with disabling headaches. He also suffered aggravating lifetime emotional problems from abuse as a child.

David's mother Leona had been appointed payee for both of them, and she served as their money manager. It was Leona Lancaster who had been paying early every month!

I thanked David for his helpfulness and asked for his mother's phone number, which he gave me. Before saying goodbye, he timidly asked, "Are we going to be evicted?"

I told him no, and assured him that nothing would change. The monthly payments would simply go to me instead of Herbert Shaw.

By the time I reached his mother Leona, David had already spoken to her, worried what was happening. Leona Lancaster was a cheerful person and said she had told her son, "I've had my home mortgage sold four times and it didn't change anything for me."

She repeated the story her son had told me, adding that there was no danger that the two would move out and abandon the property. They had lived together for five years and they liked this little house they had moved into. Anthony was able to drive and David wasn't. Anthony took care of David when he had his asthma attacks in the middle of the night. If there were ever serious problems, she would come from her home only 15 minutes away after receiving a call.

Leona explained to me how it had taken her six years to get her son a disability income, and finally had to get a lawyer to do it. Anthony, on the other hand, got disability income after only eight months, and never needed a lawyer. Both had a steady monthly income from the Social Security Administration, and their medical bills were covered.

I was satisfied that I was making a sound purchase, and sent Leona a balance verification document for David and Anthony to sign. They both signed it quickly and sent it back to me.

Ruth's problem with the note seller was solved and we completed the transaction. But if I had not checked so thoroughly about the note payor, I would have let this opportunity escape.

Art barely responded when I finished this story. Something was going on. I didn't press it, and decided to tell him a happy story about note payors:

A young man arrived at our office with a smile on his face. His name was Leo Williams and he was clearly on Cloud 9. With a twinkle in his eye, Leo said, "I'm selling my note so I can buy my girlfriend a diamond ring. I want to give it to her on Valentine's Day. I'm going to ask her to marry me."

Well, that was different! It was refreshing to be involved with love—but Valentine's Day was rapidly approaching, giving us less than two weeks to close.

We looked over Leo's well-written documents. We checked the value of the payor's house, which was fine. We got a clean title report. The long-term payment record was impeccable. The fire and hazard insurance policy covering the house was sufficient. This transaction appeared virtually flawless. We expected an easy closing.

The note payor was a couple named Kenyon. We sent them an estoppel document—which verifies the balance and stops the payor from denying that amount—and requested their signature.

The next day Natalie Kenyon called me. Tearfully, she told me her husband John had served her with divorce papers the week before. Her lawyer had advised her not to sign anything or make any more payments on the house until further notice. She said she was sorry. She would forward the papers to her lawyer.

Two days later, John Kenyon called from his mother's home where he was staying. His lawyer had told him that we intended to buy the note. He was willing to cooperate and sign the estoppel so the note could be sold. However, John's lawyer had advised him to sign nothing, and to stop the house payments until it was decided if he should pay or she should pay. So he could do nothing. He sounded depressed.

So we got depressed too. How could we close when we'd been notified the payments had been stopped indefinitely? When we told Leo, he was downcast. How would he be able to buy the engagement ring on time?

I called Natalie to see if things had been repaired. They hadn't. She began confiding in me. She told me she loved John. She didn't want a divorce. She really didn't understand why he was so angry that he wanted a divorce. She thought she'd been a good wife. She went out of her way to do nice things for John. After his father's death the year before, she helped him relocate his mother from the East Coast to a nice home nearby. Natalie hoped she'd get back together with John.

I called John to see what he had to say. He sounded sad and upset. He too began confiding in me. He told me of many bad things Natalie had done. He just couldn't understand why she'd done such horrible things behind his back and said such nasty things about him. He didn't know how he could have fallen in love with such a person.

Something just didn't make sense. I asked, "How did you find out these things about your wife?"

John said his mother had told him. That sounded suspicious to me.

I took a chance. I called both Natalie and John and asked if they would meet me at my office. Reluctantly, they agreed. However, I could sense hope in both their voices.

When they arrived they couldn't look at each other. I took charge of the conversation and carefully nudged them to talk. As they began to unfold their feelings, both were stunned to discover that John's mother had been fabricating lies!

They called her on my office phone and told her they knew what she'd done. She tearfully admitted she'd lied, explaining she wanted her son with her. She couldn't cope with being alone after her husband's death.

That confession changed everything.

The next day John and Natalie called me. They had dropped the divorce proceedings, fired their lawyers, and were living together happily. They had personally delivered the monthly note payment to the servicing agent, and assured me that all payments would be forthcoming on a timely basis. They both signed the estoppel document and sent it to us by messenger.

We were able to close the sale of the note on time.

On Valentine's Day, Leo called to tell us a diamond ring was now on the finger of his beloved. While we were still on the phone, a delivery man came into my office with a bouquet of red roses from Leo in appreciation of closing on time.

In the same delivery was a flower arrangement from John and Natalie, with a note saying, *"Thank you for helping us get back together. By the way, mother received a box of candy from the widower next door."*

Art smiled at the story, but said nothing.

"Okay, Art," I said. "I don't know what's eating you, but do you remember when you told me you'd make good on all the time I was spending with you and that I said I had something in mind when the time came?"

"Yes," he said.

"Well, the time has come. This is our last lunch session. I'm very impressed with you, Art. So impressed I'm going to do something I rarely do. I'm a note buyer, not a note seller. But you want to buy notes, and you deserve to have a good one, so I'm going to sell it to you. I'm going to sell you the Townsley note. The guy who built the school where your folks came from. And for a good price. You won't have much money left in the bank, but you'll have a nice income stream from the note payments."

Art looked shocked. "You'd do that for me?"

"Like I said, I'm very impressed with you."

I could see him fighting back his emotions.

"Look," he said. "I wasn't going to tell you this, but I've decided to go work with that Townsley, go find my roots in Ixtapa. I thought I'd have to eat into my savings. I was worried how I'd make a living there. It's so far from any seaport. Longshoring is all I know. But this note…"

I finished his sentence for him: "will give you enough to live on and then some—that handsome profit."

And that's how things worked out. I hear from Art now and then. He's doing well. He grumbles about how hard it is to keep the school open and how the poor don't get a fair shake from the rest of the town and what a taskmaster that Townsley is. In other words, he's happy as a clam.

Chalk up another story of the unlikely world of note buyers.

FAST CASH

PART TWO

The Business

FAST CASH

Chapter 5
Routine

"**H**ere's the mail," said Gloria, our executive assistant. "Oh, and here's a renewal notice for the classified ad. Want to keep it in the *Seattle Times* like it's been?"

"Let's see," I mused. "It's under 'Mortgages' and what else?"

"Well, their classifieds call it 'Mortgages/Contracts.'"

"Oh, that's right. And it's still our 'We buy notes for fast cash' ad, right?"

"That's the one," Gloria said.

"Make sure it has our website on it."

"It's right here: www.wallstreetbrokers.com."

"Okay, go ahead and renew it."

The note buying business has its routines like any other. It also has its quirks, like any other.

Our office procedure is reasonably routine. Note buying is less so. A lot less.

Our "routine" note purchase usually begins with a phone call. It could be an email, or a fax, or a personal visit, but most begin with a phone call. That's when the quirks begin.

The routine items are the steps we follow in sequence while buying a note—the steps are always the same, or at least they *should* be:

■ Preliminary agreement

▲ Due diligence (the investigation required to make a sound decision—the opposite of negligence)

● Closing

These are the three steps in buying a note. I've given each its own symbol—square, triangle and circle—because next we're going to look at three note purchases, each emphasizing one of the steps, and the symbols will announce which stage we're in.

Since each story covers an entire note purchase, we'll insert a ■ at the part where the preliminary agreement appears, a ▲ where due diligence is the key subject, and a ● where closing is what's happening.

Now let me warn you about the quirks. No two note purchases are the same. They're as individual as the people selling the note.

Here's an example of a note that relied for its success on the preliminary agreement. It's got plenty of quirks.

Peter Finch, a note seller, called me with an unusual proposal. He offered my firm a note secured by a hunting and fishing lodge on Manker Creek in the vast Copper River Valley of Alaska's rugged Chugach Mountains—*a full day's horse ride to the nearest road.*

That's not the kind of security note buyers want. But a note buyer should give fair consideration to even the strangest opportunities. So I listened carefully as part of my due diligence, but with misgivings.

▲ Mr. Finch told me the security was located approximately 170 miles southeast of Anchorage – many miles beyond the middle of nowhere. It was completely snowbound during the winter. The business that made the security valuable had a short summer-only operating season.

▲ On the positive side, the payors, Tom and Linda Chard, who operated the lodge, were dedicated and businesslike. They had a loyal and affluent clientele from big cities that was delighted with their service and the wilderness setting. The setting itself was magnificent, offering big game hunting for Dall sheep, moose, grizzly and black bear, beaver trapping, and great fishing for several types of salmon and trout. The Chards maintained their own string of mountain horses and employed licensed and experienced guides. Gold panning was available for those who caught the gold bug. Hiking and nature photography were other popular options.

▲ A client could expect to be picked up at the Anchorage International Airport, and driven an hour and a half to the tiny town of Wasilla, Alaska, for an overnight stay at a bed and breakfast whose motto is "Fish and relatives stink in three days." The next day guests are driven three and a half hours to remote Tolsina Lake on Glenn Highway. There they board a seaplane and a bush pilot flies them down the lake for forty-five minutes to Manker Creek. They land in a small side lake without a dock, wade to shore, get mounted up and ride a horse for forty minutes. At the end of the trail is the mountain lodge. It is built on five acres of private land in what was probably the site of Moose Camp dating from the 1897-98 gold rush.

▲ The lodge itself is a handcrafted log building with kitchen, dining, and lounging areas. Seventeen other structures included sleeping quarters, a sauna and hot shower. In addition to the land and buildings, the security included the string of mountain horses, saddles and tack, and various camping and construction equipment.

▲ Hearty home-cooked meals and fresh baked goods kept guests well fed. There was no electricity in any of the buildings and no inside plumbing. Despite advertising for welcomed guests to bring non-hunting companions, 95 percent of the visitors were men.

▲ The financials would tell me quite a bit about the desirability of this note. I found that the guests paid $275.00 per day for a minimum one-week stay. The lodge was usually well booked in advance each season. The Chards had paid a large down payment and signed a ten year note. They had already paid four payments. The payments were due in one annual amount each November, which gave the Chards the full season to earn the money. Mr. Finch agreed to our price, which was lower than the five other offers that other note buyers had made — *all five had subsequently turned it down.*

▲ The financial stability of the operation looked good, and we evaluated the Chards — a husband and wife team, both native Alaskans, with two small children. Linda Chard's parents stayed with them during the season because her father loves to fish and her mother helps with guests.

■ We were concerned about Mr. Finch, because he'd been promised money by five previous note buyers who didn't come through. We decided to buy it, but we wanted Mr. Finch to sign a preliminary agreement that he would sell it to us. Mr. Finch signed the agreement and faxed us a copy. We were ready to go.

■ At the last minute, we discovered that Mr. Finch was secretly negotiating with the Chards, allowing them to pay off the note at the same price we offered. The Chards came up with the money in a short time, which was a clear indication that the note was very secure. We contacted Mr. Finch and told him we didn't appreciate his actions because he had signed an agreement to sell the note to us. He tried to justify his move by claiming that he had sent only a fax to us, not the original agreement. He agreed to contact his attorney to determine whether a fax agreement is binding.

■ Meanwhile, we contacted the Chards and notified them that we had a signed agreement with the seller, and that we intended to buy the note. They were very embarrassed because they didn't know of the circumstances, and we worked it out with them on a friendly basis. Mr. Finch's attorney informed him that a faxed agreement was indeed binding in Alaska, and that settled the last of the questions.

● The transaction closed.

You can see right away that if we hadn't had a preliminary agreement signed, we would have lost the Finch deal to the Chards—after doing all that costly and time consuming due diligence.

Yes, the preliminary agreement is *supposed* to be the first step. One of the quirks of this note is that we did quite a bit of the due diligence before we got the preliminary agreement signed by Mr. Finch. That's a common problem you'll run into as a note buyer: you really don't know whether you want to buy a particular note until you have enough facts.

Now here's a note which features that very problem, and talks about the importance of due diligence.

Donny Richards, a polite East Coast gentleman, found our firm on the internet. He called and discussed a serious problem. He'd sold part of a note – 10 years' payments – seven years ago. He was under pressure for cash and wanted to sell the rest of the note. He was dismayed to discover that the institution he'd sold to was out of business. He didn't know what to do.

Such inquiries are always a problem: We never know how much time and money it will cost to trace the present whereabouts of the "partial note," as we call it, and we are even more uncertain whether we will want to buy it once found.

We make such decisions on a case-by-case basis. This note sounded more promising than most, so I decided to take the risk.

▲ We first helped Mr. Richards do some tedious detective work. Together we traced defunct corporations, mergers, and name and address changes. We slogged through a maze of transcontinental assignments and endorsements and discovered the note's part had been sold *six times*. It was now held by Great Canadian Financial.

▲ Next, Mr. Richards contacted Great Canadian Financial to see if they would buy the rest of the note. The answer was terse and absolute.

"No!" said Mr. Art Wentworth, the regional manager.

"We inherited 13 note parts as assets in a merger. We don't buy parts of notes. We don't buy notes at all."

▲ Wentworth went on to explain that the parts of notes were a headache: despite all the company's modern technology and computer systems, they were not equipped to do the bookkeeping and tax reporting involved when owning note parts. The few stragglers they had left were being hand posted. The square pegs were not fitting in the round holes. Wentworth offered to sell the part back to Donny Richards at a discount. He wanted it off his books.

Wow, that was complicated!

■ Our firm then made an agreement with Donny Richards to buy the entire note from him when he bought his part back from Great Canadian Financial. Both transactions could be completed at the same time. We got to work on our due diligence.

▲ First, we verified with Great Canadian Financial that they had possession of the original note and its six original endorsements, since they would have to endorse the note over to Donny Richards who would in turn endorse it to our firm.

▲ We then contacted Bill Lawrance, the payor on the note. He was a crusty old contractor who claimed he always paid his bills when they were due. He was understandably nervous to find out his note was being sold *again*! He told us of his woes with all previous owners of the note. No one could tell him his correct balance due – he'd even tried to re-finance once and his loan was frustrated because he got conflicting payoff figures.

"How can you have two payoff figures?" Mr. Lawrance snorted into the phone. "I've gotten such weird numbers on this note I feel like I've entered the Twilight Zone. Don't get me involved with this mess again." He was about to hang up.

"Wait, wait!" I pleaded. "I can explain the confusion. Just give me three minutes, okay?"

Mr. Lawrance said, "I'm listening. And looking at my watch."

I quickly told him that the reason he'd been given such funny figures is that *part* of the note had been sold – not the whole note. Those weird figures were amounts owing on *part* of the note. We were buying the *whole* note and everything would be consolidated again. He wouldn't get funny numbers and he could emerge from the Twilight Zone.

"They sold *part* of the note," repeated a bemused Mr. Lawrance. "Can you do that?"

"You can do that," I said.

"But you're going to get everything in one place again?" he asked.

"We are," I assured him.

He decided to cooperate with us. We were able to put all the strange numbers together and calculate the correct balance on our computers. Finally, Bill Lawrance signed the balance verification.

▲ We knew the mortgage securing the note was in first lien position on a 10-unit apartment building in New Jersey. But we certainly wanted title insurance to back up this knowledge. We decided to get title insurance from the same title company that had insured it in the past. But we also wanted assurance that there was coverage from the beginning of the note up to the date of recording our assignment of the lien. We wanted insurance that there were no intervening liens, since the note part and lien had been sold so many times before.

▲ We waited and waited for the preliminary title report. Despite numerous phone calls and empty promises, it took them six weeks to furnish the report. It was clean. This is the longest time I have personally ever had to wait for a title report. We don't know if it was typical of this title company, the snow was slowing them down, or if we just got lost in the shuffle.

▲ During the long time involved, Donny Richards was getting upset. He needed his money and did not understand about all the delays. We did a lot of hand holding and explaining to Mr. Richards during the interim. We've learned that keeping the note seller informed with the situation on a near-daily basis holds the transaction together and calms nerves, taking away the "what's-taking-so-long" mystery.

▲ While waiting for the title report to arrive, most of our due diligence was completed. We received our appraisal showing the property was worth twice as much as the note balance. We were named as first mortgagee on the fire/hazard insurance policy. It was a good deal.

▲ But as careful as we had been, we wanted to be legally protected. We hired Prescott Woolsey, an attorney in New Jersey, to review everything, especially all six of the previous sales, to make sure our note purchase would be airtight.

▲ While preparing the documents, Woolsey discovered that one endorsement was missing: it was an *allonge*—a separate piece of paper that was supposed to be inseparably attached to the original note, but somehow got removed. He contacted Great Canadian Financial and notified them of the problem. They quickly scoured their files and retrieved the missing endorsement, which, it turned out, had been accidentally sheared off between two file folders. It was wrinkled, but intact.

● The New Jersey lawyer finally got possession of all originals, got signatures of all parties, recorded the assignments of lien and got our final title insurance policy.

● The transaction closed. We paid a large attorney bill, but it was worth the legal protection due to the complexities.

Again, it's clear that without due diligence—a lot of due diligence—we'd have lost the Richards deal, not to another party, but to a failure of nerve when confronted with all the obstacles.

Technically, due diligence extends all the way up to the last minute when you sign the transaction. It's easy to understand why: the closing—signing all the required papers—is the least complicated step in buying a note, while the due diligence is the most complicated—and time consuming.

But every now and then, signing all the required papers becomes almost as complicated as the due diligence. Here's a note that had an outrageously complicated closing because of unsigned documents:

August March wanted to sell his $90,000 note. It was a good one, he told me on the phone.

I'm always a little skeptical of such seller claims, so I asked how the note was secured.

"It's a nice little piece of real estate with a deli and espresso business on it," said Mr. March. "The payors are totally reliable, every payment on time—they're a couple named Witt, Andres and Naomi. They came from the Netherlands originally and bought the place from me three years ago. They named it The Magical Bean—after coffee, I guess."

The Magical Bean was situated amid a cluster of businesses on a main highway in Cody's Corner, a Washington State town near the Canadian border. The Witts had paid $50,000 cash down on the property, with a sale price of

$140,000. They pledged the property as security for the $90,000 note to August March.

With a balance of $83,000 remaining on the note, we considered August March's offer worth looking into, so we drove to Cody's Corner for a preliminary inspection. It was quite a revelation.

▲ When we stepped into The Magical Bean, we found Naomi Witt running the business with flair: fresh coffee, good food, happy people — not a speck of dust anywhere and everything in its place.

▲ We didn't identify ourselves, but took a booth and watched the sit-down crowd and the line of customers at the drive-thru window ordering morning coffee and breakfast goodies. Andres Witt took our order and we were served sooner than we expected. Fast, friendly and efficient. The Magical Bean was clearly a going concern.

▲ With breakfast over, we strolled around Cody's Corner to size up the surroundings. The Magical Bean stood in the middle of a nice business community — a day care next door, then a dentist, car repair and fire station on one side of the street, with a tavern, grocery store and an arts and crafts business called Sunny's on the other side.

▲ We dropped into Sunny's and I instantly fell in love with an exquisite wood carving on display. While paying for it, I asked Sunny, the owner, about the deli across the street. She said it was always busy and in the mornings there was usually a long drive-thru line, but it moved quickly. And she always bought her lattés there. This was music to our note buyer's ears!

■ We liked the note and quickly signed a preliminary agreement with August March.

▲ Now we got into the details. Lots of details. March first explained that he was not the sole owner of the property. It had been a four-way split between him and his ex-girlfriend, Kay Mullins, and his two business partners, Deane and Sherry Van Donge.

▲ March told us that after the Witts bought it, Mullins and the Van Donges had transferred their interest to him, so he was now the only owner and the sole note seller. Good enough.

▲ But August March said he wanted us to move fast, as he had some medical problems and was under pressure for cash. We assured him we would.

▲ We began our due diligence, and got document copies.

▲ The first problem appeared right away. Closing the deal required signatures on all the proper documents.

● I discovered that there were four critical closing documents without proper signatures: August March had failed to get the signatures of his three other business associates 1) on the back of the note; 2) on the assignment of the security agreement on the business; 3) on the notification to the Witts, and; 4) on the notification to the servicing agent.

● No signatures, no closing. We called March and stressed that Mullins and the Van Donges would have to sign those four papers to clean up the deal if he wanted fast action—four signatures each from three people. He assured us that there would be no problem, so we proceeded toward closing.

▲ Then came some more due diligence: the title insurance report with a bizarre revelation, that Kay Mullins and the Van Donges had indeed signed one key document called the Assignment of Deed of Trust to August March shortly after the sale of the property to the Witts. But a year after that, the Van Donges pledged the Deed of Trust—which they didn't own any more—to Island Bank.

● We called March again and notified him that there was a possible delay because we needed Island Bank to release the Van Donge pledge. Now we needed a fourth person's signature.

▲ March felt there would be no problem, so we contacted Peder Johanssen, president of Island Bank. We asked if he'd release the Van Donges off of March's asset. Johanssen said he'd check into it and get back to us. After several days of telephone tag, he finally said he would release the papers as soon as we sent him a release form. We immediately sent one to Johanssen and waited for him to return it. And waited.

● In the meantime, August March called and said, "There's a little problem getting Sherry Van Donge's signature on the four papers. She's in Paris for a month—she goes there every summer as part of her school teacher's duties with a group of honor roll kids. Can her husband Deane sign her name?"

● "No," I explained patiently, "they both have to sign the papers and each signature has to be notarized. We need her signature fast, so we'll overnight the papers to Sherry in Paris and she can get them acknowledged at the American Consulate."

● Then I told March of another delay we'd run into: "August," I said, "we tried calling Kay Mullins several days in a row and she hasn't called back. We need her signature to close."

"I'll take care of it," March said, with an edge of anxiety in his voice.

He called a little later to say he'd reached Kay's mother and found that his ex-girlfriend had just gotten married to a rich man and was on her honeymoon — she'd be back in two weeks.

"But I need my money now," he said. "Will this hold up the closing?"

"Yes, it will," I said.

"Is there any way to speed it up?" March asked in desperation.

● I told him about the possibility of an "escrow hold out" where we could give him some of the money in advance and the rest after Kay signed the four documents. But we needed Island Bank's release and Sherry Van Donge's signature before we could do that!

● August was beside himself with worry, but there was no way to speed things up. A few days later, he called to say Sherry Van Donge was back home. She had fallen ill in Paris, and returned from her trip early. The Van Donges sent the notarized papers the next day. Two signers down, two to go.

● We emailed Island Bank's Peter Johanssen. Where was our release form? He replied it had been sent through the "proper channels" and we should have it soon. We finally received it a week later. Three signers down, one to go.

● A couple of weeks later I received a phone call from Kay Mullins. She was back from her honeymoon! I explained carefully that although she'd signed the Cody's Corner property over to August March three years ago, there were four more documents needing her signature—that this was basically a "clean up" of a past transaction.

● It turned out to be bad timing. A jealous male voice in the background snapped, "Kay, don't sign anything until you see my lawyer!" I encouraged Kay to see the lawyer right away.

● Kay was silent for days. We called her once more and she told us she'd signed the papers and sent them via FedEx Next Day delivery. Great!

● But the papers didn't show up. Two days later, August March called to say he had just talked to Kay again and she told him she'd finally signed the papers and sent them to us. But, again, they didn't arrive.

● Two more days later, August March called in exasperation. He said he'd finally realized that Kay was just as unreliable now as she had been when they broke up three years earlier—he was certain that she hadn't signed the papers at all.

● "You know," he said bitterly, "it's been three years

and she still hasn't even given me my car back. If we wait, it'll be another three years before she signs those papers. I'll just have to go handle this in person."

● August March drove eight hours to Kay's new home, where he met with her and her new husband. After considerable wrangling, he got his car back, and somehow convinced Kay's husband it was okay for her to sign the papers. Four signers down, no more to go.

● We were finally able to close the transaction properly, though not very quickly.

That's a spectacular—and long drawn-out—closing. I'd just as soon not see another one like that. But you can see how note buying puts you smack in the middle of the human condition.

You meet all kinds of people, and you come to like them—or maybe just tolerate the really abrasive types.

But you learn to see each note as a human interest story ready to unfold. And every now and then, one goes through without a hitch, just like you hope they all will. Here's one I really like:

As usual, our first contact came by phone, from a man named Arthur Weiss. He had a note secured by a two-bedroom rental house located on a large five acre view lot.

I had Mr. Weiss fax me some of the key documents and looked them over. The payors—two married couples, each with a half interest—had been paying the note on time for five years, a good sign of stability. The property was worth substantially more than what had been paid for it. You couldn't ask for a better beginning.

■ Without hesitation, I gave Mr. Weiss a price quote and he accepted it. We signed a preliminary agreement and I went to work.

▲ A lot of things can go wrong with a note, so I began my usual careful examination of this one. I started with the seller—Arthur Weiss. Experience has taught me that three main things can go wrong because of the seller.

- First, the seller can't find the original note.
- Second, the seller backs out.
- Or, I find a serious problem that the seller didn't reveal, such as unfulfilled agreements that could hurt the value of the note.

▲ However, as I performed my due diligence, Mr. Weiss seemed to have no problems, so I investigated the payors, Tim and Alexis Morgan and Forrest and Kathleen Galvin. Payors can stop a deal in many ways.

- They might have bad credit or a bad payment history.
- Or they may show a balance owing that is incorrect.
- Or the payors may have unfulfilled promises from the seller that make the note undesirable if we can't resolve the problem.
- And it is not unusual that the payors, upon learning of our intent to buy the note, will make a deal with the seller to pay off the note at a discount—thereby eliminating the note altogether.

▲ But the Morgans and the Galvins had none of these problems. It was at this stage that I began to wonder what was wrong. Things were going too well.

▲ So I was particularly careful about inspecting the property, which would be our security in the event of a default on the note. Problems with the property can put a sudden stop to any transaction. We might find that its value is inadequate to serve as security for the note. Or it might be an unsightly mess that has not been maintained. Or it might have an underground oil tank that could cause endless pollution liability problems. I couldn't find a thing wrong with the property that secured this note.

▲ I found myself getting suspicious. Perhaps the title insurance report would show some defect. There might be a cloud on the title—liens that can't be cleared up, or something like that. I might find that the seller doesn't have the authority to sell because a former spouse has made claims to it. Or the lien itself might be defective—some technicality could make it invalid. For example the lien might have the wrong legal description, or if state law requires both husband and wife to sign it, but only one actually signed, the title might not be eligible for title insurance. There could be all kinds of title insurance problems. But the title report came through without a single flaw. Now I really began to worry.

▲ I scrutinized every word of the note, looking for problems I knew must be in there somewhere. The usual defect is poor draftsmanship of the note which makes the note "non-negotiable." The problem is that if we buy a non-negotiable note, we probably could not be a holder-in-due-course—there's a new concept for you—which means that if any problem emerges about the note, we wouldn't be protected against claims by third parties. If the note turns out to be non-negotiable, that makes the note worth less (or worthless).

▲ But when I finished examining the documents for this note, everything was in order. The note was definitely negotiable.

▲ What about the other documents surrounding the creation of the note when the property sold? I studied the closing statement, the original purchase and sale agreement, and the escrow instructions, knowing that some uncertainty would most likely lurk there. Nothing. Everything was fine. I couldn't believe it.

▲ Aha! One last thing: fire and hazard insurance. Where was the insurance? I've seen so many transactions in which there was no fire/hazard insurance, or where the seller doesn't know where the insurance is, or where the payor won't tell you where it is. But there it was—at the bottom of the file. I checked, and the insurance was correct and in force.

● The deal closed and not a single thing had gone wrong. Success!

That's when I realized my past experience with tangled transactions had almost turned me into a cynic. I had to laugh at myself. The anxiety I went through looking for a problem with this note was as bad as actually finding one. And I had just completed a routine note. A really, truly, *routine* note.

FAST CASH

Chapter 6
Note Sellers

When I was young and just starting in the note buying business, I went to a lawyer to get some advice.

The first thing he told me was this: "Always remember, Lorelei, every note seller is a liar and a crook."

I was shocked to hear him say such a thing. What did he mean by that?

I found an explanation in a book by note buying pioneer, George Coats. To paraphrase:

> Experienced note buyers often claim that the best approach to the investigation of any note is to assume the other fellow is a crook, and then work backward from there. Depressing as it may sound, there is considerable justification for this attitude. Truth is not a matter of black and white; it's a matter of degree. Truth exists only in the eye of the beholder, and anybody can rationalize his behavior. More important, however, is the way the approach can keep your antenna tuned for trouble. Such sensitivity is valuable, because you can never be certain that someone out there hasn't figured out a new way to outsmart you.

After over thirty years in the note buying business, I understand exactly what my lawyer and George Coats were saying. Why should you look at every note seller as a crook?

There are only two reasons why anyone would sell you a note:

1) To get cash; and
2) To get rid of a problem.

What is it about wanting cash that could make your note seller a crook?

Think of the note seller's situation. He wants the cash as fast as possible. And he's willing to take a discount, to lose money, on the note in order to sell it for cash. That tells you something right away.

A note seller is under pressure. It could be something as simple and innocent as needing to buy a new car or send a kid to college. It could be something as complex and serious as paying off a gambling debt or the IRS threatening penalties over delinquent income taxes.

The pressure is there in either case. Such note sellers may not volunteer any bad features of the note because they are afraid that each bad thing will devalue the note further.

This is the kind of note seller who will tell you the payor has never been late, and then you find out that the payments are always at least three weeks overdue. This is the kind of note seller that will tell you the payor keeps the property in picture-perfect condition, and when you drive by to inspect it you find junk cars, garbage and broken toys all over the yard. When you bring such discrepancies to the note seller's attention, they always have a justification ready, just like George Coats said.

"Well, they do pay, eventually."

"Well, I haven't seen the place since just after I sold it, and it looked good then."

Cash-hungry note sellers may not be deliberately lying, but they are more than likely to taint the truth with rose-colored glasses in hopes of getting more money for their note.

People are funny with money.

And what about note sellers wanting to get rid of a problem? If there weren't problems, why would they sell their note at a discount anyway? They could have an unhappy payor who has discovered defects in the property and wants expensive repairs. Or your seller might know that the payor just lost his job and can't pay anymore. Or your seller may have been threatened with a lawsuit by the payor for failing to dig a promised new well. It could be any of dozens of problems. And your note seller might not tell you about any of them.

And then there are completely innocent people who find themselves with a note and no information about it. They could be the adult children of an elderly seller, or heirs who inherited a note, or the executor of the estate of a deceased person, or a bankruptcy trustee. They're not crooks in any way, but they have very little information about the note, yet they want fast cash at top dollar.

The worst part of the whole thing is that note sellers don't think there's anything wrong about withholding negative information. They rationalize it in weird and wonderful ways: They think, "Oh, well, you're in the business, you know there are risks, and after all, you *are* getting a discount."

Talk about withholding negative information! Let me tell you about Roger Clooney:

Our firm made arrangements with this Roger Clooney, who was a note seller from Oregon, to purchase a huge note—well over $400,000. It was secured by a motel on the Oregon coast. The beachfront property had superior value, and the payor, Jonas Haresh, was highly creditworthy. In short, it was a good note.

Clooney, of course, was in a hurry for cash from the sale of the note.

Our due diligence on this note involved two tasks: first, checking out the real estate—as you do with every note—

and, second, evaluating the personal property that came with the motel—beds, furniture, lamps, drapes – that kind of thing.

First, we ordered a title insurance report on the real estate and saw no problems. Then we ordered a Uniform Commercial Code (UCC) search of the personal property to make sure there were no other liens against the personal property. (The Uniform Commercial Code, which we'll see more of later, is a nationwide law that governs commercial transactions such as sales and leasing of goods, bank deposits, and secured transactions—including notes.)

We prepared an estoppel document for Mr. Haresh to sign that verified the balance due and mailed it to him for signature, along with a letter stating that we were in the process of buying the note.

Mr. Clooney had possession of the note, which was payable to him and no one else. A standard question we ask is, "Is the seller married?" We asked Roger if he was married.

Yes, he said, telling us his wife's name was Phoebe.

When we received the personal property UCC search results, we found an old lien on the motel. It was signed by both Roger and Phoebe. We checked into the lien's status and found that it had been paid off long ago. No problem.

Our attorney prepared the final closing papers for both Roger and Phoebe to sign. We were prepared to close as soon as we received the signed papers.

Almost immediately, Roger called in alarm.

"Phoebe has nothing to do with this transaction," he snapped.

"We have to have her signature," I said.

"If you do, that's a definite deal killer," said Roger, "I won't sell you the note if you need her signature."

"But Mr. Clooney," I said firmly, "Washington is a community property state. We have to have her signature."

Roger testily reminded us that the motel was located in Oregon, which is not governed by community property laws.

"It's silly to demand Phoebe's signature," Roger huffed. "Her name's not on the note. Besides, she's with her sick sister in England for two months. She's just not available to sign any papers."

He asked me to re-do the papers and send them to him for his signature only.

Wow, talk about a disaster waiting to happen!

We've seen this kind of thing before. There's always some plausible justification, but behind all the talk there's trouble.

So, over the years, we've developed a standard policy to require both spouses to sign, *unless we have official documents to prove it's not needed.*

In this case, we knew that Phoebe long ago had *some* interest in the motel because she'd signed that old UCC lien on the personal property.

Phoebe might be able to make some claim to the note if we bought it and paid all the money to Roger and none to her.

There was no way we would buy that note without Phoebe's signature. We told Roger. He was livid.

The next day, I received a call from Jonas Haresh, who had questions about the estoppel document we sent for his signature. After going through all his questions, we got to chatting about the motel on the coast. Haresh mentioned it was too bad about the Clooneys' divorce.

"Divorce," I repeated.

"Yes," he said, "after I bought the motel, Phoebe left and moved in with her sister in Portland."

I immediately called the title insurance company and explained what Haresh had told me. I asked them to check records in Multnomah County where we found that the sister lived to see if there was a pending or completed divorce. A couple of hours later, the title insurance company furnished documents showing that, indeed, a divorce was pending and there was a restraining order preventing the husband from selling any assets without court approval. The title insurance company had missed this important fact because the divorce was in one county and the motel in another.

We contacted the divorce lawyers for both Roger and Phoebe. After weeks of haggling, they finally agreed to sign the papers and split the proceeds. Now we were able to close the transaction.

Think of the mess we averted. And how close we came to it.

Was Roger Clooney a crook? Not really.

Was he a liar? Yep.

Most problems with the seller are of this sort, hiding bad news.

Here's another way it can happen, and it involves a job in the note industry we haven't encountered before, that of the *note broker*, someone who finds notes for sale and connects them with someone who buys notes, and does it for a commission:

One of our favorite note brokers called with a $40,000 note for sale. His name was Nat Miller. Although Nat was relatively new to the business, we had bought several extraordinarily good notes from him and expected another.

Nat described the note, which was being sold by a man named David Mostel. It was secured by a dry cleaning business, Clearway Cleaners, in a nearby town at its busiest intersection—a perfect location.

The note did not include real estate, just the business, so we'd call this one a "business note," but it had everything we look for: a large down payment on the business, about a year's worth of payments—we'd say the note was "seasoned" for about a year—and the payment record was perfect.

The note payor, Ralph Stanley, had managed the business for Mostel prior to buying the business, and thus had considerable experience. The payor's mother, Natalia Stanley, a woman of substance, guaranteed the note. It sounded great.

We made an offer of $34,000 and Mostel accepted. We signed a preliminary agreement and began our due diligence.

Nat Miller furnished the necessary documents, but told us there was one condition: Mostel had told him that we absolutely must not contact Ralph Stanley or he would not sell the note.

That's one of the reddest of red flags in a note deal.

Miller knew this was unacceptable practice, but begged us to make an exception: Mostel had explained that Stanley was a childhood friend. Stanley would feel very uncomfortable about paying anyone except the bank where the two of them had made the original arrangement to service the note payments. Stanley's monthly payments were set up as automatic withdrawals that went directly to Mostel's bank account. Mostel expressed deep concern that we not upset Stanley.

I told Miller that it only made us want to contact Stanley all the more.

"Something is very wrong here, Nat," I said. "We've got to find out what."

"How can you be so sure?" asked Miller.

"The story doesn't wash," I said. "Stanley will have to send his payments to us after the note sells, so why would Mostel be that concerned about keeping it from his old friend before it sells?"

"Look," said Miller in his best cajoling voice, "you're being too hardnosed. I've spent a lot of time with Mostel, and I trust him. It's just a peculiarity of this note. There's nothing wrong."

"We routinely contact the payor, Nat," I said firmly, "*especially* if the seller tells us not to."

Miller was convinced that the deal was sound.

I wanted to cultivate this eager young note broker, so

I finally told him that we wouldn't contact Stanley unless we cleared it with him first—but emphasized that I still felt Mostel was hiding something.

I began a regular check-out: I inspected the documents and sent Kay, our staff attorney, to examine the location.

Things began to check out perfectly: we got proof that the down payment and the monthly payments had been made on time. Miller even provided us with the financial statement of Natalia Stanley, the wealthy guarantor.

Maybe Miller was right.

But then we contacted Leonard Uchida, owner of the property where Clearway Cleaners was located—the land-lord—and explained that we were interested in buying the note. I asked what he could tell us about the Clearway Cleaners.

"Don't buy it!" Uchida barked.

"Oh?" I said, taken aback by his tone. "Why not?"

"That blasted cleaners has spilled toxic waste on my property. Contaminated it all to hell. I'm suing Mostel and Stanley both for the cost of the cleanup."

"How much is that?" I asked.

"A hundred-sixty-thousand dollars," Uchida said bit-terly.

That's four times more than the amount of the note.

"Well, thanks, Mr. Uchida," I said in parting. "You've been very helpful."

I had Kay examine the court documents of Uchida's lawsuit. It was exactly as he had said.

I then called Nat Miller and explained what had hap-pened.

"Nat," I said, "nothing on earth could convince me to buy that note."

He was stunned. When he could speak again, he only said, "Well, chalk one up to experience."

It's not uncommon to run into this kind of deception in note sellers, but it is uncommon to run into calculated attempts to swindle you. This is something you have be alert to catch:

A note broker named Dan McGill contacted us for a quote. He said he had a relatively new note for sale.

Relatively new? Hmm... I asked, "How new?"

"Well," said Dan, "only two payments."

That could be a caution sign, so I asked about the property being offered as security.

The note, he said, was secured by valuable acreage that had sold for $80,000 in a resort area in eastern Oregon. I knew the place, and knew land values there were substantial. So far, so good.

"What about the down payment?" I asked.

Dan said the payor, a woman named Judy Meyer, had made a cash down payment of $32,000—40 percent—and was paying the seller the remaining $48,000 on the note.

That reassured me, so I offered $42,000, a good cash price for the note, and McGill accepted. I signed a preliminary agreement for our firm and began our due diligence.

Dan McGill immediately faxed me a few documents. He was emphatic that his client—the seller—Sam Stephens, wanted fast cash.

I reviewed the documents and noticed there was no closing statement on the sale of the acreage. I called up the note broker and said, "Dan, there's no closing statement. Can you get it for me?"

"There isn't one," he said.

"Why not?" I asked, now on guard.

"Look," said Dan, "a lawyer prepared all the documents, but Stephens and Meyer closed the sale of the property themselves."

That wasn't just a caution sign, it was a roadblock. Without a closing statement, I couldn't verify that Judy Meyer had actually made a cash down payment of $32,000.

If you can't verify the down payment, you're asking for trouble.

I asked Dan McGill to get a copy of the canceled check, showing that Judy Meyer had paid $32,000 to Sam Stephens as a down payment on the property.

The next day Dan called back and said, "Judy didn't keep a copy of her canceled check because she didn't foresee any problem with the transaction. But she said she'd talk to you and help out any way she could."

So I called Judy Meyer. The first thing she wanted to know was when Sam Stephens would get his money. Then she apologized for not keeping a copy of her $32,000 canceled check. She was extremely helpful, and even offered to take the papers to Stephens for his signature to save time.

When I put down the phone, all the warning lights began to flash in my mind.

Why was Judy Meyer being so cooperative? Payors usually resist helping in the sale of their note—sometimes they even become hostile and try to buy the note out from under you.

Judy Meyer would get no money for helping me buy Sam Stephens' note. In fact, it would cost her substantial time and effort to take the papers for his signature.

There were too many things that just weren't right.

It made me draw up a list of all the suspicious features about this note:

- I couldn't verify the amount or even the existence of the cash down payment.
- No real estate agent was involved in the sale of the property.
- There was no verifiable real estate commission paid.
- There was no record that normal real estate closing costs were paid.
- The transaction wasn't closed by a disinterested and legitimate third party closing agent.

- There was no evidence of title insurance when the property sold.
- Real estate taxes weren't paid. It was highly irregular that taxes were not current at closing.

I was now extra careful in my due diligence, scrutinizing everything for any other irregularities. While inspecting the documents, I noticed that the seller and payor in the past had used the same street address. I checked out the address and found it was a private mail service.

That was too much. I called Sam Stephens and asked about it. He told me that he'd sold other properties to Judy Meyer. It turned out she was a longtime friend of his.

That was enough for me.

Without doing any more work, I contacted Dan McGill and told him I was not interested in the transaction. The note might have been perfectly legitimate, but there were just too many danger signals. I revoked our preliminary agreement for cause.

McGill was mad. He thought I was being too picky. Maybe so. But I wasn't going to buy that note.

Did I avoid a note that would have gone bad? Did I miss a golden opportunity? Were Judy Meyer and Sam Stephens perpetrating a fraud? Were they perfectly honest?

I'll never know. But I can say that this was *probably* a phony deal.

Don't get the impression that note buyers are totally defenseless against phony deals. We're not. Every now and then we can turn the tables on deceptive sellers. Here's a prime example:

Our firm ran an ad in the community newspaper of our favorite seaside getaway spot, Washington State's Sandy Shores. We did it more to be neighborly than expecting any real business, but one day Nancy Taylor, a Sandy Shores resident, called our office with a note for sale.

Nancy was a real estate agent. She and her husband Jim offered us a note secured by a second lien on an 8-unit apartment they had built on a desirable ocean front lot. They had been receiving payments on the note for two years. The apartment building itself was only two years old, having been brand new when they sold it. The apartments were all occupied with renters, Nancy told me. She gave me a copy of the rent roll with the names of each renter, when the rent was due, and all the necessary information.

This was beginning to look good. The payors, Heather and Bill Hobart, made a substantial down payment, got a first lien loan from the bank and the Taylors accepted a second lien note for the remainder, which was the note they wanted to sell. The Hobarts had even made extra payments over the two year period and reduced the balance owing by $20,000. Heather Hobart also affirmed that all the apartments were rented.

This was beginning to look really good. We signed a preliminary agreement with the Taylors and began our due diligence.

We first obtained a copy of the closing statement from the sale of the property and found that the second lien did not appear.

We always treat that as a warning. It usually means that we have a "Silent Second" on our hands—a secret second lien that the first lien lender does not know about. I asked Nancy Taylor about it and she assured me it was not a silent second, and that the banker, Tad Erickson, knew all about it.

So I called Mr. Erickson to verify Mrs. Taylor's statement, and sure enough, he said he knew the Taylors and the Hobarts very well and knew about the second lien note. Mr. Erickson said the bank was not concerned about it. It was not a silent second.

That seemed a little odd—both the fact it was not listed on the closing statement and that the bank knew about it but didn't seem to care. So, I looked through the first lien documents and found nothing that prohibited a second lien. It seemed okay.

We checked the Hobarts' credit, which was impeccable. Heather held a good-paying secretarial job and Bill was a high school teacher with 17 years excellent service. I thought, "He's so squeaky clean he's probably a Boy Scout leader." Heather, I noticed, was listed as being formerly known as Heather Taylor, the same surname as the property seller.

"Oh, well," I thought, "Taylor is a common name. It's probably just a coincidence."

Now we wanted to get proof that the payments had been made on time including those extra payments totaling $20,000. Nancy and Jim Taylor said they would get us that information.

While waiting for that, we got the tax assessor's valuation of the property, which showed a very high value for the property, enough to leave substantial equity to the second lien.

It looked like a very good deal, so we decided to buy the note.

We sent the Taylors the closing papers to sign, but Jim Taylor called us back and said they couldn't sign one of the warranties.

I asked which one. Mr. Taylor said it was the one which warranted that the seller and the payor have no business or personal relationships other than the purchase of this property.

I asked why they couldn't warrant that, and Jim Taylor said, "Because Heather is Nancy's daughter."

I had suspected that in some corner of my mind. It made me edgy about this deal, because experience says that sales between relatives often result in problems. I asked, "Why didn't you tell me she was your daughter?"

"You didn't ask." Jim Taylor replied.

I thought, "Am I supposed to ask every note seller whether the payor is their daughter?"

This was not looking good. But it wasn't necessarily bad. I decided to reserve judgment until I got the inspector/ appraiser's report.

I got it the next day. Kathy Bennett, the inspector/ appraiser we hired, told me the property was worth what the assessor valued it at—if the apartments were all rented. But it appeared to be a vacant building, she said. Signs of neglect were everywhere, she said. Litter on the grounds, piles of sand that had drifted into the laundry room, she said. She could find no indication of occupants.

Now I was worried. I tried to get the phone numbers of the 8 tenants listed on the rent roll Nancy Taylor gave me. I found that not one name had a phone number.

I contacted a neighbor next to the building and he assured me that no one had lived there for months.

I was worried no more. I was angry. At that point I was sure that the Taylors were trying to dump an empty building on me by selling me a note they knew would go into default and force me to foreclose on it.

I could see it all now. The Taylors built the apartments but found themselves unable to pay off the construction costs. They immediately arranged a "sweetheart" sale to the Hobarts, the daughter and son-in-law with their perfect credit, in order to get a bank loan for their immediate needs.

The Hobarts couldn't get a loan for all the money Taylors needed, so Nancy Taylor, with her real estate knowledge, took a note for the shortage and secured it with a second lien on the property.

The Hobarts wouldn't even have to actually pay on the note. The Taylors could keep it as an "ace in the hole." If things didn't work out—which they didn't—they could always sell the note for fast cash and get their money that way.

The Taylors figured that the note buyer would foreclose and get the building. It probably didn't seem so bad to them, just a convenient way out of a scrape.

I cooled off and thought it all through.

What would the final outcome be? It was clear that I would never get the money just by repossessing the property. But the Hobarts had other assets that I could take. Under the laws of Washington State, if I didn't recover all my money from taking the property back, I could collect the rest—the deficiency—from the Hobarts' other assets.

Ah, *deficiencies!* A little-known facet of law that protects people like me.

Therefore, buying the note wasn't really as risky as it seemed. If I couldn't get all my money from the building, I would be delighted to get the rest from the Hobarts' other assets. This note was definitely collectable! I knew I could get all my money if I bought this note.

Now the question was, do I want to? Did Bill Hobart know the deadly consequences of deficiencies?

I knew from experience that most people, both sellers and payors, believe that in a foreclosure, all I could do was to take the property back. They did not know that I could collect the deficiency from the payor's other assets.

So I called Bill Hobart at his school and informed him of the situation. I explained, "As long as the Taylors keep the note, they aren't likely to sue you for any deficiency, because you're family. But if I buy the note, I have the right to sue you and recover any deficiency from your other assets. Do you understand this?"

He didn't. He was shocked silent. Now I could tell that he was just going along with somebody else's plan. His wife Heather and her mother Nancy were obviously the ones behind the deal.

I told him I would not buy the note unless he approved.

The next day, an older couple came into our office, introduced themselves as the Taylors and said they wanted to cancel the deal, even though they had signed a preliminary agreement they couldn't back out of.

Nancy Taylor was shaking with fear that we weren't going to let her out of the deal. She evidently had not known about deficiencies either, and how deadly they can be for note payors. I couldn't believe that she would have put her daughter and son-in-law in such a position had she known.

I didn't press the matter and revoked our preliminary agreement for cause, allowing the Taylors to keep their note. I doubted they would try to sell it to anybody else. I also figured the Hobarts would never trust them the same again.

It's true that I could have bought that note and collected the money. But did I really want to end up going after a respected high school teacher and his working wife and take a substantial amount of their life savings?

Absolutely not. Even in a tough business like ours, sometimes it's better to be a little lenient and not give in to greed.

Why do I feel that way? Well, I more often run into better examples of humanity, and that gives me a more benevolent feeling about the others.

Here's a different side of note sellers:

We weren't prepared for the bizarre turn of events that followed this routine inquiry.

A man named Gilbert Cash called our firm for a quote on a note he wanted to sell. It was a $200,000 note that had been paid down to a balance of $95,000, and the security was good, so we quickly offered $85,000, what we thought was a fair price.

Cash accepted, came into our office, signed our preliminary agreement, and delivered a very thorough package of documents. Things looked in order, so we started working on our due diligence.

The next call we got about the note came not from Gilbert Cash, but from his sister Annette Harbin.

"My brother shouldn't sell his note," she insisted. "He

needs the steady income. You have to understand that he was in a bad auto accident and has a steel plate in his head. If he gets that money all at once, he'll just squander it and then what will he do?"

Alarmed, we called Gilbert and asked him about his situation.

"Yes, I was in an accident," he said. "But I'm able to take care of myself. It's my money and Annette has no business telling me what to do with it. She's always meddled into my business. Let's go ahead with the deal."

We were disturbed by his sister's insistence that he not sell the note, but went ahead with our due diligence, checking everything out.

Then we got a call from Gilbert's *mother*, Juanita Cash. "You know, my son needs more money than you're offering. I think he's not using good judgment. In fact, after the accident, I wonder if he's using any judgment at all."

Now we were worried. I didn't like the attitude of his sister and mother, insinuating that my firm wanted to make a profit from a disadvantaged person.

I checked around the industry to see what other note buyers would pay, and found that our offer was top dollar. No one would pay more for this note.

So, I called Gilbert once more and told him his mother was concerned.

Same response: "It's my money and my mother has no business telling me what to do with it. And if they think I'm mentally incompetent, let them try to get me committed!"

"Do you believe they really think you're mentally incompetent?" I asked.

"I'm not sure," said Gilbert Cash. "But they might."

"Could you ask your lawyer if he'd give us his opinion?"

"Sure," said Cash, and the next day we got a call.

Cash's lawyer was noncommittal about the price, his

client's mental competence, and his client's ability to make a decision about selling the note.

Perplexed, I talked to our staff attorney Katy and asked what we should do. She suggested that when such questions arise, there is one sure way to answer them: have the note seller examined by a qualified doctor to determine his mental competency.

It's a real insult to ask of a note seller, but I reluctantly asked Cash if he would submit to such a test, realizing how humiliating it could be.

He laughed. "Sure, I'll take the test."

By chance we had recently bought a note from William Burroughs, a respected physician who dealt with geriatric patients. I called and verified that he was qualified to administer such a test that would meet a court challenge if necessary.

So, Gilbert and Dr. Burroughs met at our office, and spent an afternoon in the conference room.

"He's fine," was the doctor's conclusion. "He knows who he is and where he is. He knows his date of birth. He knows what the date is today and what day of the week it is. He knows who's President of the United States. He knows who the two previous Presidents were. He answered all the other questions correctly. There's nothing wrong with this man's mind. I consider him to be mentally competent."

Dr. Burroughs wrote out a lengthy report of his findings.

Gilbert smiled. "Now I'm the only one in my family that can prove they're sane."

Although it cost us $1,000 to have Dr. Burroughs administer and certify the test, we knew it could save us many thousands if Gilbert's family ever challenged his mental competency. It was a minor investment to prevent a potentially big problem.

We quickly completed the transaction.

We don't know if our sane note seller squandered all the cash or not, but somehow I doubt it.

Chapter 7
The Balance Owing

"**W**hat's the problem?" asked Gloria. "I could hear you muttering to yourself all the way out in the reception area."

"It's the balance owing on this confounded Jenkins note," I snorted.

"What's the matter with it?"

"Everybody's numbers are different. The seller says one thing. The payor says another. The servicing agent says another. And my numbers don't agree with any of them!"

"All four possibilities," mused Gloria. "That's really messy. I'm going to stay out of your way until you get that one cleared up."

"Good idea," I said, submerging back into my problem note.

Believe me, I wouldn't get so bothered about the balance owing on a note if it wasn't so important.

But think about it: the balance owing is what you're buying. That's what you're paying good hard cash for. If the balance you *think* you're buying isn't the balance you're *really* buying, you could lose big.

You could just take the word of the note seller that the balance owing is stated correctly. In the last chapter we saw why that's not such a great idea.

You could just take the word of the note payor that the balance owing is stated correctly. You've also had a few hints that the note payor gets nothing for helping you out with correct numbers, and could even become a competitor who tries to buy the note out from under you.

You could just take the word of the bank or the collection agent or whoever the servicing agent is that the balance owing is stated correctly. They make more mistakes than you might think.

So it's my highest gold-plated mega-priority on every note to make sure I know what the balance *really* is.

Let me illustrate:

A few years ago, an elderly man named Walter Lane contacted my firm with a note to sell. He told us he had something very important to do with the money, and emphasized that he was 90 years old and not getting any younger.

He sounded more eager than desperate, so I began to tell him what documents to send me in order to get a quick bid. The talkative old-timer broke in to just about everything I tried to tell him, explaining that he wanted the cash to pay his grandson's tuition at the Delphian School in Oregon.

That seemed a little curious—it must be *some* high school!—but I went on and told him to send me the note and several other documents, particularly the bank's payment record for the last two years.

Mr. Lane jabbered on and on, telling me all about his grandson Ben: the boy started out shy and introverted and completely turned around because of this great boarding school. I listened patiently, but reminded him that my list of documents was essential for me to give him a good bid.

Mr. Lane promised to send me the necessary items right away, but not before he explained in great detail how his relatives had been so impressed by Ben's progress, they pooled their money—originally intended for the boy's college—to put him through three years of the very expensive high school. I thought that was admirable, but hurried him to get off the phone and get the documents if he needed more money that quickly.

When I finally got dear Walter off the line, I was utterly charmed by the man's chatty enthusiasm.

The documents came in right away and the staff and I checked them out. We examined the note, the property and the payment record. The payor, an export company executive named Donna Gerber, was solidly creditworthy. Everything was in order. To my surprise, Mr. Lane had even included a letter from his doctor confirming that he was sound of mind—a nice touch from someone his age who was looking for money in a hurry. It made me smile.

Now I set out to verify the balance. First, I ran an amortization schedule on our computer. That gave me what the balance should be if all payments had been exactly as called for on the note.

Then, I checked the current payment record from United Commercial, the bank that was servicing the account. Their balance was a couple of thousand dollars higher than my figures showed! That was a sure sign the note was delinquent.

I called Mr. Lane, who assured me the note payments were current. He also chewed my ear some more about his wonderful grandson Ben. The boy was now 17 and self-confident, the old fellow told me, and he had one more year of this costly high school before starting college. He'd won a full scholarship to a good university, which really tickled the sweet old guy. But paying for this last year of high school was hard. Grandpa had this one last disposable asset, a note, which was the only way to pay the tuition. And grandpa was certain that the note payments were current.

I didn't think Mr. Lane was hiding anything, but I didn't take any chances. I checked the entire five years' payment record, and found that the bank had not posted the first three payments on the note. I could only guess that Mr. Lane had received three payments from Donna Gerber before United Commercial became the servicing agent, and the account had been set up incorrectly five years ago, a common occurrence.

So, I called Ms. Gerber to verify the balance. Donna acknowledged sending the first three payments directly to Mr. Lane. The mystery was solved, or so I thought. I immediately furnished her an amortization schedule indicating what we figured the balance was.

To my astonishment, Donna called back and angrily told me it was dead wrong. In no uncertain terms she explained exactly how she inherited a great deal of money the year before and paid an extra $10,000 directly to Mr. Lane.

Donna practically shouted, "My balance should be ten thousand dollars less than what you figured!"

Chastened, I meekly asked Ms. Gerber to send me a copy of her canceled check. She did, and it was just as she said. The bank had not been informed about this large balloon payment.

Well, I called Mr. Lane again and asked how he could have ignored such a big payment.

"What do you mean?" Walter asked indignantly. "I certainly didn't ignore it. I sent it to the school right away!"

"No," I said politely, "I understood that *you* knew about it. Why didn't the bank know about it?"

"Ask Donna," Grandpa huffed. "She's the fancy executive. Telling the bank is her job. I took care of my job and paid for that school."

Well! I could see where I stood! No point pursuing that line of questioning. At least everybody now agreed what the balance was.

I had Gloria send Donna a balance verification, and she thanked us profusely for being so careful in checking things out.

I gave Walter Lane a new bid, which he accepted. We closed the deal and I wished his grandson Ben well.

Things aren't always so easy to figure out. Every now and then a deal gets so complicated you wonder if it's really worth the work it takes to figure out.

My firm recently had the opportunity of buying an unusual note—secured by vacant land in a residential area. The property was on beautiful Bainbridge Island in the Pacific Northwest's Puget Sound—an empty lot in an expensive subdivision.

It wasn't just a vacant lot, either: two neighbors, the Thomases and the Beringers, had joined together and bought the empty lot between their two homes. This gave them both a larger yard and the satisfaction that another house would never be jammed between them.

The two neighbors had signed the note "jointly and severally," which means each was responsible for the entire payment of the note, even if the other did not pay anything. As it turned out, the Thomases were fastidious about payments and very creditworthy, while the Beringers were careless with their payments—generally a day late and a dollar short.

Puget Central Bank was collecting the payments for the note seller, an elderly woman named Winona Garville. Upon inspecting the payment record, we saw that the Thomases sent their half to Puget Central on the first of the month, while the Beringers paid the other half at the middle of the month, an arrangement the two neighbors had made between themselves.

However, when we ran the figures through our computer, we saw that the bank's calculation of the balance due was about $1,000 more than it should be. It seems the bank's computer was not too accurate when posting two payments in the same payment period. This was clearly Puget Central's fault.

We contacted the bank to straighten out the records. To our dismay, Puget Central notified us that all collections were being transferred to Oceanic Credit Group, a professional collection company in Florida. It seems that Puget Central had made no money collecting payments on private notes and contracts, and decided that their contract collection department could no longer justify its existence.

So Puget Central would no longer be servicing the account, and had notified its customers to pay Oceanic Credit Group. That put us in a bind. Our transaction hadn't closed, so we had no authority to tell Puget Central to transfer the collection to Wall Street Brokers.

That wasn't all. Mrs. Garville, the elderly seller, still had control of the note, and rejected Oceanic Credit Group as a servicing agent. She didn't want her collections made by any out-of-state outfit. Instead, she authorized a local company, Accurate Accounting Center, to collect the payments for her. She had trusted friends there, so that's where she wanted her payments to go until she sold her note.

That suited us just fine. Many professional contract collection companies are also in the business of note buying. Once they find out we're going to buy a note, some become automatic competitors with an advantage. They have the records, the documents, and the balances, and can delay or frustrate our purchase so they can buy the note. We didn't want it in the Florida firm's hands either.

But Puget Central had already turned the collection over to Oceanic Credit Group, which, in its turn, had sent payment coupons to the Thomases and the Beringers.

I contacted both the payors, telling them that our firm intended to buy the note, and when it closed, they'd be notified to send the payments to Wall Street Brokers' contract collection department. I also told them that the balance they owed should be about $1,000 less than Puget Central's records, which made them happy.

However, I didn't know that Mrs. Garville had sent the Thomases and the Berigners written instructions to make their payments to Accurate Accounting Center, which had also sent payment coupons—showing the bank's higher balance.

The Thomases and the Beringers, needless to say, were confused. Who do they pay? And whose balance was right?

I called them again and explained the situation, but they were skeptical.

The Thomases decided not to pay anyone until they were sure the balance was correct. But the Beringers sent their half-payment to Accurate Accounting Center—another complication.

Finally, as a last resort we hand-figured the entire payment history. We still came up with an amount about a thousand dollars less than Puget Central's.

By this time, the Thomases and the Beringers were getting annoyed. We decided to close on our balance, not the bank's. Payors don't complain about a wrong balance if it saves them money. And it was right as far as we were concerned.

We finally closed the transaction, retrieved the Beringers' half-payment, and sent legal proof to all parties that we had purchased the note. Now we had authority to tell the payors to send their payments to our contract collection department.

After the dust settled, both the Thomases and the Beringers signed a document verifying the balance that we had calculated.

Puget Central Bank, Oceanic Credit Group, and Accurate Accounting Center all closed out their contract collection of this note.

So you see, settling on the balance owing can be a real trial. But the balance on some notes is so complex it makes even rocket scientists scratch their heads.

One day a woman named Janet Desmond came into my office, wanting to sell a note that was a year old and had four more years to run.

The note was on her home in an exclusive community, which she had sold for $1.2 million. The home was only a short walk from that of one of the richest men in the world—a very prestigious neighborhood.

Janet Desmond's average-sized home had been lavishly remodeled and professionally decorated, but it was actually a so-so home in a hot-shot neighborhood.

The buyers of the home were a professional couple, Matt and Phyllis Wilson, both with high paying jobs. They had paid $300,000 cash down from the sale of their previous home. It was important to them to move to this expensive neighborhood for social reasons. However, when they applied for a bank loan to buy the house, they got only $600,000, half of the sale price.

That meant they had to ask Janet to accept a second lien and take a note for the $300,000 balance due at 12 percent interest, which was the normal interest rate at that time. I listened to her description of the note, and it sounded quite ordinary.

Then Ms. Desmond told me that even though the Wilsons were a high-income family, they seemed to be living on the edge. Because of the large monthly payment to the bank, they wanted to keep the payments on her note as low as possible.

She had accommodated their wishes, but in a way that made it an unusual note. She had set the monthly payments at $1,500, *which is only half of the $3,000 monthly interest*. In other words, the Wilsons weren't paying enough each month to even cover the interest, much less the principal.

That means instead of owing less every month, the Wilsons *owed more*. Paying a note down is called amortization, so this is called *negative* amortization. It's not common, but it's not completely unheard of.

However, it means a major headache for a note buyer like me. I no longer have a routine job in figuring the balance owing, I have to do some fancy mathematics to make sure I've got the numbers right, and in a negative amortization they can get pretty weird.

The weirdest result is this: every month the Wilsons were paying *nothing* on the $300,000 principal, and only $1,500 (*half* of the interest), so after five years of making payments, they would still owe $300,000 plus another $90,000 of unpaid interest! It sounds crazy, but people do it.

So when the five-year note was finished, the Wilsons would face a huge balloon payment of $390,000! And they would have already paid $90,000!

Personally, I think that gambling everything on being able to come up with such a huge balloon payment in a few years is a fool's game—especially for people already living beyond their means.

Then things got even weirder. Janet gave me a copy of the amortization schedule for the note—a table showing the monthly payments and final payoff amount.

"My good friend Darla at Lake-East Realty had her computer run this out for me," Janet said. "See how the balloon payment at the end is $422,500? This note is really valuable. I hope you can give me a good price."

Wait a minute. I had just calculated the balloon payment to be $390,000. What was Janet talking about?

Examining the amortization schedule carefully, I realized that it had been calculated using *compound interest*, not simple interest. Simple interest is the standard in the note buying industry.

What's more, the schedule showed the interest being compounded monthly, not annually. That was highly unusual. It meant that the $1,500 unpaid interest would be added to the principal balance every month, so that the Wilsons would pay interest on interest *monthly*.

I quickly scanned the note once more. I could find no mention that Janet had the right to charge compound interest, monthly or otherwise. I wondered if the Wilsons knew they were paying monthly compound interest.

"Did the Wilsons agree to pay this way?" I asked, holding up her amortization schedule.

"Oh, certainly," she assured me.

Maybe so, but a good note buyer checks out everything.

So I called Matt Wilson. The conversation began simply enough: I wanted to get an agreement about the balance due on the note, the $422,500 balloon payment, and the note's payment terms. Things deteriorated rapidly when I asked for verification in writing that he and his wife had agreed to the interest being compounded monthly.

Matt Wilson said, "I don't agree with that balloon payment amount and I don't know anything about monthly compounding on our note. And I'll tell you right now I won't pay any kind of compound interest, monthly or otherwise."

I tried to explain that he and his wife were already paying according to Janet's monthly compound interest amortization schedule.

He got the mistaken impression that I was trying force it on him as the prospective new note owner.

He became so furious I couldn't get across to him that I was simply trying to verify what Janet had already done. He quickly became completely uncooperative. And then he became extremely rude.

I gave up that try.

Things didn't look good for Janet Desmond's note.

I called her for a long talk. I explained that nothing in the note said she had the right to compound the interest at all, and certainly not monthly.

"But the computer printed the schedule," she said, as if that meant something.

"Your friend probably didn't understand and just took whatever the computer came up with first," I said, trying to be polite. "She should have selected a simple interest amortization schedule."

"Oh," she said, confused. Clearly, Janet was no expert on interest rates.

"But this is the important thing," I went on, "Matt Wilson is absolutely firm that he will not pay compound interest. You have to realize that he is not obligated to. So your best course is to change your amortization schedule to simple interest. And that means you'll get a lot less money at the end of the five years than you thought."

"How much less?" she asked, alarmed.

"Thirty-two-thousand-five-hundred less," I said. "The balloon payment based on simple interest is $390,000. That's all you're entitled to."

Janet was jarred but not distressed. "Okay," she said slowly, "if I do what you say, how much will you pay me for the note?"

"The negative amortization is a substantial risk," I said. "The best I can offer is $250,000."

Janet looked grim and thought about it for several minutes. Then she accepted my heavily discounted offer. So we signed a preliminary agreement—not so "preliminary" after all that work—and started working on the closing.

I figured out, by hand, the very complicated future payment stream and came up with a firm balance owing. I double and triple checked it.

I mailed the new payment schedule to the Wilsons asking for their signature on the estoppel document, which verifies the balance owing. I enclosed a note explaining that everything was now correct and proper.

Matt Wilson remained rude and uncooperative and refused to sign the estoppel.

Normally, I won't buy a note if the payor won't sign

an estoppel. It creates too much potential conflict over the balance owing. But I had spent so much time on this note and knew it so intimately that I bought it anyway.

For the next four years, the payments came in every month right on time.

Then one day the balloon payment came due, and I got a call from Matt Wilson asking very politely if I would grant an extension on the huge payment.

It seems that all those years the couple had been "house poor." They didn't go on vacation. They didn't buy new clothes. Everything they had went for the house payments and basic survival.

Phyllis Wilson was so tired of the situation, she convinced Matt to sell the house and move to a more affordable place. They came to the conclusion that living in a prestigious neighborhood wasn't worth sacrificing their hard-earned income.

I granted the extension, while musing to myself, "Why is it always the blankety-blank bad-tempered payors who later ask me for favors?"

Oh, well, at least the note paid off: as soon as the Wilson's house sold, we received the balloon payment in full.

Problems with the balance owing can have unexpected consequences. Try this one:

Jason Parks, an ambitious young man who had plans to start a new business in Atlanta, came into our office one day with a note for sale. It was secured by an apartment building. I examined the note and thought I recognized the payor's name. It was a foreign name and reminded me of the payor on a note we had purchased three years earlier.

I looked in the old file and found that it was, indeed, the same person—a good payor named Manfred E. Schärig. The documents showed what you'd expect, an excellent credit rating, spotless payment record, that sort of thing, and then my mind drifted to a vivid memory of buying that note. Well, actually, it was of Manfred.

It was only a brief meeting, but I remembered him as tall and fit, a personality as strong as his body, and speech heavy with a European accent—I couldn't tell if it was German or Swedish. I remembered him being very polite. I fleetingly thought it was too bad he was married. There was something about him….

The note seemed attractive, too, so I reviewed the supporting documents in detail and discovered some irregular extra payments that Jason hadn't calculated.

I contacted Manfred to let him know that we were considering buying the note on his property and to verify the balance with him. He suggested that we go over the figures together, and he came to our offices with his payment records.

Yes, it was the same man, I saw, and my memory of him was right. Tall, strong, exuding confidence and certainty, yet mannerly and thoughtful. I studied his face for a moment, admiring the smiling blue eyes that softened his well defined, almost craggy features.

We got to work on the note and found that my balance was correct, but Jason's wasn't. Manfred owed less money than Jason had shown. I felt the instant urge to protect Manfred's interests.

In order to prepare the estoppel document verifying the balance owing, I had to ask him a probing question:

"Are you married?" I said, hastening to add, "If you are, your wife will have to sign it, too."

"No," he said, looking right through me with those sparkling eyes, "I'm not married."

"Good!" I replied, then covered my tracks. "It will save time and make the estoppel easier."

Then came a routine question: "Manfred, are there any unfulfilled promises made by the seller or are there any property defects?"

His face darkened. "Yes," he said quietly. "In fact I have a list here."

He brought out a sheet of paper filled with bold hand-writing—in some other language. I couldn't make head or tail of it.

"This first item is a list of the repairs Jason promised, but he hasn't done them yet. And here are seven repair bills that he hasn't paid. But this is the most serious thing: we have a bad construction defect on the roof and Jason hasn't done anything about it."

Suddenly, the note looked problematic.

I said, "Manfred, I don't want you to sign my usual estoppel document verifying the balance until Jason resolves these issues. Let me call him and work it out."

Early the next week I told Jason of the problems, and advised him that I could not buy the note until he got the bills paid and made the necessary repairs to the building. He didn't seem very happy about that.

A couple of days later, I got a call from Manfred asking to come to the office for some advice.

When he arrived he looked worried, and quickly took the chair in front of my desk. "I took notes," he began.

I was puzzled, "Notes about what?"

"Two people called me yesterday. They're note buyers like you. Here are their names and phone numbers. They both said Jason had offered to sell them the note on my apartment building."

I just nodded. "It happens all the time, Manfred. He's shopping the note."

"But I'm concerned that one of these people will give Jason the money before he fixes the problems. Is there anything I can do?"

"Yes, there is." I advised him to see his lawyer about filing a notice against his property so it would be "of record" that bills needed to be paid, repairs made, and defects in construction remedied. That way if anyone wanted to buy the note, it would show up on the title report.

Several days went by and I heard nothing from Jason, so I carried on with my due diligence. Late one morning I called Manfred to check on his fire and hazard insurance. He cheerfully located the papers in his files and we went over the details. It only took a few minutes to determine that everything was in order. I was ready to say goodbye when Manfred said, "Would you like to have dinner with me tonight? There's a nice place right on Puget Sound."

Things were obviously changing. Maybe Manfred was beginning to feel about me the way I felt about him. When he came to pick me up that evening, he seemed more attentive and considerate than usual, but the conversation on the way to the restaurant and during a fine dinner remained down to earth and ordinary. Was I mistaken?

"Let's go for a walk along the waterfront," Manfred said, his eyes twinkling. I wasn't mistaken. He took me by the hand and after we had strolled along listening to the waves lapping the shore, he kissed me! Just like that! And then he took me home, the perfect gentleman all the way. At my door he politely said goodnight and departed with a smile.

Well, I was beginning to figure him out. He could be flawlessly proper or all business, but he had definite feelings about me. And as things got worse with Jason and his note, they got better with Manfred and his interest in me.

I knew Jason was now off to Atlanta to get that new business started. I called Manfred to see if he had filed the notice as I advised. There was still a chance that someone would buy the note without checking it out, and that could land Manfred in a lawsuit. Manfred said he had. Then he asked, "Do men wear wedding rings in this country?"

I got the message. I gave some offhand reply like, "Some do, some don't," but I knew what he was getting at. That was just his way. Now I knew things had changed a lot.

Several days later after we talked about the title report on Jason's note, Manfred asked with a twinkle, "How do you ask someone to marry you in this country?"

I just smiled and said, "You send a certified letter."

We both broke up in laughter.

That was as close to a formal proposal as I ever got, but shortly after Valentine's Day we were married.

The marriage was a better deal than any amount of money could ever be.

That was many years ago.

We're still married.

Oh, and I never did buy Jason's note.

Chapter 8
Foreclosures

"Look at all these files," said Larry Stevens, shaking his head.

I looked up at my father and said, "What about them? That's the foreclosure files. I'm archiving the old ones."

"There must be a dozen foreclosures here. That doesn't say much for our handling of problem notes."

"For the last two years?" I said. "Dad, that's not much more than six every year. How many big note buyers do any better?"

"When you look at it that way, I guess it's not so bad," he said, setting the files back in the sort box. "I've always looked on foreclosures as a disappointment. I can't help thinking we should have worked something out with the payor."

"Don't beat yourself up, Dad," I said. "You've saved more defaults from foreclosure than anyone I know."

There are all kinds of reasons payors stop paying on a note. And there are all kinds of things a note buyer can do to prevent or solve such a default. We at Wall Street Brokers pride ourselves on handling defaults to avoid foreclosing on the property.

> We've learned to listen very carefully to note payors, because they may not understand how serious their situation is, and a few words can make a big difference.
>
> Sometimes they're just down on their luck for a little while, and something like eliminating balloon payments, or waiving unpaid payments, or getting additional security, or even increasing the interest rate and lowering the payments will put things back on track.
>
> Sometimes you don't have to do anything: the payor goes through a rough period and comes out the other side, then brings the payments up to date without any urging. Doing nothing is the right thing in that case.
>
> We've also found that if you grow tired of a delinquent note and just want to get out of the picture, you may be able to sell it for cash. We don't like that path because the prices are low and buyers are hard to find. And when we do sell a delinquent note, we always sell it "without recourse" to avoid guaranteeing the note payments.
>
> But, when everything else fails, we take the available legal remedies, the most common being foreclosure. And, like everything else, there are many kinds of foreclosure.

Here's one of the kind that we really dread:

Gary Fredrickson was a disabled person with a modest income, but he managed to buy a $25,000 home with an ocean view in southern Oregon. His down payment came from a $5,000 whiplash settlement in a car accident that had reduced him to a social security disability recipient.

He bought it from a local couple, Dan and Phyllis Barnaby, who financed the remaining $20,000 on a first lien note at $150 per month. It was a nice affordable situation for this payor's meager income.

Two years later, the Barnabys ran into financial troubles and filed bankruptcy, listing the note as an asset. The bankruptcy trustee, George Otto, offered to sell the note to our firm. We noted that the property had increased in value to $35,000. The payment record was perfect.

But the rest of the note was far from it. It was what we call a *"frustrating first"*—a first lien with plenty of security, but lots of other problems: the Banarbys' note had several junior liens payable to Gary's ex-wife that resulted in Oregon's child support enforcement department attaching the title.

We knew we wouldn't lose our money because our note was secured first. The junior liens were subordinate to our position. But we also knew if Gary Fredrickson quit paying we'd be stuck notifying and finding the junior lienholders to wipe them off the title.

We bought the note, and Gary Fredrickson paid us for several years.

He lived frugally on his social security income. He enjoyed walking his dog on the ocean beach. He was a heavy smoker who enjoyed an occasional beer. He spent long hours doing volunteer work for the local community. He became an icon of this small town—a "local yokel" that everyone liked and knew. He chewed the fat with the local residents, pausing intermittently to cough.

One day, while going through our accounts, I noticed that his showed up delinquent. That was odd. Not long afterward, Rudolf Terfel, his attorney, sent us a letter informing us that Gary had passed away. Terfel said in closing that he'd notify us soon about the disposition of the property.

We mourned the loss of such a fine person, but we weren't concerned about the note. When a payor dies and there is equity in the property, the payments are normally kept up.

Four months later, Terfel sent us another letter. Gary Fredrickson's estate was insolvent. The property might not sell for enough to pay all liens. Terfel asked if we'd be willing to accept a "short sale". A short sale is when the creditor (that would be us in this case) releases the property for less than the balance due in order to get the property sold and clear title.

There was only $9,000 left on the note, so we didn't think a "short sale" would work on such a tiny debt. How much would they be short? No one knew the current market value of the property and there was no sale pending.

My husband Manfred had a business trip to Oregon, so I asked him to take a side trip to the former Frederickson property and inspect its condition. When he came back he disgustedly reported that it looked like a junkyard, trashed out, with an abandoned van and an inoperable bus with "Jesus Saves" painted on the side.

The home's inside was strewn with garbage, the roof leaked, and parts of the floors were rotten. Some windows were replaced with cardboard and walls were tilting. It was obvious Gary Frederickson had possessed neither the mental nor physical ability to care for the place.

Cleaning up such a disastrous mess would be prohibitively costly. The old saying "It should be remodeled with a bulldozer" was appropriate. We discussed the problem in a staff meeting. If we did bulldoze the house down, the vacant lot might be worth more than the lot with a wrecked house. We checked a few land-only sales in the area and found fair prices. So we stood a good chance of getting paid what we were owed if we took the property back and tore Gary's sad place down—since his estate was insolvent, no money would be coming from its other assets.

Our only alternative was to take the property back and tear the house down, much as we regretted it. We hoped to break even.

Then we had to face the irritating problem of locating all those junior lienholders. It wasn't easy. They had scattered to the four winds. We even hired a private investigator to find the ex-wife who'd moved across the country to Vermont. It took two months of searching.

Finally our attorney completed the foreclosure and we got the property back. We tore the house down, cleaned up the lot and sold it quickly.

Much to our relief, the price we got not only wiped out the costs, but also yielded one of those handsome profits!

Not every foreclosure has such a tragic cause and sad consequences. Some of them are actually uplifting, in a bizarre kind of way. Like this one:

One day my firm received an inquiry from the neighboring state of Idaho. The caller, a Mr. Nathan Reed, wanted to know if we bought second lien notes and would we give a quote on a transaction involving a business property?

Yes, I told Mr. Reed, we buy second lien notes. But sometimes business notes are too complicated for us to give an instant quote over the phone. We would have to examine all the documents, inspect the property, and interview the payor in order to come up with a price.

The note, explained Mr. Reed, wasn't actually on a business, it was on real estate only—a warehouse used by a businessman named Bergman who was the payor on the note.

That simplified matters, I replied. But when Mr. Reed told me the warehouse was in Troutville, a small town far from population centers, I told him we would still have to look it over and talk to Mr. Bergman before offering a price.

So, Mr. Reed sent us the necessary documents, which we examined. It looked like something we might be interested in, so I asked my husband Manfred if he'd like to take a little trip combining business and pleasure—neither of us had been to that part of Idaho and we could use some time away from the city.

When we arrived in Troutville I found that the warehouse was situated on a state highway among similar buildings and small business offices. The concrete warehouse was well maintained and had no structural problems that I could detect.

The fact that it was in a small remote town was the major strike against it: In the event I ever had to repossess the property and sell it to recoup my losses, how likely would I be to find a ready buyer out here?

I would be able to offer Mr. Reed only a deeply discounted price, but in the event he was agreeable, it looked like a fair deal—if the payor proved to be reliable.

So we went to talk to Mr. Donald Bergman, the payor. I was pleased to find that he and his wife owned and operated three furniture stores in the region and been in business for thirty years. They used this building to warehouse some of their furniture and kept the property in good condition.

"We're workaholics," Mr. Bergman told me. He was a vigorous, likeable man in his middle fifties.

"You'll have no problem receiving payments," he assured me.

The payment record showed he'd always made his payments on time.

I later asked Manfred his impression—he's a very shrewd judge of character and has an almost eerie ability to spot a phony.

Manfred just said, "He's a good solid man."

That was good enough for me.

The Bergmans had a small equity in the property—not much, really—so the price I offered Mr. Reed for the note was discounted almost 50 percent.

I explained to him that this kind of property was something of a white elephant in a small town. He understood and accepted our offer. We closed the deal.

The monthly payments came in regularly. I kept in touch

with Mr. Bergman by telephone for the first few months, and during a conversation he told me that there had been a fire in one of his buildings, but it wasn't the one on which we held the note. The other building and its contents were a total loss. I expressed my regrets and didn't give it any further thought.

Not long afterward, however, Mr. Bergman called me and said he thought he might have to file bankruptcy. I was floored. How could that happen?

Through a serious clerical error, it seems, he had let his insurance policy lapse. The building that burned had contained $200,000 worth of inventory that he still owed money on. The loss put him in a terrible financial position.

I liked Mr. Bergman and spent many hours on the phone with him going over his finances and offering suggestions that could keep him out of bankruptcy.

The next few months went by without any payments from Mr. Bergman. It was clear that we would have to repossess the building. If he fought it, that could make my life miserable and ultimately force him into the bankruptcy court we both wanted him to avoid.

So I contacted him with a suggestion that could help us both: I asked him for a *deed in lieu of foreclosure.* Instead of going through the messy legal trauma of repossession, he could simply *sign over the deed* to the property to my firm and *we would continue paying* the first mortgage while looking for someone to buy the warehouse.

By agreeing, he would sacrifice his modest equity in the property—a loss for him—but could avoid a serious stain on his credit rating if he could stay out of bankruptcy.

I was aware that if Mr. Bergman filed bankruptcy, the bankruptcy trustee would have the power to reverse his deed in lieu of foreclosure to me, but the equity was so small that I was willing to take the calculated risk that the bankruptcy trustee would not find it worthwhile.

Mr. Bergman faced this heavy test of character with

dignity. "Go ahead," he said. "I'll sign the deed." I was deeply impressed by his integrity.

I made an appointment to meet him at the building two days later—I had to go alone this time; Manfred had other business to tend to.

I got to the place in Troutville at the proper time, but Mr. Bergman didn't show up. Forty-five minutes went by. I worried that something had gone wrong. After more than an hour, Mr. Bergman arrived with profuse apologies for being late. He had been tied up in a meeting trying to pull his business back together.

Now to get the documents prepared. In the Yellow Pages we found a lawyer whose office was right down the street from the warehouse building. There weren't many lawyers in this little town, so I felt lucky until we walked into the offices of Mr. Edward Campbell, attorney at law. He was at least 90 years old. He couldn't hear us very well. He shook a little. But he said he would take care of it. Mr. Bergman and I were not so sure.

However, a week later Mr. Campbell sent us all the papers perfectly done. My firm now held the deed to the warehouse property. We had avoided the usual turmoil of foreclosure, but now had a warehouse on our hands.

I went to the only real estate agency in town, where Ben Taylor, a very professional man with a big cowboy hat, listed our warehouse for sale. He was cheery and helpful, but had a wait-and-see attitude about ever selling the property.

Within a short time, I got a call from a man named Jonathan Walters who was renting the building next door to the warehouse we had repossessed. He had found out about our warehouse while talking to Mr. Bergman and said he was interested in buying the building.

I referred Mr. Walters to our real estate agent Ben Taylor and we quickly sold the property for substantially more than we had paid for the note. We were so happy with the sale that I told the escrow agent to hold out enough cash to buy Ben Taylor some fancy cowboy boots to go with his hat.

When everything was done, I called Mr. Bergman to thank him for being such an honorable man. By not dragging us into a conflict, he had made it possible for my firm to cover its losses quite nicely.

We will always remember him.

That's a rare foreclosure because it wasn't a foreclosure at all—it was a deed in lieu of foreclosure. Most are a little more contentious. Like this one:

The first sign of trouble was the missed payments. The note had paid promptly since we bought it three years earlier. It was a good note, secured by a motel and restaurant on a busy highway in the little desert town of Columbia, in Eastern Washington. But now, nothing.

We called the Dunromin Motel and Café to find out what was going on. An unfamiliar voice, a man who refused to identify himself, answered the phone and gave us the news every note buyer dreads: the payor, Dwane Patel, had left the country. Skipped out.

Why? Well, the main highway through Columbia had been diverted, and the motel was losing customers. The facility slowly crumbled and Patel just couldn't make it any more. He moved to England.

Shocked and alarmed, we began the long and frustrating process of foreclosure. While the decaying Dunromin Motel and Café sat vacant, we announced a foreclosure sale open to all bidders.

The announcement had one good result: Tina Moore, a local woman who worked as a paralegal in a law office near the Dunromin, called and said she'd be interested in buying the property after the foreclosure was over, if we got it back. At least we had a lead to recover our money.

Thursday, the day before the foreclosure sale, I left our Seattle office for eastern Washington to witness it. While crossing the Cascade Mountains on Interstate 90, I got a reminder that where there are high peaks, cell phones don't always work. My calls to Tina Moore didn't even get out of the antenna.

However, a little later while I was driving through an open valley beyond the crest, an anxious Tina called and got through. She told me that two suspicious men had been poking around the Dunromin property for about an hour. Tina's uncle works at the Riverside Motors car lot right across the street, and has a full view of the motel.

I figured they were a couple of the soon-to-be-ex-owner's cohorts, which spelled real trouble. I was about to ask Tina to keep them from taking anything when the Interstate curved to hug a granite cliff and my cell phone went completely dead. Mountains!

The two strange men were not completely unexpected. When there's a motel foreclosure, payors typically try to salvage—let's be blunt about this—*steal* as much personal property as they can before they lose the real estate.

They steal the televisions, gardening tools, supplies, furniture, air conditioners, vacuum cleaners, maid carts, towels, cleaning supplies, telephone systems, and so on – property not extremely valuable, but expensive and difficult to replace.

 We had taken precautions against this very eventuality by filing Uniform Commercial Code claims (UCC's) on all the Dunromin's personal property.

Since the two strange men had no legal right to take anything from the motel, I called the Columbia police when I finally found a pay phone at the Elkhorn Rest Stop some twenty minutes after Tina called me—it's lucky I keep quarters in my car. It's unlucky it had started to rain.

While I got drenched at the pay phone, the Columbia

police hemmed and hawed, and didn't seem too interested in my predicament. After five minutes of pleading, I got them to agree to stop by the motel and ID the two men. They agreed to ask the men to not take anything until I could show up with my legal papers.

After a tense and rainy drive into increasingly barren desert, I finally reached Columbia and saw a huge moving truck in the motel parking lot. I pulled my car right behind it to block the way out.

I got out of my car into a pelting rain and confronted the man who turned out to be Dwane Patel's Chinese silent partner, Andrew Chin. We stepped under the motel's eaves for shelter, where he politely introduced me to his elderly Guatemalan father-in-law, Arturo Gama, who spoke little English. Chin told me they'd driven nearly a thousand miles from Southern California to recover some of their investment, and were dead tired.

Chin told me that when the police responded to the scene, he had gone to rent a truck and Gama was taking a nap. They awakened Gama, asked for ID and waited for Chin's return, then told them politely to wait for me, which they did.

I spoke intently to Chin, showing him my legal documents, especially the UCC filings, and explaining that he had no right to take anything, even if he was the key backer of the man who'd run out on both of us. I asked for his agreement to not take anything.

Chin was at first outraged, then disappointed, but finally gave in. I don't know if it was the police scare, me physically blocking the truck, their being tired from their 16-hour drive from California, the fact they'd likely need two trucks instead of one, or whether it was raining cats and dogs and they didn't feel like loading up all that stuff—but we parted amicably.

I was stressed out and dead tired myself. After briefly walking around the sadly run-down motel, I went for a quick dinner so I could get to bed early. When I paid the bill and went to leave, there was the Chinese/Guatemalan pair again! I said goodbye once more and drove down the block to check into the Northstar Motel—the Dunromin was shut down, of course.

I had barely finished checking in when Chin and Gama came up to the counter and broke into a big smile. Chin joked that they were probably staying in the room next to mine (they weren't), and we said goodbye a third time that Thursday.

I got up early Friday morning and went to the court-house for the foreclosure sale. I took a seat in the lobby of the courthouse and learned a lot about noxious weeds for the next hour. Noxious weeds are a real problem in some counties!

Finally, our lawyer, Jim Elliott, showed up, and Tina Moore popped up a few minutes later. Our time arrived, and our lawyer went through the foreclosure procedure, offering the property to the highest bidder. Nobody made a bid, so ours won, and we got the property back—for $70,000 less than what Patel still owed on our note, because that's all the place was worth in its present condition.

Then my lawyer and I did the local courthouse shuffle, going from here to there, recording documents, paying fees, getting "official stamps" and so on.

At last, the foreclosure was over.

Then came the problem of retrieving our money. Tina Moore came forward, telling me she wanted to buy the motel property, remove the buildings and lease it to the owner of Riverside Motors, the car lot across the street where her uncle worked.

I had lunch with Tina and her husband, Tom, and then went with them back to the Dunromin to get into a few units and see how they looked—not of much interest because she was just going to have them removed to make way for an auto sales lot. While Tom inspected the exercise room, Tina and I talked about the terms and conditions and price of a sale.

We came to a tentative oral agreement. I gave her the keys for safekeeping, and to allow her to thoroughly inspect the property over the next few days. I trusted Tina because of our previous contact and the obvious fact that she was a pillar of her community.

Tina checked around and was surprised to find how expensive it would be to clear the property. She then made a written offer for $50,000 less than what I expected. I didn't like it, because we would actually lose money at that price. Impasse—we wanted $50,000 more than she wanted to pay.

We had to think fast. Thank goodness all the personal property was there. There were 45 new televisions, new sets of furniture and brand new microwaves, plus much else. There were snow plowing machines, washers, dryers, towels, cleaning supplies, gardening and building tools, and building materials.

We made a deal with Tina that she could have all the personal property. She accepted and held a huge "motel yard sale" where she collected more than $20,000 in cash.

Furthermore, because our bid was $70,000 less than the balance Dwane Patel owed us, we had a legal right to obtain a deficiency judgment against him. I offered to assign our rights to Tina and allow her to pursue payment from Patel. Since she worked at a law office and had a nice boss who would help her for free, she agreed.

So, together with the money she got from the personal property and the hope she could collect over $70,000 from Mr. Patel, Tina was happy. She bought the property for more than she wanted to pay, but the extras made it all worthwhile.

So, even the problematic foreclosures can have tolerable outcomes. Trying to make the best of a foreclosure is not easy, though. It requires hard-headed business sense and soft-hearted human kindness mixed in proper proportions. The trouble is, you never know what the proper proportions are while you're in the foreclosure process. In fact, sometimes a foreclosure can make you downright obsessive. Like this one:

A long-time family friend called me out of the blue. I'd known John Richie and his wife Martha since childhood. They were old friends of my father Larry, who sold them their first note back in 1954. They'd been buying notes for over 50 years.

I asked John about the recurring health problems I knew he'd had over the past year. He'd been hospitalized several times. At one point, the doctor didn't think John would make it. But he did, against all odds. He was home recuperating, many thanks to Martha's loving devotion and good cooking.

"Lorelei," John said, finally broaching his real purpose. "I've got a note that I'd like to sell."

That's odd, I thought. John *selling* a note? Note buyers like John usually hang onto them. They buy notes – they don't sell notes.

That piqued my interest, so I asked him to tell me what he had in mind.

"It's a problem note, Lorelei. I'll just be honest with you. I bought it four years ago from a guy named Archibald— he's the original seller of the property. It had been paid on for three years before I bought it, so the note is seven years seasoned."

"That's good, John, not bad," I said.

"I know, but here's the problem: there hasn't been a payment for over six months. The payor is a lady named Patty Payne. She owes $25,000."

"That's a lot, John," I said.

"I know, and it's weird. She paid every payment on time for six and a half years, and then poof—nothing."

"What do you mean, nothing?"

"She's vanished. I wrote her several letters. Nothing. I even drove to her house twice. It looks vacant. Heck, it looks a *mess*. When I checked, the fire insurance had been canceled.

"Lorelei, I need to get out now and get some cash. I don't want the hassle of foreclosure and fixing up the house. My health isn't good and I don't need stress."

"Not exactly my kind of note either," I half-joked, "but let me look into it and I'll call you next week."

I don't usually buy delinquent notes because of the lack of a most important legal protection: *holder in due course status.* If Patty Payne had legitimate gripes about why she quit paying, I would not be protected. She could get out of paying all or part of the money, and I would lose money.

But, experience has shown me that the longer the note is seasoned, the less chance that the payor is likely to try such shenanigans. A seven-year-old delinquent note wasn't likely to give me that kind of trouble.

That weekend I drove to the property in the Mountainview Terrace area of Tacoma. As I neared the address, the worst house on the block stood out, and, yes, it was the one!

I got out and looked around. This cosmetically-challenged house was definitely vacant. Newspapers covered the porch and a thicket of envelopes and magazines stuck out of the mailbox. The front lawn was overgrown and garbage littered the back.

Then something incongruous caught my eye. The front and back doors were brand new, and expensive. That made no sense at all.

I checked next door, where a large family lived in a tiny house. They only knew that a crew had painted and carpeted the interior about six months earlier. Nobody had been there since.

This was getting totally bizarre. I left and sought out a local real estate agent who specialized in selling and buying "fixer-uppers" in the area. He knew the house.

"It's okay," Denzel Williams said. "But the layout's not so great. It's a two bedroom, but you have to walk through one of them to get to the bathroom."

I sighed and asked, "What would you pay for this house, in its present condition, if I were to sell it to you?"

"Figuring my fix up and sales costs, I couldn't pay any more than $60,000. If you put it on the market, you might be able to get $70,000 tops."

I thanked Mr. Williams for his help and asked several other local real estate agents to double-check comparable sales.

The consensus was that the price was on target and the land with no house was worth $40,000. I didn't like the fact there was no fire insurance, because I knew the difficulty and expense of insuring a vacant house in poor condition. I reasoned the land would cover the $25,000 Patty Payne owed on the note, even if the place burned down.

The next day I received the paperwork from my old friend John Richie and agreed to pay him $17,000 for the delinquent note. I chuckled when he and his wife came into my office to pick up their money and endorsed the back of the note "without recourse."

"Yes," John said, "I remember twenty years ago when you taught me to always write 'without recourse' if I sell a note so I don't have to guarantee the payments. I sure don't want to guarantee anything on this one!"

"It's no prize, alright," I admitted. "But I'll get all the money one way or another, plus interest. With all the lawyers I work with, another foreclosure isn't going to bother me. I just have to keep eating nails for breakfast, like my father taught me."

John laughed and said, "You're already tough as nails, Lorelei. But you're a softie when it comes to helping out friends. We appreciate you taking this problem off our hands."

The Richies left with their check and I owned a delinquent note.

And a mystery.

Where was Patty Payne? And why did she vanish?

I've foreclosed on a lot of payors who didn't have any equity and didn't care if they lost the property.

But I never saw anyone with seven years of equity suddenly quit paying. If Patty Payne had problems, she could sell the property and get lots of money—not just disappear and abandon her nest egg!

I had to find her. My executive assistant, Gloria, and I went to work. We checked public records. We called an ex-husband. We called ex-employers. We called neighbors. No one knew anything. She was just missing.

"Hey," I wondered, "Is she a real Missing Person?"

I called Pierce County Missing Persons and asked. No, she wasn't listed. On a whim, I asked if I could report her as missing and got the answer I expected: "Sorry, Ma'am. You can't report her missing because you're a creditor. We can't take reports from creditors. It has to be family or a personal friend. Goodbye."

"But she has equity!" I protested to the dialtone.

I told my lawyer to go ahead with the foreclosure. He sent legal papers to Patty Payne's last known address in Mountainview Terrace—all the law required. She had to pay up or lose the property.

Nearly two months later I received a check for three payments on the note. It was written by someone named David Lloyd. The address was near the state capital of Olympia. There was no phone number.

It didn't matter. The check wasn't even close to being enough to stop the foreclosure. Then why did it arrive?

The deepening mystery got to me. So, on a Sunday I drove to the address on the check—Foster Drive in Tumwater, Washington. I knocked on the door and a woman answered.

"Are you Patty Payne?" I asked.

"I am," she said.

"I've been looking for you for months."

"I know," she replied, and invited me in.

We sat in her living room where she brought some tea. Finally, the mystery unfolded.

"I remarried two years ago," she began. "My name is Patty Lloyd now. We moved here from the Tacoma house."

She saw me looking around at the packing boxes and other signs of moving.

"They're foreclosing this house too. But we're moving back to Mountainview Terrace."

My jaw dropped, but I just let Patty Lloyd go on.

"Oh, yes. I know it sounds unlikely. Just hear me out. Last week we were down in the dumps, very low. Then a man named Sam O'Conner contacted me. He invests in real estate. He found out about the foreclosure on the Tacoma house and hired a private detective to find me. I told him this house was also in foreclosure, and he bought it from us, just like that. Now we have money. We can pay off all the back payments on our Tacoma house next week."

Patty Lloyd then told me why she had been so hard to find. Shortly after she married and moved to Tumwater, she and her new husband took in Patty's ailing mother.

They rented out the Tacoma house for nearly a year, and when the renters left, the place was trashed. They'd just started to remodel the place when Patty was seriously burned in a cooking accident and hospitalized for four weeks.

Her husband David took charge of the finances.

Patty came home to heal up and resume caring for her mother's heart disease, but despite all medical treatment, her mother soon died.

Almost simultaneously, her husband David had a series of mild strokes, and Patty was totally absorbed taking care of him for the past six months.

This incredible streak of bad luck was behind everything. David had not made the payments for the past six months, even though he assured Patty that everything was taken care of. She was unaware that his impaired memory had blotted out their financial well-being.

She finished: "Two weeks ago I went back to the Tacoma house and found the foreclosure notice in the mailbox. Until then I had no idea the payments were late. I only had enough in the bank for three payments, so that's why we didn't send the whole thing. I thought we'd lost everything. Then Sam O'Connor saved us, bless his heart."

The Lloyds paid off their delinquent payments and I stopped the foreclosure. They're back in Mountainview Terrace with a new lease on life.

If they can keep it up for seven more years, their note will be paid off.

For me, it was never just about the money, but I knew I'd get it back one way or another. I'm glad it was *this* way.

FAST CASH

PART THREE

Technicalities

FAST CASH

Chapter 9
Details

"'The Devil is in the details,'" said Gloria, standing in my office door waving a newspaper. "This article says what you just said five minutes ago."

"I'm sure reporters say it too," I muttered to the papers on my desk.

"No, I mean everybody's saying it these days. Do you think more people are reading the fine print?"

"No, I don't," I said, looking up at her.

"Oh? What, then?"

"I think more things are happening that weren't even in the fine print."

"You're still upset by that Nordway note."

"Of course I am," I said.

"There's no way you could have seen that coming."

"That's what I'm talking about. But it doesn't make things any better."

The note business has many rewards, money being the most obvious. But, once you've mastered the intricacies, it's just plain fun.

Until something like the Nordway note sneaks up on you, that is. This is one of the best (or worst) examples of the pitfalls you can never be prepared for in this business. It's the archetypal example of "the Devil is in the details."

Nearly four years ago our firm bought a large note. There was nothing unusual about it. We bought it from an immigrant named Dominic Todas, a bold businessman who took one risk too many. He had suffered financial reverses and needed fast cash—the most ordinary reason that people sell their notes.

The note itself had been created when Mr. Todas sold one of his homes to a couple, Fred and Thelma Nordway, for $300,000. They paid $100,000 down, leaving $200,000 on a note secured by the property.

When Dominic Todas came to us with the note, the Nordways had been paying regularly for two years. We did our due diligence and saw no problem.

We wrote to the Nordways and asked that they sign an estoppel document that verified the balance and stated that they didn't have any rights, claims, defenses or offsets against the note.

We wrote that we were assuming everything in the estoppel was correct, and that if we didn't hear from them by our scheduled closing date, we would presume that the estoppel was true and correct.

We didn't hear back. We knew that in the real world payors often won't sign an estoppel document, but will almost always tell you if anything is wrong with it. And besides, we had Mr. Todas' written warranties that there were no rights, claims, defenses or offsets against the note.

So we went ahead with the closing and gave Dominic Todas his fast cash.

Regrade National Bank, which we knew well, had serviced the note for Mr. Todas, so it made sense to leave it there. We agreed to take over Todas' half of the small servicing fee and the Nordways continued to pay the other half. Regrade National held all the original documents, including the note.

The Nordways paid without any problem for three years. Then they missed two payments in a row. We called them. They wouldn't talk to us and referred us to their attorney, David Barstock.

To my shock, Mr. Barstock told me he had instructed his clients that they should not make any more payments. The remaining balance of $170,000 would never be paid.

"Why?' I asked, flabbergasted.

The answer was completely unexpected: The Nordways had discovered contamination on the property that had also migrated underground into a neighbor's property. It was in the previous location of an exterior heating oil barrel. The barrel had been removed many years earlier when Mr. Todas converted the home to natural gas heat. The Nordways had the soil tested before putting in a new garden and the results came back showing heating oil residue.

But, we told Mr. Barstock, the Nordways did not give notice of any such claims when we sent them the estoppel document.

Mr. Barstock then sent us a copy of an agreement between the Nordways and Dominic Todas saying that if they discovered any contamination on the property they could pay for cleaning it up and offset whatever they paid against what they owed on the note.

An offset!—the nemesis of note buyers. It's a deduction from the balance that a payor can claim under certain circumstances. Most are like the Nordways' claim, to pay the cost of fixing some problem with the property. But the law protects note buyers from offsets with a special status called "holder in due course." If you follow all the rules as a note buyer, you have this special immunity from offsets. But, as we were about to find out, even the most bulletproof legal protections can have holes in them.

The agreement between the Nordways and Dominic
Todas was news to us. We dug in our file and could not find
any such agreement. Had we known about it, we certainly
would not have bought the note. We had those written warranties from Mr. Todas stating that the Nordways had no rights
or claims other than what was included in the note or recorded
at the county recorder's office.

But despite what we believed, there on our desk sat a
copy of the agreement sent by David Barstock. Dominic Todas
never disclosed that he had this agreement with the Nordways.

We knew that Mr. Todas was broke, so there was no
sense in trying to collect from him for violating his warranties.

But we felt untouched by this claim anyway. We called
Mr. Barstock back and told him that we were a holder in due
course, immune from such claims. We asserted that the
Nordways couldn't refuse to pay us because there's nothing
on the face of the note about their side-agreement with Mr.
Todas. We emphasized that we bought this note for value, had
no knowledge of the Nordways' claims, and were a holder in
due course.

Mr. Barstock wouldn't budge from his adamant re-
fusal to instruct his clients to pay, so we were forced to seek a
court order. We hired an attorney, Roberta Dix, who filed a
lawsuit on our behalf to foreclose the Nordways' property.
We accelerated the note—making it due and payable in full as
of the day's date—and pressed our legal action to collect on
the note, basing our claim on the fact that we were a holder in
due course.

When Mr. Barstock responded on behalf of the
Nordways, one of their defenses was that we were *not* holders
in due course—because we did not have possession of the
note, Regrade National Bank did. You can't be a holder in due
course without physical possession of the original note.

That was terrible! Not because Mr. Barstock was
wrong, but because he was right. You can't be a holder in due

course without physical possession. We were about to go to court and lose $170,000 because our own servicing agent, Regrade National Bank, had physical possession of our note.

The day before before our court hearing, we got to thinking. It was one of those "don't pick the lock, take the door off the hinges" kind of things. If the problem was that the bank had the note, why don't we go to the bank and get it?

We went to Regrade National and they gave us our note, no questions asked! Of course, they were unaware there was any legal action about it.

When we went to the courthouse the next morning, we quietly slipped the note to our lawyer, Ms. Dix. She was shocked for two reasons: one, she herself should have thought of such an obvious move, and didn't (obviously, Mr. Barstock hadn't either); and two, the documents she had filed didn't include the fact that we had possession of the note.

That could lose us the case, even though we now had physical possession of the note—a judge can only rule on the record before him, so our lawyer couldn't argue on the new evidence.

How many of these shocks would we have to endure? We had to get our new evidence into the written record somehow! But there was no way to stall the hearing.

Judge Anston Jones entered the courtroom and opened the hearing. As expected, Mr. Barstock argued that we weren't a holder in due course because we didn't have possession of the note.

But Ms. Dix replied, yes, we were a holder in due course, because Regrade National Bank—as our agent—was holding the note for us. So possession by the bank should be deemed to be possession by us.

Judge Jones was very interested in our case and had prepared by careful study of the Uniform Commercial Code and other applicable law. He ruled that because the Nordways were paying half the service fee, the bank was a *dual agent*, not just our agent. Therefore, we were not a holder in due course because the bank held the note for both of us.

In desperation, Ms. Dix said to Judge Jones, "My client told me just before the hearing that they do have physical possession of the note. Here it is, your honor."

She handed it to the judge.

Mr. Barstock looked aghast.

Judge Jones scheduled another hearing to allow time to complete the record with this new evidence.

That hearing never came, because the Nordways knew they were going to lose. We had possession of the note.

We entered into negotiations and they agreed to pay us off. We received a cashier's check from the Nordways in the full amount owing.

If that doesn't make it clear why note buyers need to get the original note, nothing will.

Someone always asks me during my presentations, what happens if you *can't* get the original note? Good question. We've already talked a little about how to locate a missing note. But sometimes the note really *is* lost. Then you have only one reasonable alternative: create a replacement note.

How do you do that? With great difficulty:

One day an attorney named Dale Cole called with a huge note to sell. He told me he was handling the estate of Juanita Smith, a young single mother who had died on the operating table. That alone was enough to catch my attention, so I listened further.

Mr. Cole sketched the situation: The young woman had been lucky enough to inherit a house some time earlier, which she had sold to Larry and Nancy Arnold, reliable payors who were now making monthly payments. The regular monthly income had supplemented Juanita's own salary and allowed her and her two daughters to live comfortably, even though they were a single-parent family.

The note had been her main asset. The estate now needed to liquidate the asset for cash. The note was secured by a beautiful home and the Arnolds were impeccably credit-worthy.

Mr. Cole and I settled on a cash price and we signed a preliminary agreement. He sent me all the documents he had. We proceeded with our due diligence, investigating the merits of the note. Everything looked fine until we asked for the original note. As is common in cases involving a deceased person, no one knew where the original note was.

We couldn't go any further until the original was found. To solve this crucial problem, Mr. Cole and our office worked together on a thorough search for the missing note. We looked in all the usual places and all of the *un*usual places.

- The servicing agent didn't have the note,
- nor did the original property closer (the person who closed the original sale of the house from Juanita to the Arnolds).

These are the most common parties who might have a note if it turns up missing. We even looked in the estate's court file. It wasn't there.

The note was lost and no one could tell us its whereabouts. Now we had only one viable option: the Arnolds had to supply us with a replacement note with their valid signatures on it.

Mr. Cole wrote a lawyerly letter to the Arnolds telling them the note was lost and asking them to sign a replacement note and accompanying documents. The Arnolds never responded.

After a couple of weeks with no reply, Mr. Cole sent the Arnolds another letter—this time via certified mail—asking that they sign the papers because the estate needed to sell the note for cash. Mr. Cole received the certified receipt signed by both of the Arnolds. Now we knew they had received the letter.

Still no response.

I told Mr. Cole that I would personally contact the Arnolds. I telephoned several times and only got an answering machine. They never answered my numerous calls.

Mr. Cole was getting discouraged.

We had no idea why they weren't calling back. I asked Mr. Cole if he knew any reason why the Arnolds were stonewalling us. He didn't.

Then I asked, "Do they know Juanita's two little orphans need money?"

Dale Cole was silent a long moment, then said, "You know, I was being so efficient with my request that I never mentioned *why* we needed to sell the note."

"Let me handle this," I said.

I wrote to the Arnolds and told them the whole story:

Juanita was in her late 20s and overweight. She had gone to Founders General Hospital in Seattle for a medical procedure, stapling her stomach to help her lose weight. A hidden heart condition emerged during the surgery, and she died despite the best medical response. Now her two young children, age two and four, were orphans. Their father had died two years earlier. Now their only hope was to get a replacement note so that the estate could sell it and have sufficient money to care for them.

I included a replacement note for the Arnolds' signatures, as well as affidavits.

A few days later I received the signed replacement note and other papers. Nothing else came in the envelope—no explanation, no comment.

Only what we needed.

We went ahead and bought the replacement note, the estate had the money it needed, and the children were provided for.

I sent a "thank you" to the Arnolds, indicating the appreciation of all people involved in the transaction. Their

[handwritten note: BANKRUPTCY NOTES — buyer cannot be a holder in due course]

only response was sending the monthly payments on the note for several years, until they finally paid it off.

So, the sad details of Juanita's orphaned girls prompted a replacement note that gave the story a happier ending.

Now back to offsets. As we saw with the Nordway note, offsets are details that just invite devils by the dozen. My firm ran into another problem with offsets that, if anything, is even more complicated.

In the middle of a recent July, a bankruptcy trustee named Kirk Nethercutt contacted me, asking for a bid on a note in one of his bankruptcy cases. I've bid on many bankruptcy notes, and knew that I was getting into a maze of technicalities. I submitted a bid anyway, knowing that the potential rewards outweighed the risks. Here's how it happened:

The bankrupt person in this case was a former tavern owner named Kevin Moran. He had owned the land, building, equipment and business of his Oakwood, Oregon tavern. The business was highly profitable until he made a fatal error.

One summer, a familiar crew of migrant workers came to town, and, as usual, enjoyed slipping into Kevin's place, downing a few too many, and having a good time brawling with anyone who cared to join in.

This year they broke the place up more than usual. Most of these itinerant workers were Latino, and Kevin got so mad at them that he swore he'd never serve Mexican-Americans in his tavern again—and he swore it in public.

The next thing Kevin Moran knew, he got sued for violating the civil rights of Mexican-Americans—racial discrimination. Customers kept coming anyway, but Kevin was buried in legal expenses far in excess of his earnings. There was nothing to do except sell his tavern fast.

Kevin found that a local man, George Thomas, was willing to pay $210,000 for the package of land, building, equipment and business. George borrowed the $50,000 down payment and gave his lender a first mortgage on the property. George then gave a second mortgage for $160,000 to Kevin, secured by the tavern property—and, as a "good faith" gesture, George gave Kevin a mortgage on his personal residence (which had no equity), and that solved things for a while.

George ran the tavern successfully. He faithfully paid Kevin every month.

However, Kevin lost his discrimination suits and the payments from George were no longer adequate to cover his expenses. When the next summer arrived, Kevin finally threw in the towel and filed bankruptcy.

Kirk Nethercutt, the court-appointed bankruptcy trustee, found that Kevin Moran's estate had only one sizable asset: George's $160,000 note, which had to be sold to satisfy claims against the estate. Nethercutt sent out a request for bids on the Thomas note and that's where I came into the picture.

Notes from a bankruptcy suffer a legal defect that lowers their value tremendously: the law specifies that the buyer of a note through operation of law—as in a bankruptcy proceeding—cannot be a holder in due course. As you saw with the Nordway note, that privileged status is designed to protect note holders (it works in almost all cases—we fell into one of the rare exceptions because we didn't have physical possession of the note).

However, the bankruptcy defect turned out to be merely redundant: the Thomas note was defective when Nethercutt got it. It contained an offset clause. It stated that if Kevin Moran didn't pay the tavern's bills, George Thomas could pay them and subtract the amounts from his payments on the note to Kevin. An offset of any kind makes a note "non-negotiable" under the Uniform Commercial Code's rules.

"Non-negotiable" is a technical term that could be confusing. It does *not* mean "non-saleable." It just means that

" NON - NEGOTIABLE " =2f ...

the note doesn't meet all the legal tests to assure its value when transferred.

The owner of a non-negotiable note by law cannot be a holder in due course. So the Thomas note disqualified any note buyer from being from a holder in due course even before Kirk Nethercutt took it into his bankruptcy files.

As if that wasn't enough, we found that George's note had more problems: its security was poor, since it was a second lien, and another note had first claim on the property in the event of a foreclosure.

Then we found that Nethercutt did not know the exact balance of the Thomas note. Worse, he had no payment record, and therefore no proof whether George had made all the payments on time, or even whether he had made them at all.

It also turned out that George was not creditworthy because of some unpaid business taxes. And then we found that George was also three years behind on the tavern's real estate taxes. This was looking very bad.

However, further investigation revealed that George was current on the first mortgage and had kept the business running profitably since he bought it.

My conclusion from all this? The note was risky. But even risky notes are worth something. So we made a very low bid on this risky note. Our bid was so low that we didn't expect to get it.

However, two months later Nethercutt called and told us we were the highest bidder. So we agreed to buy the note for our low price.

Now we had to go through a long, drawn-out legal process. Nethercutt had to notify all of Kevin Moran's creditors, wait for any objections, and then get a court order signed by a federal bankruptcy judge to sell us the note.

While we were waiting for the final word, Nethercutt told us that George Thomas was interested in paying off his note at a deeply discounted price, thus saving himself a lot of money. Since there was still time for George to top our bid, we could still lose the opportunity of buying this risky note. So we resigned ourselves to the fact that we might not get it if George or anyone else offered more money for it.

This is typical of the notes a bankruptcy trustee has for sale: complicated and risky, with a payor—a note buyer's major competitor—also wanting to buy it.

So we played a waiting game. The bankruptcy trustee finally got the court order approving our bid, and after the appeal period was over, we bought the risky note.

How did the Thomas note come out? It eventually paid off and we made a handsome profit on it. But I strongly advise anyone to avoid such risky business.

Note buying has enough pitfalls without tempting fate: possession of the original note, holder in due course, non-negotiability, recourse—oh yes, recourse.

Remember the story in the last chapter about Patty Payne and our search for her? And remember that we bought her note from our friend John Richie, who endorsed it "without recourse?" Well, recourse is another devil of a detail:

Many years ago, a real estate agent named Sandy Wallace contacted us from California with a note to sell. It was a "deferred commission."

Sandy had sold a large multi-million dollar parcel of property that earned her a very large commission. She couldn't get her commission in cash, however, because the buyer of the property, Garrett Jordan, had put everything into a tremendous down payment.

Instead, Mr. Jordan signed a secured note to Oceanside Real Estate Company, where Sandy worked. The note had small monthly payments and a large balloon payment due a few years down the road.

When we began to look into the note, we first found only good things: Mr. Jordan, the buyer of the property was very creditworthy. He had paid a huge cash down payment. The property value was very high.

Then we discovered that the seller, Servando de la Garza, had taken a first lien for the balance due. That meant Oceanside Real Estate Company's note for the commission was secured by a second lien. If anything went wrong with the first lien, we could lose everything. That made us very cautious.

We told Sandy that we would buy the note, but only if her boss Mr. Appleby would agree to sell the note *with recourse*. That means that if Mr. Jordan did not pay the note, Oceanside Real Estate Company would have to pay us. Sandy said she would speak to Mr. Appleby and get back to us.

The next day she called and confirmed that Mr. Appleby agreed to sell the note with recourse. With that obstacle out of the way, we bought the note.

Oceanside Real Estate Company prepared the endorsement on the back of the note, and it said, "For valuable consideration, pay to the order of Larry Stevens and Lorelei Stevens." It was signed and dated.

The endorsement said nothing about recourse. But the law says that such an endorsement is with recourse.

We were satisfied with the endorsement because we understood that it guaranteed that Oceanside Real Estate Company would pay us if anything went wrong with the note.

A few years went by with regular payments. The note looked good. But then Mr. Jordan quit paying the note. The value of the property had drastically decreased and Mr. Jordan was in financial trouble. It was clear that he would not be able to pay the note, so we asked Oceanside Real Estate Company to pay it.

Oceanside Real Estate Company refused, claiming they had not guaranteed the note. We could not understand their position, so we were forced to begin a legal action to collect.

As our lawsuit progressed, a strange story unfolded. Unknown to us, Sandy had sold us the note because she was ill with cancer and desperately needed money. She had asked Mr. Appleby to sell the note to help pay medical bills and he agreed. But, we discovered she had never spoken to him about guaranteeing the note – she simply didn't bring it up. Sandy died while the note was still being paid, and we were unaware of all this.

Now our lawyers asked pointed questions of Oceanside Real Estate Company's Mr. Appleby. He admitted that his office had prepared the endorsement. He admitted he had signed it, but he claimed that he didn't know about the law of recourse. Although he was a licensed real estate broker, he said he 'didn't know that if a note fails to state that it is endorsed *without recourse*, the note seller automatically has endorsed the note *with recourse*. He felt that somehow he had been tricked into guaranteeing the note.

In the end, Mr. Appleby's attorneys advised him of the law and he paid us. We gave the note back to him, and we endorsed it *without recourse*. Mr. Appleby was hoping that he could salvage something from Mr. Jordan now that he owned the note again.

This incident made us realize that licensed real estate brokers might not know this simple law – and that even lawyers sometimes forget it.

So we established the policy of always addressing the subject of recourse in writing on every endorsement. If the note seller sells with recourse, that's the way it is written. If the note seller sells without recourse that's the way it is written. We don't leave the endorsement silent.

We learned quite a lesson from this recourse situation. Even trained and experienced professionals may not know recourse law. Our simple practice saves note sellers unexpected cost and embarrassment, and prevents misunderstandings. Just another detail.

Here's a detail that really had the Devil in it: our careful attention to recourse detail backfired and landed us in trouble. *Big* trouble.

Back in the early 1980s our firm considered the purchase of a risky note from a Mr. Clarence Owens. The risk stemmed from the property that secured the note, which was not up to our standards. We felt that the only way we could protect our money was to have Mr. Owens sell us the note "with recourse."

He was agreeable, but a question arose about a very technical legal point in such a purchase: If a note seller sells us a note with recourse, does the law consider that a *loan* from us to the note seller?

It might be considered a loan because the note seller has the final liability for paying us back.

The legal question was this: if it was a loan, and our return on the note was higher than our state's usury laws allowed, would we in effect be charging illegal interest?

Since our return on the Owens note would be higher than our state's usury laws allowed, we asked Diana Gleed, an attorney who specialized in usury. She searched the legal library and told us there was *no case law* on our subject in Washington State.

Case law is the collection of reported court decisions on a particular subject, as opposed to statute law, which is written by the legislature. Case law interprets what statutes and regulations mean.

But in Gleed's opinion it was obvious that the purchase of a note guaranteed by the note seller was *not* a loan, and our return by definition could not be usury.

Gleed wrote to us: "The holder of the note who sells same and who is obligated on recourse is subject to a portion of the Uniform Commercial Code, which states the endorser 'will pay the instrument according to its tenor at the time of his endorsement to the holder, or to any subsequent endorser who takes it up.' Thus, it appears that the endorser's debt would be that shown on the face amount of the Note."

She concluded usury did not apply.

So we quit worrying about it and bought the note from Mr. Owens. We even wrote into the documents a safety clause: "Sale: It is understood and agreed that this transaction is not a loan."

Mr. Owens also clearly knew that he had to pay us if the payor didn't pay. We had no reason to believe there was any legal problem.

The payor paid for about two years, but then the payments stopped. Because we had a note with recourse, we asked Mr. Owens to pay. Mr. Owens refused. To our distress, he filed a lawsuit against us for usury. Exactly what we had worried about.

Mr. Owens complained that his sale of the note with recourse was a loan of money by us to him, and that we had charged him an illegal rate of interest.

Mr. Owens hired a lawyer who was expert in litigation and usury and felt confident that his claims would stand up in court.

That left us no option other than to assign our lawyer Richard Strunk to the case. It went to trial and we won. The trial court found that there was no subterfuge or scheme by us to collect usurious interest from Mr. Owens. We won a judgment against Mr. Owens for more than $50,000 plus attorney fees and costs.

Mr. Owens filed an appeal. Then the Court of Appeals of the State of Washington reversed the trial court's decision. The appeals court came to the opposite conclusion and ruled against us.

Now the court awarded Mr. Owens a judgment against us for nearly $50,000. The judgment we had obtained earlier against Mr. Owens was canceled. Instead of him owing us money, we now owed him.

We appealed to the Supreme Court of Washington State. But the high court denied our request and refused to hear our case. So the decision stands.

There was no further appeal. We had to pay Mr. Owens. So we paid him. When we handed over the certified check to Mr. Owens' lawyers, we were unhappy about the loss, but glad to have the case over with.

We lost a lot of money on this note. We lost the money we were ordered to pay Mr. Owens; we lost the money we paid our lawyers for their fees; we lost the court costs; we lost a portion on the money we'd originally paid Mr. Owens for the note. Mr. Owens even got the note back from us.

Much to our chagrin, case law in Washington State now says that the sale of a note with recourse is subject to the usury laws of the state as between the note seller and note buyer. Unless there is an exemption, any recourse sale of a note could subject a note buyer to serious usury penalties.

Many lawyers since have told us they would have advised us the same as Diana Gleed. Most of them also told us that the court decision was a bad one, but that doesn't change anything about our loss.

We learned a hard lesson. When there is no case law on an issue, lawyers can only give us their best guess. A substantial portion of the business of buying, brokering and selling notes is in frontier areas of the law.

This is definitely a risky business. It's not for the faint of heart.

FAST CASH

Chapter 10
Rush

"**H**ey, it's Dennis," Gloria called to me. "On line 1."

I picked up the phone and said, "How's our favorite singing cab driver today?"

"Ready for pickup and delivery," came the cheery voice. "Got any fast jobs today?"

Dennis Roberts is one in a million. He's president of the taxi driver's guild (which is a children's charity). He's a character actor you may have seen on television. He's a professional Santa Claus. He's a notary public. And, he asserts, he's a future note buyer.

We got to know Dennis because of our motto, Fast Cash: in order to get documents signed in a hurry, we frequently have to use a taxi service as our courier.

When we first met, it was by chance: the taxi dispatcher radioed Dennis simply because he was available. I have to admit that the big brawny man who walked into my office startled me (I'll let Dennis explain that himself in a minute), but we hit it off famously. Now we request him every time.

Dennis tells it best. In fact, he wrote up the story himself and sent it to a newsletter publisher in the note industry who ran it in his next issue. This is what Dennis wrote:

The call came in early on a Monday morning.

Seattle Yellow Cab's central dispatcher snapped, "I have this all-day job here, Dennis. They have papers to be picked up from the court house, go get signatures, that kind of thing. Want it?"

"Sure," I replied. "Work is work."

"Okay, see the lady at Wall Street Brokers. Corner of Fifth and Wall Street."

It was a nice address uptown. When I walked into the office, I instantly recognized the look on their faces.

I'll admit I'm a burly guy, and some people do think I look like a cross between Santa Claus and a biker-bar regular. And it's true that people stare at my shoulder-length hair and Indiana Jones hat. But I win them over.

"Hi!" I said brightly. "I'm Dennis Roberts, the singing taxi driver. I'm here to pick up those papers at the court house for you."

The lady introduced herself as Lorelei Stevens, President of Wall Street Brokers. She did a pretty good job of not staring while she explained her business—buying seller-financed notes. I would be courier for some very important deals today.

Then she said I looked like a character actor in the movies.

"Good guess," I said. "I *am* a character actor. Ever see the television series *Northern Exposure*?"

"Sure," she said.

"I was in several episodes. Been in others, too. And I've been a professional Santa Claus during Christmas seasons for years."

That went over well. I could see that Lorelei had decided I was okay for the job, so I asked about the tasks of the day, where I had to go, what to get, who to see.

"Before we do that," she said, "are you really a singing cab driver?"

"Absolutely."

"Sing me a song, then."

I gave her my best Elvis impression with his rendition of *Jingle Bells*. The whole office applauded when I was done.

Then Lorelei mapped out the day's work.

And what a day's work it was. First I drove to the municipal courthouse, got certified copies of several judgments Lorelei needed, plus tapes of important testimony.

Then I dropped those papers off at a lawyer's office and picked up some others and took them to Lorelei. She gave me some more papers to take to another lawyer's office.

Then came the surprise. Lorelei told me the next stop was a nearby town up north where I would go to the homes of two ladies, first Glenda and then Katie, who were both selling notes to Wall Street Brokers. They were elderly and neither could get out of their house for business. Lorelei explained that Glenda's note was a first lien and Katie's was a second lien, and told me what I needed to do with each.

So, I threaded my way through heavy traffic to Glenda's house and knocked on the door with her papers—and her check—in my hands. She was very cordial and said Lorelei had called and told her about me. She invited me in and to my delight she played the piano for me. Then she asked me to sing her a song, and accompanied me in *When Irish Eyes Are Smiling*.

When the music died away, Glenda thanked me for the song and turned to the business papers.

"Well, everything looks in order," she said.

Glenda then whispered in a conspiratorial tone, "You know, Dennis, I was always taught never to trust anyone when it came to money. So I have a special favor to ask."

"What's that?" I wanted to know.

"Take me to the bank so I can make sure Wall Street Brokers' check is good."

I kept from laughing out loud, and said, "Sure. We have to go there anyway to get the papers notarized, remember? Come on. Let me help you to the cab."

At the bank we spread all the papers out on a counter. "What do I need to sign?" Glenda asked.

I had all the details fresh in mind—being a cabbie gives you a good memory for details like street names and routes to avoid. Street smarts. So I showed her the exact pages where her signature was required.

When she skipped one, I politely turned the page back and said, "This one, too, please."

When all the signatures were done I made sure that all the papers were notarized by a bank official, just as Lorelei had instructed. I gave Glenda her cashier's check, she made sure it was good at the teller's cage, and put it in the bank.

Then, as we started back to the cab, Glenda said, "Dennis, let me do something for you. There's a hamburger stand across the street. Let me by you a burger. It's the least I can do for your kindness."

That was touching, I thought, so we went over and ordered burgers. I got a deluxe, the works. Glenda got a barebones burger and bun, no frills. I felt a little guilty, but ate mine with gusto.

When I dropped her back at home, Glenda wanted me to sing for her some more but I told her I had another stop to make before the day was done.

This one was to Katie O'Brien's. She's very old. Lorelei had called and told her the singing cab driver would be there, so she was expecting me. Her grown children lived across the street, and I was supposed to have them come over to have one of them notarize the papers—and listen to a song. So with a house full of people, I sang *Danny Boy.*

Katie signed all the papers and I gave her the money in a cashiers check. The O'Briens wanted me to stay and sing some more, but I had to rush to the title insurance company to drop off the papers. It was a race against time.

When I got there, they sent me to the wrong office. When I finally got to the right desk, it was just in nick of time.

I got back to Wall Street Brokers with copies of everything, all the papers signed in the right places.

"Well, you did everything perfectly," exclaimed Lorelei. "You're good at this."

"Yep," I said smiling.

We'd both had a lot of fun that day.

Since then, I've been Lorelei's Wall Street Brokers courier many times. She took a special interest in me, talked me into getting a notary license so I can do the work myself.

Every time I see Lorelei, she gives me a personal five-minute lesson about buying notes. I'm learning a lot. I may do some note buying myself one day.

Hey, gotta go. The dispatcher just called in with another fast Wall Street Brokers job.

Isn't Dennis a hoot? Now I know you're going to scold me, giving free note buying lessons to the most unlikely people. Like Art Morales the longshoreman (he's doing fine in Mexico, but found that helping with a school is a lot more work than he expected). I feel there are some people who just have that extra spark. It makes you want to mentor them a little.

But Dennis Roberts didn't need a lot of mentoring. He's one of our trade secrets—his sunny outlook and ready taxi help us live up to our Fast Cash reputation.

We're fast, but not always in the same way. One of our note deals that didn't need a courier ended up with a whole new meaning of "Fast Cash:"

The newlyweds breezed into my office with a note for sale. It was the groom's nest egg, ready to hatch the cash for a home.

Everything was in order. I reviewed Luke Aronson's complete file, arrived at a price, and signed a preliminary agreement with him.

"The deal should close in about two weeks," I told him. I singled out the original note and said, "Be sure to keep this original note in a safe place because you must deliver it to me when I give you your cashier's check."

During the following two weeks, everything went as expected. The payor, Johnny Craig, was very cooperative, and, I discovered, worked at an auto body repair shop only a few miles from my office.

In each of several telephone conversations, I reminded Luke to bring the original note when the time came. We finally made an appointment to close the transaction. Luke and his bride Heather would drive the 100 miles from his mother's home where they were staying while he got his financial affairs in order.

On the big day, the Aronsons arrived at 4:30, signed all the papers, and gave us the note. Only it didn't look like the original! I held it up to the light, I looked at the back of the note and felt for indentations, and then examined it with my magnifying glass.

"This is not the original note," I said in surprise. "I can't release your check until I have the original note."

Luke went pale and his hands started shaking. Heather stared wide-eyed and helpless.

"Let me go down to my truck," Luke said. "I may have mixed it up with some other papers."

The Aronsons bolted downstairs together, only to return in less than five minutes in utter dejection.

"It's not there," they mumbled.

I thought fast.

"You had the original with you before. Are you sure it isn't in your truck?"

"I'm sure," Luke replied.

Heather reluctantly volunteered, "I cleaned out his truck for him a few days ago."

I asked her, "Did you clean out any papers?"

"There were a lot of papers and I put them all in a garbage bag." She was on the verge of tears.

"And the original note is not in the truck now?" I said, my mind racing. "Why don't you call your mother and ask if she can find it where you've been staying?"

Luke dashed to the phone, dialed his mother, and waited for an answer. The phone rang and rang. There was no answer.

I told them, "Look, if you can't find the original, you know where Johnny Craig works. Go get him to sign this replacement note." I handed them the replacement note and other accessory documents to be signed.

Luke and Heather exchanged nervous glances. "There's a problem," Luke stammered. "We don't have any money. We were counting on that check."

"Well, you'll have the check as soon as you return with the replacement note."

"You don't understand. We don't have *any* money— not even enough for gas back home."

A tense silence filled the room. It was right before closing on a Friday before a three-day weekend. I had an urge to help these young people, and I had nothing but instinct to go on.

"I'd be willing to loan you $100." I took a $100 bill out of my wallet and motioned to Heather. I thought to myself, that's a new kind of Fast Cash, but what I said out loud was, "Here, go get yourselves some dinner and calm down."

Heather said, "But, we can't pay you back tonight."

"Then I'm just going to have to trust you." I didn't

make them sign anything. I just pressed the $100 bill into Heather's hand and said, "When you finish the paperwork, come back for your check. I've got a pile of work to do before the holiday so I'll be here until 10:00 tonight."

Four hours later they returned, jubilant. They found Johnny Craig and got him to sign the replacement note, along with the necessary supporting documents. I handed them the check and two very happy people left my office.

Oh, yes, I received a crisp $100 bill in the mail a few days later.

Most of our demands for fast cash (and faster cash) come from note sellers, but a few are goaded on by others:

I was busy doing an appraisal on a complicated note when the phone rang. A woman with a croaky voice spoke, but I couldn't understand her. At first I thought it was a crank call. Then I could make out a few words (barely): she said her name was Judy, Judy Barnes, calling from Salt Lake City.

She wanted to sell a note she'd carried from selling her beauty salon. I told her that I could barely understand her.

She apologetically told me she had a vocal cord disease and would try to speak more clearly.

"I'm in financial straits," she rasped. "And my boyfriend just dumped me. I've got a lot of bills stacked up. Would you be interested in buying my note?"

"Sure, we're interested," I said, "but I need a few details."

I must have asked the poor woman to repeat herself three or four times for each sentence she uttered, but she was finally able to make the basics clear to me: She had a business note with no real estate involved. She had sold her business to a woman named Mary de Crespo for $150,000, with $75,000 cash down. The new owner was highly creditworthy and a good businesswoman. She had increased the business enough to remodel the entire shop. Her payments were all on time with no problems.

Judy concluded our conversation saying, "I have to be honest with you. I'm also considering selling the note to someone else. I'll let you know....But before I do anything, I need to talk with my lawyer."

"OK, Judy," I said. "When you're ready to make up your mind, let me know and we'll get right on it."

About a week later she called back. However, her voice had deteriorated to the point that I couldn't understand exactly what she was saying.

We agreed we'd communicate by e-mail, which was more successful. Several e-mails later she decided to sell the note to us. She signed an agreement to sell the note and we began our due diligence.

First, we called Mary de Crespo and told her we were going to buy the note.

"Oh, but you can't!" she replied. "Judy already sold the note to someone else!"

"What?" I blurted.

"That's right," said Mary. "She was here a couple of weeks ago with the woman who bought the note, somebody named Maureen something. Judy went around the salon saying she owned this and that and the other. I don't understand why she said she owns this stuff when I bought it from her. All she has is a lien on it."

This required some quick thinking.

I asked Mary in careful terms, "Did you receive anything in writing from Judy saying she'd sold the note?"

"No. But another thing: Judy still owed the landlord $5,000 and we got stuck paying for it! That was her obligation!"

I thanked Mary for the information and told her I'd call again after I'd straightened things out.

In an instant I was on the phone to Utah Precision Escrow—the agency collecting the payments—asking about Judy's note.

A polite young man said he'd go check the file. He came back with the answer I expected: "All payments still go to Ms. Barnes and we have the original note here in her folder. We have had no notice of her selling the note."

Just as I thought. Judy had tried to sell her note to someone else and it fizzled on her. But now we had a problem. If we bought her note, we'd face the matter of that $5,000 payment to the landlord. Mary de Crespo certainly wouldn't sign any statement saying she agreed with our figures for the balance on the note until the $5,000 was cleared up.

I e-mailed Judy asking about the landlord and got no answer. Four unanswered e-mails later, I asked bluntly if she still wanted to sell the note. That got a quick reply: "Of course I do. I've still got those bills to pay."

After a brief discussion she agreed to reimburse Mary de Crespo for paying the landlord.

With everything now in order, we finalized the papers and FedExed them to Judy. We heard nothing back for more than a week.

Then a man named Eric Beebe called our closing department, saying Judy Barnes would sign her papers soon. He just wanted to know when the money would arrive and how it would get to Salt Lake City. We figured he was a friend who spoke for Judy because she was unable to speak at all any more.

I called him back asking who he was, and he said he was her lawyer, not just a friend.

"I'm really sorry I was remiss in not identifying myself," he said. "I had just returned from a long courtroom day. I must have been preoccupied. And Judy's voice has actually improved. Now let's get to your business."

He went over a couple of details he wanted changed and urged us to get Judy's money quickly.

We worked fast, got the papers to Mr. Beebe, and— to our amazement—he returned the papers by UPS the very next day, all properly signed and notarized. That struck us as highly unusual. Most lawyers delay closings and take their time getting papers back to us.

We wondered why Eric Beebe was so prompt.

While we were wondering, Eric called and wanted us to wire the funds the next day—the first of the month. He said that Judy was desperate for the money and needed it immediately. He stressed that it was very important.

I told him we understood that Judy had a lot of bills to pay and agreed to act fast.

"But," I emphasized, "Judy needs to get us the wire instructions by noon tomorrow if she wants the money the same day.

We called Judy. No answer. We e-mailed her. No answer. When we closed the office for the day, Judy had not replied. Same thing when we opened for business the next morning.

Shortly after 9 a.m. our time, Eric called us in a panic. Time was running out. He called Judy. I called Judy. No answer. We didn't get the wiring instructions. Odd for somebody in such a hurry.

The deadline passed. Then Judy called. It was after three o'clock. She apologized, saying she'd been asleep all day. The medications for her voice problem knocked her out. She asked what our e-mails were all about, and why we needed wiring instructions.

I explained that we needed the wiring information for same-day delivery of her money.

"I'm sorry we couldn't reach you," I said. "I know you have all those bills to pay and it's the first of the month, so I took it upon myself to wire it to your attorney. I hope you're not angry."

She laughed. "I'm not angry."

"You're not?"

"No! You did the right thing. Those bills I was worried about are all Eric Beebe's! I owe him a pile for legal work he did last year. It was him that wanted the money in a hurry."

Well, once you get the reputation for fast cash, people expect you to be fast for any reason at all.

Not long ago, a personable man arrived at our office with a bundle of documents. His name was Dan Jacobs and he had a note he wanted to sell fast.

He plopped the documents on our front desk and cheerfully began telling us his life story. We listened politely with one ear while scrutinizing the papers. We immediately saw that this note was well secured by a first lien mortgage on valuable real estate, so we listened to his tale with both ears.

Dan Jacobs explained that a year earlier he'd sold the property securing the note: a house, outbuildings, and 17 acres where he'd operated a recycling business for over 15 years. His was the only recycling business in his small rural county and people had fondly come to call him "The Junkman."

The small county consisted entirely of one forested island, and was inhabited by a colorful assortment of loggers, fishermen, and other close-to-the-earth types. It was a tight-knit community and everyone knew "The Junkman." They had gotten into the habit of simply dropping things off at his place and even calling him to come pick up their castoffs. Dan Jacobs didn't have to pay for advertising, as the small community's newspaper was interested in protecting the environment and occasionally ran free ads for his recycling business. He was a permanent fixture.

Over the years, Dan bragged, he had become quite well off. He told us that the recycling business was a great way to get rich. "All you have to do is bend over and pick money off the ground," he laughed.

But one day, Dan lamented, the bending over got to him—he slipped a disc in his spine and even back surgery couldn't restore the strength of The Junkman. His recycling career was over. He sadly put his business and its property up for sale.

To Dan's surprise, the first offer came from a long-time employee, Dave Plunkett. Dan patiently explained to Dave that he needed $150,000 in cash as a down payment. No problem, said Dave. In a few days he came back with a cashier's check in the amount of $150,000. How an ordinary employee could come up with such an amount of cash was a mystery, but the money was good and Dan sold out to Dave, taking a note for the balance of the sales price.

Dave Plunkett smoothly took over the business and did as well picking money off the ground as Dan had. His note payments had been on time for just over a year now, and the balance owing was less than 60% of the sales price.

This looked like a very good note indeed. We gave Dan Jacobs a preliminary quote, and he sheepishly told us that he had tried to sell his note to another note buyer, Reed Repetto, who had offered him a bit more money than we did. Repetto, however, never got the deal started and Dan was tired of waiting.

We happened to know the reason: Repetto had left for his annual African safari and would be gone for another 10 days. We knew Repetto would be very interested in this note, so we had to move fast.

We did our due diligence: checking the payor's credit, getting the property appraised, and reviewing all the legal documents.

We discovered a few interesting tidbits from the title report. Good old employee Dave Plunkett had borrowed $100,000 of the down payment from Peter Taylor, a private investor who lived near The Junkman's business. Mr. Taylor carried a second lien on the property. It was clear to us that if

Mr. Taylor found out we were going to buy the first lien, *he* would want to buy it.

Now we had two potential rivals to contend with!

After discussing the sale of the property with the real estate agent who sold it, the escrow closer who closed the deal, and surrounding property owners, we found that the other $50,000.00 of the down payment had been paid by Dave Plunkett's rich father-in-law, Conrad Wingate!

We knew if Mr. Wingate found out the first lien was for sale, he might insist on buying it.

Now we had three potential rivals to beat!

This was a place to take an unusual risk. Normally, we check with the payor to verify the balance, but in this case we couldn't. We didn't want the "news" that the note was selling to get out. We knew we had to work with speed.

This is definitely not a move the inexperienced should attempt. There is a fine balance between the "haste makes waste" theory and the "dotting all the I's and crossing all the T's" theory. You don't want to be aced out by the competition, but you don't want to act so quickly you do an incompetent job that could result in financial loss either. But we were prepared for the risk and we decided to take it.

Now it was a race with time.

Reed Repetto would soon get back from his safari and undoubtedly tempt Dan Jacobs to discard his transaction with us for more cash!

Peter Taylor, the second lien holder, would love to get his hands on that first lien note!

And Conrad Wingate would instantly jump at the chance!

We drew up the final papers and had them hand delivered to Dan Jacobs for his signature. We immediately transferred the funds, ready to disburse them. Dan Jacobs delivered the original note to us and we recorded the assignment of the first lien mortgage. The deal was closed.

All that in a matter of two days.

Fast Cash.

That's us.

Sometimes circumstances trip up your reputation, though:

Some months ago, a local man named Max Longhorn III contacted our firm with a note to sell. He told us the basic facts of the note and it sounded good. The payor, an elderly lady named Mildred Smith, had paid every payment on time for over fifteen years. The real estate securing the note was nearby in Seattle and had skyrocketed in value. It was a dream note with a dream payor. To boot, it was small in size – only $17,000.

We agreed on a price, signed a preliminary agreement, and began our due diligence.

Right away, we discovered the note to be a little unusual. It was part of the estate of Max Longhorn III's grandfather, which in itself is not unusual. Max was the executor of his grandfather's estate. Max Longhorn I—Grandpa Max— had passed away the previous year. As executor of the will, Max had power to liquidate the note and distribute the cash to the estate's four heirs, which is what he had decided to do. Notes from the liquidation of an estate are not exactly everyday items, but they're also not that unusual.

It was after Max sent me a copy of his grandfather's death certificate that the note began to seem peculiar. While studying the death certificate and other necessary papers I immediately saw a potential problem.

I called Max and told him, "Your grandfather died in Idaho, not Washington. The real estate securing the note is in Washington. That's going to complicate things."

"It's ok," Max replied. "My attorney in Idaho completed the probate and I'll send you copies of all necessary papers."

"That's probably not enough," I told Max. "You might also need to do an ancillary probate in Washington state."

"Ancillary probate? What's that?" he asked.

"Ancillary just means supplementary, secondary, that sort of thing. It amounts to a mini-probate to supplement the one you did in Idaho, except this time under Washington law. Your Idaho probate clears the estate where your grandfather died, but not where his real estate is. We probably won't be able to get title insurance in Washington without it."

Max was surprised, but when we checked with the title insurance company, the answer came back in no uncertain terms. In order to obtain title insurance for our firm's purchase of the note, an ancillary probate must be conducted in Washington.

Now Max began to fret about the amount of time and money it would take to fulfill this irritating requirement, especially considering the small amount of money the note involved.

We contacted the chief underwriter at the title insurance company and made our case. He reviewed the Idaho probate papers and after much resistance finally agreed to waive the requirement for the ancillary probate—but only if all four heirs would sign the papers.

Thank goodness! The time and money for an ancillary probate would be eliminated!

Or so we thought.

We got busy with the final details, which included readjusting the balance owing on the note. We discovered a discrepancy during routine scrutiny of all the documents.

While going over Grandpa Max's amortization schedule, we admired how he regularly checked off his payments as they came in. That's how we noticed that the payor, Mildred Smith, had made extra payments during the last year of Grandpa Max's life. But when he checked off these extra payments, he hadn't refigured the balances, which meant that about $3,000 in principal that had been properly paid hadn't been subtracted from Mildred's balance owning.

So we re-figured all balances, and Mildred Smith signed a verification that she owed $14,000, not $17,000. Therefore, we had to reduce our price accordingly to buy the note.

We were wrapping things up smoothly when we received the papers from three of the four heirs. But one last heir, James Lutz, refused to sign the papers. Instead, he wrote a lengthy letter making all kinds of ridiculous accusations and rejecting all efforts to avoid an ancillary probate.

Max asked me for advice. We brainstormed and thought and talked. We considered ways to convince the other heirs to pay Lutz extra money to get the deal through.

But in the end Max said disgustedly, "I know what's going on. That little jerk is holding out because he wants to buy the note himself."

"Are you sure?" I asked. I had run into this many times before, but I wondered about Max, who had no experience in note buying at all. How could he be so sure?

"He's my step-brother," Max said. "I grew up with Jimmy, and he's always figuring an angle. If there's a way to mess somebody up to gain an advantage, he'll do it. He wants that note for himself. I just know it. But he's not going to get his way this time."

We agreed that Max would notify Jimmy Lutz that if he did not sign the papers within one week, an ancillary probate would be paid for and finalized. Once finalized, the executor would have full power to sell the note without the signatures of any heirs. The cost of the probate would be subtracted from what all four heirs would receive.

Lutz still refused to sign, and sent back a letter with even wilder accusations—and veiled clues that he indeed wanted to buy the note himself.

So Max had to pay for the ancillary probate. All heirs received their quarter of the proceeds, minus one-quarter of the cost of the probate! Holdout James Lutz got less money than he would have if he'd simply cooperated. His holdout scheme failed.

We weren't so speedy this time.

PART FOUR

Reality

FAST CASH

Chapter 11
Pressures

"What do you make of this, Dad?" I asked, plopping a large file on the desk of Larry Stevens, founder of Wall Street Brokers.

"What is it?" he said, sizing up the inch-thick folder.

"The Murdock note. Another one of those oddball deals I should have refused on the phone."

"What's wrong with it?"

"Everything in the world is wrong with it."

"Then why did you agree to look at it?"

"I don't know. Something about it just seemed like we could make it work. Now I don't know."

"What do you want me to do about it?" my father asked with a little smile.

"What you usually do," I said. "Give me good advice."

"Sit down," he said. "I'm going to give you the same advice I always do."

"You always tell me to figure it out myself."

163

"I always tell you that you're the one who can figure out what to do with these goofy deals that no one else will take."

"But that's no help," I retorted.

"Sure it is," he said, his smile getting bigger. "You've always had a good gut feel for things. It must be intuition or something."

I sat staring at him, perplexed.

"Here," he said, handing back the file. "Go sit at your desk and try to remember why you said 'yes' in the first place.

As usual, he was right. I did remember why I said "yes" in the first place, and we bought the note—which produced the handsome profit we were looking for. The note buying business has so many twists and turns, you just have to go on gut feel every now and then.

I remember one that was a sure loser, but look what I did anyway:

Many years ago, a sad note seller named Joshua Dole contacted our office. He had tried to sell a note, but could find no buyer. We were his last hope.

The problem was that his note was secured by a third lien. Note buyers heard "third lien" and wouldn't even talk to him about it. They thought he must be naïve or foolish to have accepted a note with a third lien—it was too risky standing in line behind a first and second lien.

But Dole was no amateur: he was a real estate broker who had sold a large and valuable apartment building belonging to PacNorWest Management Associates, and took a note secured by a third lien on the property for his real estate commission. The property had been bought by Quandary Properties, a limited partnership that took over the payments on the first lien and signed a second lien to PacNorWest for the balance due.

PacNorWest subsequently sold the second lien to one of our firm's competitors, Gothamgate Mortgage Company. The first thing Dole did was to contact Gothamgate to see if they would buy his third lien, but they refused to even discuss it. Dole then contacted other note buyers and they all turned him down.

When he contacted us, he explained that the value of the apartment building had declined since he sold it to Quandary. The balances due on the first lien and the second lien owing to Gothamgate left little equity in the property to secure Dole's third lien position. He realized we would most likely reject his note, but decided to inquire with our firm anyway. He really needed fast cash—he'd fallen on hard luck and hadn't sold any real estate for a long time. He had bills to pay and no income.

I took the time to review the papers, more as a courtesy than anything. I knew the apartment building was insufficient to secure the note. The values in its area were declining rapidly. I saw the title report showing a third lien position. Dole openly told me that Gothamgate had declined to buy this one. I felt like I was probably wasting my time, but had agreed to give it a cursory review and so I kept my word.

Then I looked at the real estate commission note. It had been signed by Gonzalo Peabody, PacNorWest's general partner, who had the legal liability for the partnership's debts—and a reputation for not paying his debts. He had signed the note on behalf of the limited partnership, a group of doctors who were his real estate investors.

However, I was surprised to find sixteen other signatures on the note. They were the signatures of all the doctors and their spouses. It was highly unusual for a note from a limited partnership to be signed by the general partner *and* all of the limited partners. Dole's lawyer had insisted that all the partners sign personally because of the precarious third lien security position the real estate broker took for his commission.

Those sixteen signatures changed my mind instantly, because I realized that *by signing the note, each and every one of those sixteen creditworthy people had obligated themselves to personally pay the entire amount of the note!*

Now it made no difference to me that the property would likely end up in foreclosure, because I knew that these sixteen payors would pay the note. I wouldn't have to gain possession of the property in the event of default—I could simply demand payment because these sixteen payors were personally liable.

The **personal liability** of the payors is often overlooked when making a decision whether or not to buy a note. But that's something I never overlook. To have 16 creditworthy payors is any note buyer's dream, regardless of the value of the property!

We bought the note from Dole, fully expecting the property to go into foreclosure.

A year later, the apartment building's value had even declined further. Gothamgate started a foreclosure to re-take the property. If we wanted to protect our third lien position on the property, we would have to pay the first and second lien, which, of course, we had no need to do in order to get our note paid.

Gothamgate completed the foreclosure after much time and expense, and ended up with the property but they still had to pay the first lien. They wiped us out and left us with no lien on the property.

At the proper time, we wrote to the sixteen payors and asked them to pay. We received several phone calls from the payors indicating that they'd lost the property and our third lien position had been wiped out. They told us they didn't have to pay now and they didn't own the property any more.

We explained to each caller about "personal liability," which means they were liable to pay whether or not the property maintained its value. Each caller was surprised, thinking that since they'd lost the property they didn't have to pay us. Like most payors, they didn't know about "personal liability."

The sixteen payors retained an attorney who advised them they had to pay the note. So we received a payoff check a few days later for the entire amount owing on the note.

A couple of weeks later, I had occasion to discuss the property with the property manager at Gothamgate who had called about another matter. He cried the blues about how much time and money he lost by re-taking the PacNorWest property. He apologized for having no choice but to wipe us out, thinking we had lost everything.

I told him we got paid in full.

He only said, "Sure you did," thinking I was joking.

I said nothing. I just smiled to myself.

I don't tell everything I know.

Here's another example:

The caller was not unusual. Tom Rogers wanted to sell his note because he needed fast cash to pay off the IRS for back taxes. Many—if not most—note sellers call because of a financial pinch.

The note was on a business that Tom Rogers had owned, a gas station franchise that he sold to an immigrant from West Africa, Mr. Aziz Kwame. The new owner had paid a large down payment and signed a note for the rest.

It looked like a good deal with the big down payment, and Mr. Kwame had good credit. Tom Rogers gave me a payment record that looked perfect.

I began my due diligence and called the IRS about Tom Rogers' debt to them, so I could get accurate figures to pay off his taxes. The revenue officer told me they had seized the payments on the note, having told Mr. Kwame to send all payments to the IRS. However, the officer said, the IRS had received no payments.

That was a shock. I called Mr. Kwame and he admitted he had not paid. The note was five months behind. Tom Rogers didn't know that Mr. Kwame was not paying, because he had received the seizure notice from the IRS and assumed the payments were going to the government as ordered.

Oh, rats! Did I really want to keep on wasting my time on a deadbeat? But something made me want to know why Mr. Kwame had not paid. It was that intuition talking to me again. I couldn't grasp why an immigrant wasn't paying the IRS according to the seizure. It was so unusual my curiosity had to be satisfied.

So I asked Mr. Kwame and he said it was because of some irregularities in the sale of the gas station to him. It seems that Mr. Rogers had left some unpaid bills that Mr. Kwame had to pay. Mr. Kwame had offsets and had intentionally not paid.

It took a while, but I arranged an agreement between Mr. Kwame and Mr. Rogers. Then Mr. Kwame signed an estoppel, and we had the protection we needed.

We bought the note and paid off the IRS. Everybody was happy and Mr. Kwame was routinely paying on time. He even kept in touch with me, telling me how he wanted to build up his gas station, even put in a deli to attract more customers. He was full of energy and ambition. If anyone could make the gas station pay, it was him.

One evening I was watching the news and there was Mr. Kwame, saying he was suing the oil company that franchised the gas station to him. I gave it no further thought. Mr. Kwame had paid on time every month for 3 years.

Then one day I noticed he was three months behind on his payments. I called his gas station and the person who answered told me Mr. Kwame didn't own it any more, that the oil company had taken the station back. The person told me that Mr. Kwame had settled his lawsuit out of court for $2 million. Mr. Kwame had departed and nobody knew where he was.

If I wanted our money, I would now have to deal with the oil company. We had a lien on their business, recorded both at state and county levels, so our position was solid. I wrote to their lawyers and told them that Mr. Kwame had disappeared still owing our firm $100,000.00 on a note.

The attorneys replied that they had settled the case for an undisclosed amount, and gave Mr. Kwame all the settlement money. He was supposed to pay us, they said. But he didn't, I said.

The oil company lawyers realized they had made a mistake, and began legal action in federal court to collect our money from Mr. Kwame. They couldn't find him, but they did find his lawyer, Jerome Washington. Kwame had paid $100,000 to Mr. Washington for his legal services, and it was still in the Attorney Trust Account.

The oil company filed a motion to attach Mr. Washington's Trust Account to pay us, but the federal judge refused. She did issue a restraining order against the absent Mr. Kwame to stop spending money until he paid us off. That wasn't much comfort, because a restraining order doesn't do any good if you don't know where your payor is or where his bank account is.

Then I realized I probably did know where his bank account was. I looked through my file and found a copy of Mr. Kwame's first payment. I always make a copy of the first check we receive from each payor. There it was. I told the oil company lawyers to contact Mr. Kwame's bank and inform them of the restraining order. The account contained ample funds to pay us off.

Mr. Washington evidently contacted his client somehow, because he asked us to accept a discount for the payoff. We refused to accept a discount and refused to release the lien on the business until we were paid in full.

Mr. Kwame then paid everything except for $750 unpaid interest. After more negotiations he finally paid that last amount and the note was paid in full.

Most of our demands for fast cash come from note sellers, but a few are goaded on by others:

Ten years ago, our firm bought a good note, secured by a commercial building located in the center of the small Northwest farming town of Owen. It was as solid a note as you're ever likely to find.

The payor, a local man named Hal Jones, ran a thriving family restaurant in the building and was well-respected in the community. He had purchased the property for $400,000 and made a hefty $100,000 down payment, leaving a balance owing of $300,000.

Hal's Café did well and Hal paid like clockwork. After ten years of timely payments he brought his balance down to $250,000.

Then one day not long ago Hal called us. His voice sounded flat and empty.

"What's wrong?" I asked.

"I'm not going to pay on my note anymore," Hal said. "I'm burnt out. I'm through with the café ."

"What?" I said in disbelief.

"I've got things set with my lawyer to close the café and file bankruptcy. I just wanted to give you two weeks notice."

"Two weeks?" I was stunned.

"Two weeks."

I had feared this would happen. We knew that Hal had divorced his long-time wife Joan a couple of years back and soon married an Owen schoolteacher named Mary. Hal kept a good relationship with Joan because of their kids, but most of his attention was devoted to Mary.

Things changed, especially in the business. Joan wasn't there anymore to handle all the details of running a restaurant and Mary wasn't interested. Customers no longer saw Hal watching over them all the time. Little repairs didn't get done.

Then big repairs didn't get done. We'd heard reports from Owen that things were going downhill, but we didn't know how badly.

We had to think fast. Two weeks isn't long. We didn't want to end up with an abandoned building, with Hal in bankruptcy. The insurance premiums alone would eat into our profits, as it's difficult to get a decent premium on a vacant building! Selling an abandoned building wouldn't command nearly the price of an up-and-running business.

We did some quick checking and confirmed our worst fears. Hal had really let the place fall into shambles. The property value had fallen to little more than half its previous level. It was worth only $250,000, while ten years earlier it had been worth $400,000! Our security had shrunk to the same amount that Hal owed us.

Then we discovered that the fire insurance had been canceled and the insurance company hadn't notified us. This deal was getting worse and worse.

We didn't have many choices. The only realistic solution was to find a new buyer for the property and arrange a "short sale"—we would accept less than what we were owed to avoid the even worse problem of getting the property back. But we couldn't do that in two weeks.

A small town property like Hal's Café might be on the market for months before a buyer came along. We needed Hal to stay there and manage the place until it sold.

But Hal wouldn't do it. He was happy to be out in two weeks. What to do?

While looking over Hal's note, it came to me.

I called Hal and asked, "Do you realize that if you file bankruptcy, you'll drag Joan into bankruptcy with you?"

He was stunned. "But Joan gave me a deed to the place when we divorced," he said. "How can she still be liable?"

"You divorce your spouse, you don't divorce your creditor," I told him. "Just because you and Joan are divorced doesn't change the fact that Joan is just as liable to us as you are, Hal."

"This is over my head," he muttered. "I'll have to ask my lawyer."

An hour later Hal called back. He was all humility.

"I don't want Joan bankrupt," he said. "What do I do?"

We had him list the property with a local realtor named Carol Sharpe and agreed to negotiate a lower note balance to get the property closed. We agreed to let Joan off the hook whenever the property sold, and Hal agreed to stay "for awhile."

I also told him I needed to reinstate the fire insurance, and asked him for the name of a local agent.

"Talk to Lila Olsen," he said.

I did. While I was explaining the situation to her, Lila stopped me.

"Wait a minute," she said. "I know someone who wants to run a restaurant."

"Who?" I asked.

"I don't know if I should mention this, but a young man I know may be interested."

"What's his name?" I pleaded.

Long pause. "Let me give you his mother-in-law's name and number. They own a little deli just behind Hal's Café. They've been growing so much they're looking for a bigger space."

So I spoke with Hazel Conrad, the mother-in-law. She was a little wary.

"It's true that Jason has really made the deli take off," she said. "He has the best head for business I've ever seen and he's still under 30. But I don't know, he's been talking about leasing the Big Burger place two blocks down on Oak Street. He might already have an agreement."

"Would you at least tell him about it?" I asked. "Hal's is a better location, and think about this: he'd be a property owner."

Hazel agreed. I immediately called Carol Sharpe and gave her the name and number of Jason Mann.

I don't usually do this, but I drove to Owen and called unexpectedly on two businesses, Hal's Café and Jason's Deli. At Jason's there was not a crumb on the floor, and nothing out of place. It was truly organized. The customers were bright and happy.

At Hal's I found the roof leaking into buckets next to people eating dinner. In the parking area, garbage lay strewn about. Egg from teenager pranks remained plastered on the windows.

I dropped in unexpectedly and introduced myself to realtor Carol Sharpe and Jason and his family, including his wife Sara. I explained to all that I was not the seller, but the note holder. But the seller owed us as much as the asking price—and that we were willing to lower our note balance if we could get a quick sale and a decent down payment from a responsible, organized operator with the determination to make a good future for the place. They took that in as I watched the possibilities light up their eyes.

I'd hit pay dirt. I knew instinctively Jason was the right person to take over Hal's. Though he and his relatives had little cash, I felt they could increase the income in no time. Jason could see the enormous potential in Hal's Café.

We began the process. I worried that Big Burger would make Jason a sweeter deal, but they didn't. It took about three weeks and lots of negotiating, but Jason made a decent offer and the sale finally closed.

Hal could now tell the Owen townspeople he sold the place—a more honorable outcome than filing bankruptcy and forcing his ex-wife to do the same. Jason and his family took over Hal's Cafe and overhauled it in less than a month. Now it's spotless and we're hearing reports that the food is better than ever. Ironically, Hal and his wife Mary have become regular customers.

SHORT SALES

Well, once you get the reputation for fast cash, people expect you to be fast for any reason at all.

Every note buyer dreads the words, "short sale." A short sale is one where the sale of a property doesn't bring in enough to pay all debts.

It's obvious that lien holders get stung in short sales, but they may agree just to get rid of a problem property or because a sudden change of circumstances gives them no choice.

My firm unknowingly got caught in one of those "sudden change" situations several years ago.

It began when Rick Blevins, a note owner, called and asked if we'd buy his share of a note he owned with three partners. We buy "fractions" as such parts of notes are called, so I asked him for details.

Blevins was one of four partners in a company called Assisted Living Enterprises, which owned a substantial property in Spokane, Washington, called the Viewpoint Apartments.

The complex consisted of 35 apartment units and four townhouses. It had been appraised at $1.8 million, with a cool million owing on the first lien to a Canadian life insurance company.

Blevins owned one-quarter of a $400,000 note secured by the apartment complex—a second lien that left only $400,000 in equity on the property.

That looked risky to me. Blevins was open about his reasons for selling: "I'll be completely honest. The property value of the area might be going down. I want out because it's just too risky for me in my current financial condition. But for someone else it could be a good thing."

I visited the property and found it to be average in every way. It was well maintained and enjoyed relatively good occupancy rates. Encroaching development was part industrial, part retail—some good, some bad.

It was risky but acceptable. We bought Blevins' 25% share of the note at a huge discount, and crossed our fingers we'd get paid according to the terms.

The payor was a real estate investor named Jay Simpson, who paid—sometimes a week or two late—every month for three years. Then the note came due in full. Now the trouble began.

Mr. Simpson was unable to make the balloon payment, and asked us and the three Assisted Living Enterprises partners for a one year extension. We all agreed, and charged him a small fee.

Jay Simpson started having problems when the economy changed. He owned too many properties that had failed to meet his income expectations. He put the Viewpoint Apartments on the market. We got word that another creditor won a lawsuit and obtained a $650,000 judgment against him in Idaho. Simpson's real estate empire was turning into a house of cards.

A year passed and Jay Simpson had still not sold the Spokane apartment complex. He asked us for another year's extension, but had no money to pay an extension fee. We and the other three note owners refused to grant the extension, but told him, "Keep the property on the market and we'll see what happens."

Occasionally I spoke to Converse Properties, the real estate office that had the apartment complex listing. Roland Evers, the Converse agent, said the property was ok. The market was ok. He'd shown the place a dozen times or more. Just no buyers yet, but one could arrive any time. Every time I called Evers, it was the same story. He was working on it. But nothing yet.

Then one day, out of the blue, we received a letter from Jay Simpson saying he'd sold the property and it would close in three days!

However, there wasn't enough money from the sale

to pay off all the obligations. Would we be willing to grant him a $60,000 discount?

There it was, the dreaded "short sale."

I was unwilling to grant the discount, but knew that I had to gain concurrence from the other three noteholders. We had a written agreement with them stipulating that "majority rules" on any decisions to change the terms of the note—including accepting a short sale.

The attorneys for the Assisted Living Enterprises partners haggled with Simpson and wrote us that they'd granted a $45,000 discount. They'd asked their clients, who'd agreed.

Gee, a $45,000 discount to the note payor, Mr. Simpson. What a gift! Since we'd gotten such a deep discount when we bought our quarter of the note, we were still making a handsome profit. No one likes giving away $45,000, but it was our view that it would be better to nurse the deal through than to end up with the property and pay a million dollars to the Canadian life insurance company to protect our position.

But something bothered me. Why did Mr. Simpson wait until three days before closing to ask for a short sale? His timing seemed too hasty for someone dealing with such a large amount of money.

I called Mr. Simpson's office and asked to see a copy of the title report. It took two days and several requests before I received it. The sales price was enough to pay off our lien in full!

Then why was a short sale necessary? It appeared that a month earlier, Simpson had placed three liens on the Spokane property.

One of the liens—for $60,000—was payable to Simpson Management, Inc.! It appeared Mr. Simpson didn't have enough money in one pocket to pay himself in another pocket!

There were two more liens, each for $20,000, to private individuals unknown to us. Simpson wanted to pay these preferred creditors instead of us, when we were recorded first!

This rubbed me wrong. Mr. Simpson had maneuvered a way to reimburse himself and his friends partially at our expense.

I contacted Assisted Living's lawyers with the evidence, and they were sheepish they hadn't looked into the matter more carefully, due to the time constraints. They wrote a strongly-worded letter saying no discount would be granted.

Simpson then called Assisted Living's lawyers and pleaded. He needed reimbursements to cover his outstanding loans which had been made to feed the complex. He sent financial information about the complex to the lawyers. He pleaded. He whined. We were holding up the closing. Every day was costing him big money because of interest accruing.

Assisted Living's lawyers finally caved in a couple of days later and agreed to the $45,000 discount. This left a bad taste in all our mouths, but at least the transaction would close and we wouldn't have to worry about taking the place back in a foreclosure.

The real estate commission was $95,000. It would likely be the real estate people who would pay the $45,000 if we blocked the sale. But we didn't think it was fair to Roland Evers, the hard working real estate agent who'd been trying to sell the place for more than two years. Evers deserved his money. So we abandoned any idea of having the discount taken out of the real estate commission.

We knew we were being "had" but went along with it anyway, just to get rid of Mr. Simpson and his problems. We didn't like it, but the Assisted Living partners outvoted us, so we acquiesced.

The next day Mr. Simpson's secretary called and said the $45,000 wasn't enough relief. Mr. Simpson didn't want to pay the $1,800 in late charges which had been included in the payoff figure. Would we please contact the lawyers and get this eliminated?

We wouldn't. We didn't. The deal closed the next day.

FAST CASH

Chapter 12
Quirks

The first thing I saw when I came to work that morning was the photo lying on the reception desk. I was expecting it. My husband Manfred had agreed to a side-trip in his business travels to take this picture. It was clipped to the work folder of a new note we were looking into. It's routine for us to document the security for a new note with a photo.

But what this photo showed was totally unexpected: It was a house—no, it was a *shack*—in such terrible condition I couldn't imagine anyone living in it.

"We can't buy that note!" I said to the room, then sheepishly realized I was the first one there this morning. I walked away from the offending photo and went to work at my desk.

In a few minutes I heard our founder Larry Stevens—my dad—striding by the reception desk. His footsteps stopped abruptly. He said sharply, "We can't buy that note!"

He poked his head into my office and said, "Did you see that thing?"

179

"I saw it," I said, trying not to visualize the wretched place.

"We can't buy that note."

"We won't," I agreed.

Shortly after Dad settled into his own office, Gloria came in and walked by the reception desk. A few seconds later she called out, "We can't buy that note! Lorelei, we can't buy this note!"

"I know, I know. We won't."

Then my husband Manfred walked in and cheerfully said to Gloria, "Did you see that thing I took a picture of down in Oregon?"

"How could I miss it?" she replied. "It's hard to believe that's the Conrad property."

"Oh, that's not the Conrad house," Manfred said, picking up the ugly photo. "This is an old dump I saw about half a mile away. The Conrad place is beautiful. I just put this here to make everybody wake up this morning!"

Three voices joined in chorus: "Manfred!"

As you've seen by reading this far, the note business is positively peculiar.

Can it get any more unusual?

Oh, Yeah!

When the call came in from Mexico, I was surprised to hear the voice of Gloria Steinberg. I remembered well the note she had sold us twenty years earlier. She and her husband had retired, moved to Mexico, and were renovating a hotel they had bought on the Pacific oceanfront. They needed fast cash. She had another note to sell.

It was a huge note, secured by a 101-year-old brick building in a historical district of downtown Seattle. We inspected the building, which had substantially increased in value since the note was created. This sturdy structure on valuable downtown land provided far more security than we needed.

The five year payment record was perfect. The payors, Harold and Miriam Horowitz, were stellar. The title was clean. The property was insured for hundreds of thousands of dollars more than the balance owing on the note.

It was an ideal note with great profit potential. It was one any note buyer would love.

Mrs. Steinberg agreed to sell the note, but only if we could guarantee she would receive money by an exact date less than a month away. She had a deadline with the contractor doing the hotel renovation. That was fine with us, and we assured her she'd have her money by the deadline.

"Is this one of those 'too good to be true' notes?" I wondered.

Normally we would contact the payors, Mr. and Mrs. Horowitz, to sign an estoppel document to verify the balance due. However, we knew that there was a great likelihood that if the Horowitzes found out the note was being sold, they'd contact the Steinbergs and try to pay off the note at a discount. So we decided to take a calculated risk and not to contact the payors until after closing.

As the deadline drew closer, one morning I was joking with Gloria about what a good note it was. I laughed, and said, "Wouldn't it be odd if the building was somehow destroyed—what if it burns down right before the deal closes?"

Silly me.

A couple of hours later, my office started rattling and shaking. We all panicked and ran under the door jambs! It was an earthquake! For thirty seconds that seemed like an eternity we kept our balance and said our prayers.

After it stopped and we regained some of our composure, we went to the office television—the "Rattle in Seattle" was 6.8 on the Richter scale! Big one!

The greatest damage was in the historical area of down-town! But we couldn't get any specific information about the Steinberg building. Confusion reigned.

I received an e-mail from Mexico—would we still buy the note, Mrs. Steinberg asked. I thought we still could buy it, but wanted to be sure there was no obvious earthquake damage. My dad walked to the building and reported that things looked fine. What a relief!

We e-mailed all documents for Mr. and Mrs. Steinberg's signatures.

Then an unexpected problem stopped us in our tracks. The recorder's office had sustained enough earthquake damage to be declared a public hazard and was shut down. There was no guarantee that the building would be repaired in time for us to meet the deadline. The whole deal was in jeopardy.

On top of that, the Steinbergs had no way to notarize the documents. The American Consulate near the Steinbergs' hotel was closed for two weeks because of a Mexican holiday, and their notary was unavailable.

This was getting to be impossible!

But that evening, Mrs. Steinberg got to chatting about her quandary with a distinguished-looking restaurant guest in their hotel.

The guest said his name was Cyril Coates and stunned her with the announcement, "Madam, it so happens that I am an attaché with the American Consulate. My notary seal is here in my briefcase. Where are your papers?"

So he notarized the documents! One problem solved.

But another set us on edge. The only courier service from the Steinbergs' area had promised to deliver her documents to us a day before the deadline. But severe weather diverted their flight to Cincinnati.

Now we didn't know what to worry about most. Were we a bundle of jitters because of earthquake aftershocks? Or because severe weather would wreck our deadline?

Deadline Day, and the Steinbergs' papers didn't arrive!

For our part, we had the money ready to disburse. A little luck was with us, too: the recorder's office re-opened in the nick of time. But there was nothing to record. When we went home from work that day, we thought the deal was dead, even though we had lived up to our end of the bargain.

The next morning the documents arrived. We thought it had all been for nothing. We had missed the deadline.

An hour later an email arrived. The Steinbergs had convinced the renovation contractor to extend their obligation one more day because of the extreme circumstances.

Overjoyed, we went ahead and closed the transaction. We owned the note.

Now, we had one last thing to do: contact the Horowitzes and let them know the note was sold.

I called David Horowitz, who was a well-known Seattle attorney and civic leader. I explained that the Steinbergs had sold their note to us and we had mailed a written notice to him. Mr. Horowitz immediately said, "Well I hope you know that your note was drafted poorly. It's a problem note."

Oh, no! You can't imagine anything worse than buying a huge note and having the payor—a lawyer, no less—tell you first thing that you have just bought a *problem note*.

After surviving the Seattle earthquake, the shut down recorder's office, the severe weather, the consulate on holiday, etc, etc, we closed the deal and found out it's a *problem note*! Oh no! My heart sank.

I asked in the calmest voice I could muster, "Why is it a problem note?"

"Those stubborn Steinbergs would not allow me to make extra payments! We've been arguing about it for years!"

When I got my voice back, I said, "Mr. Horowitz, let me assure you that you can pay as much as you want every month!"

In the end, it turned out to be a better note than we anticipated—we got our money back plus our profit much faster.

Okay, you can see that sometimes after everything goes wrong, everything goes right.
Can it get more unusual?
Oh, yeah!

A while ago an attorney named Ragnar Blomsted called my firm seeking to sell a note. He was the court-appointed bankruptcy trustee for the assets of a Mr. Tory Wells, and the assets included the note he wanted to sell.

We routinely receive inquiries from bankruptcy trustees, because we've built a good reputation with them. They know about us and rely on our long experience in these complicated transactions.

It may seem unreasonably risky to buy notes involved in a bankruptcy, but they're no different from any other note when it comes to risk—the note *payor* is not the bankrupt party, remember.

So, when Mr. Blomsted called wanting to sell Mr. Wells' note, we agreed to take a look at it.

The note was secured by real estate; a gas station and mini-mart were part of the property. It had originally belonged to Tory Wells, but was put up for sale by bankruptcy trustee Peter Savidge, who originally handled the case. Mr. Savidge was later killed in an automobile accident and Mr. Blomsted took over.

Mr. Savidge had sold the property to HamCoPacific, Inc., a company run by Samuel and Rebecca Hamilton. HamCoPacific had paid one-third down and maintained a perfect on-time payment record since the purchase, more than a year.

However, Mr. Blomsted was unable to provide us any further information about HamCoPacific or the Hamiltons because he had not been involved in the case from the beginning.

This lack of information was a danger signal, but we were lucky enough to know the real estate agent who sold the property, a bright and friendly woman named Sandy Cubin. We contacted Sandy and she sent us copies of the sales documents.

After examining them, we could see that the file wasn't detailed enough to meet our company's normal standards of due diligence. We couldn't establish the financial status of HamCoPacific or the Hamiltons and we couldn't determine the income of their gas station and mini-mart. We had no way to get anything more.

We had to make a decision.

Our conclusion was that this note was too risky for our company. But my dad, my husband and I knew the real estate was excellent security, and that we as a family were willing to accept the personal risk—at a low enough price.

So we personally made a deeply discounted offer, only 50 cents on the dollar, which amounted to $93,000. We guessed that someone else would submit a higher offer to the trustee, but that was the most we were willing to venture. Mr. Blomsted as trustee was legally bound to accept the highest offer, so we just waited for the outcome.

When the trustee notified us that our offer of $93,000 was the winning bid, we were happy, but we wondered a little whether we had made the right decision. The other bidders obviously thought it wasn't worth $93,000. We could only hope that we were right and they were wrong.

We had won a very complicated note.

Consider all the steps:

• Tory Wells, the original owner of the gas station and mini-mart had filed for bankruptcy.

- Then Peter Savidge, the original court-appointed trustee, sold the real estate and business to HamCoPacific, Inc., the current payors, who had paid one-third down and signed a note for the remaining two-thirds balance owing.
- The payor was a *corporation*, which is another danger signal because we could not hold the Hamiltons individually responsible for their corporation's debt.
- Then, shortly after the sale, bankruptcy trustee Peter Savidge was killed and the court appointed Mr. Blomsted in his place.
- Mr. Blomsted received the payments on the note for more than a year, but then...
- decided to liquidate the estate, which was when he contacted us seeking to sell the note.

We realized just how complex this transaction was, so we hired Gene Sakowitz, a bankruptcy lawyer, to help process it. Mr. Sakowitz had long experience with Mr. Blomsted and held him in the highest regard.

We split up the work, having Mr. Sakowitz handle the court documents while we did what due diligence we could.

Mr. Sakowitz's first task was to obtain a court order allowing the sale of the note. Then he had to find the old court order that authorized the sale of the real estate and business to the present payor. Without that, we may have bought a note with claims against it.

To our shock, Mr. Sakowitz couldn't find such a document anywhere.

Despite this alarming development, we had to put up the $93,000 right away. Failing to honor a winning bid such as this is a sure way to ruin your business reputation permanently within the close-knit bankruptcy trustee community. So we sent a cashier's check to Mr. Sakowitz to give to Mr. Blomsted in person.

When Mr. Sakowitz tried to deliver the check, Mr. Blomsted refused to accept it, saying that he didn't want it in his possession in case something went wrong with the deal and it didn't close. Blomsted told Sakowitz that this was his last case as a bankruptcy trustee and he didn't want any loose ends.

Now we were really worried.

Mr. Sakowitz kept the $93,000 cashier's check in his case file folder—for another two-and-a-half months, which is how long it took to finally close the deal.

At last the necessary court orders came through, and we finished up the transaction. Mr. Blomsted accepted the check and we were done. We had bought the note.

While we were tidying up the file, we noticed that Mr. Blomsted's office was practically next door to one of our family's new (and unintended) investments: my dad, my husband and I had repossessed a BigBurger restaurant in a note default, and had no choice but to keep it open under new management to protect our security. So here we were, reluctant moguls in the fast food business. I decided it would be a friendly and amusing gesture to send Mr. Blomsted a coupon that entitled him to a free hamburger and milk shake at our family's eatery.

We shortly got a letter back from Mr. Blomsted with our coupon returned. The letter graciously informed us that a bankruptcy trustee cannot accept gratuities of any kind.

I was so embarrassed! Then Mr. Sakowitz received his copy of the letter. He called to let me know that Mr. Blomsted had just been appointed a federal bankruptcy judge, and reminded me that it was a position with extremely strict ethics rules.

Now I was totally embarrassed! But after smarting from the humiliation for a few days, I began to doubt the common sense of anyone thinking that a respected bankruptcy trustee would sell out the law for a hamburger and milk shake. Soon the whole office was laughing about it. We apologized to Mr. Blomsted who laughed about it too—and said he'd visited our restaurant on his own and thought the burgers were just fine.

A month later, our family got a surprise request from an escrow company for the assumption figures on our note. HamCoPacific, Inc. was going to sell the property to a group of three highly credit-worthy married couples. Along with the request came all the financial information that we had previously been unable to get.

If we approved, our corporate note would be assumed by three wealthy couples who would take personal responsibility for the debt. They were "dream payors." Overnight, our weak corporate note had turned into a Cinderella transaction as sound as any we've ever seen.

The family met and approved the assumption. On the basis of the new business ownership, we borrowed the amount we had paid for the note, $93,000, securing our loan with this newly strong note. So we had no money in the note anymore. Our only obligation was to pay back our lender—even in the event no further payments came in on the note, a highly unlikely situation. We would receive a hefty cash flow for the next nine years.

Thus a highly dubious note ended up being the best deal of the year. How's that for a quirk?

If that's not odd enough, here's a prickly cultural war that puzzled us for weeks:

A young couple approached us to sell a large note under pressure of a substantial debt to the IRS. They were an enterprising Korean-American couple, Jerry and Grace Kim, who had sold both the real estate and an associated fast food business to an older Korean-American couple, George Pak and his wife

Dorothy. The Paks paid a 65% cash down payment, and signed a note to the Kims for the balance due.

The Kims and the Paks had maintained a good relationship since the sale. Mr. Pak had personally delivered the monthly payment check to Jerry Kim on the due date each month.

Everything looked good, so we began our investigation. The lawyer who had closed the sale, Thomas Choi, was a long-time associate of mine. I called about the transaction and told him we were buying the note and asked for copies of backup documents.

Then we got a surprise: Mr. Choi told me that the Paks had recently made arrangements with the Kims to pay off the note at a discount, and had hired him to handle the money and paperwork.

This was very upsetting but not unfamiliar. As in many previous situations, our note deal was about to vanish—one of the common hazards of note buying. Payors often insist on buying the note themselves at a discount when they discover that it's up for sale.

The next day Mr. Choi called and told us that even though the Paks had gone so far as to begin re-financing their house to get the cash, the Kims and the Paks got into an argument and their deal fell through.

Now it appeared that our vanishing note deal was back on track. However, the argument was a bad sign. There was a problem in the deal somewhere, and nobody had told us what it was. Even worse, Tommy Choi didn't know what it was either.

So, I contacted the Paks. We'd sent them an estoppel document for signature, verifying the balance due and that they had no claims, defenses, rights, or offsets against the balance due.

Mr. Pak told me he was mad at Mr. Kim and he would

not sign the estoppel. I asked about the nature of the problem, but he wouldn't tell me. That raised a red flag.

I didn't want us to buy a note and then endure a costly fight with the Paks about an unresolved problem with the Kims—especially when we didn't know what the problem was. So I tried several times to get Mr. Pak to tell me what the problem was, but he just wouldn't do it.

Finally, I contacted Michael Yoon, the Korean-American real estate agent who represented the Kims when the property sold. Mr. Yoon told me that the problem was Korean tradition. It is the custom for a younger man to always show respect for an older man. It even extends to such things as a younger man surrendering his seat on a bus to any older man who gets on. The older man in this transaction was middle-aged George Pak, who had requested that the younger man, Jerry Kim, perform some minor repairs to the property. Mr. Kim refused, an act of extreme rudeness by Korean custom. Mr. Pak was outraged. He didn't get the repairs he had asked for and he had been affronted by a younger man. Thus their relationship collapsed. Mr. Pak decided not to pay off the note at a discount.

Grace Kim, seeing a good offer disappear, urged her husband to apologize, but Jerry obstinately refused. He did not see any reason to make the repairs and felt there was nothing to apologize for.

I then contacted Richard Kang, the Korean-American agent who represented the Paks when the property sold. I asked what the cost of the requested repairs would be, and found that the problems could be fixed for about $5,000.00. So, I went back to the Kims and told them that my firm would still be interested in buying the note, but for $5,000 less than our original offer.

Even with this lowered price, we knew this was a risky situation, since it is not wise to buy a note when you have notice that there are problems. However, we had investigated this note thoroughly and knew that the repair issue was the only problem. We took a chance and bought the note without the estoppel, knowing full well that we would have to handle any problems that arose after we paid the Kims for the note. We instructed the Paks to make all future payments to us.

However, Mr. Pak sent his first payment of $10,000 to Mr. Choi, the closing lawyer, instead of to us. Mr. Pak instructed Choi that he had offsets and to hold the money. I asked Tommy Choi not to send the money into court and to give us some time to work out the problem.

I immediately went to work solving the problem. We sent a certified request with a deadline for the Paks to inform us of his demands. Pak replied with a list of minor repairs, totaling $5,500.00. We were relieved the problems were not much more than we expected. We agreed to pay the $5,500 and sent a new estoppel document for the Paks to sign, just to make sure there would be no further demands. Mr. Pak told me he would be happy to take the money, but he would not sign anything.

My father, Larry L. Stevens, who is in his early 70s, invited Mr. Pak to our office to make an agreement. Pak arrived, but was very rude to my father, and in a harsh voice repeated that he wanted the $5,500 but would not sign anything.

My father thought a moment.

Then he said in his most authoritative voice, "Now listen, young man, I demand some respect."

The next day the Paks—George and Dorothy—signed the estoppel. We gave them the $5,500 to use for repairs.

Things don't usually get as culturally sensitive as that, but some notes just seem to insist on growing from strange to stranger.

Can it get even more unusual?

Oh, yeah!

Not long ago a note broker named Rita Carlson faxed my firm some information about a rural New Mexico property of 400 acres with 2 houses, one occupied by the owner, the other rented out.

The owners, Ronnie and Lydia Warnick, had purchased the property from a family named Barrett on contract three years earlier. Now the Barrett family wanted to sell the contract.

A real estate contract is like a note and a lien combined. In a real estate contract, the payor doesn't get title to the property until it is paid off. That's important to the seller, but for me, buying this contract was much the same as buying a note.

What concerned me about this contract was its complicated ownership. It was owned by four heirs of John Barrett (the original property owner): three adult children and a minor child—and there were two ex-wives serving as representatives of their deceased former husband's estate. The first wife, Eilene Barrett, representing the adult children, wanted to sell. The second wife, Tanya Barrett, representing the minor child, did not.

In short, I was being asked to buy three-fourths of the Barretts' position in the real estate contract.

This is not an unusual request, but I wanted some details before going further. I found that John Barrett had been killed in a tragic accident some years earlier. He had loved his remote desert home and was buried on a lone mesa at the back of the property. According to his will, the property went to his four children in care of their two mothers. When the estate emerged from probate, the Barrett family jointly decided to sell the property after finding a suitable buyer in Ronnie and Lydia Warnick, who found it the perfect isolated haven from their frequent world travels on business. The Warnicks had faithfully paid on the contract for three years.

The first wife, Eileen Barrett, and her three grown children—two sons, John Junior and David, and a daughter, Annette, now living in various parts of the nation—were deeply religious and happily involved in church activities. Together these three heirs decided to sell their part of the contract and place the funds in control of their mother Eilene, who had decided to donate some of the funds to their church.

The second wife, Tanya Barrett, wanted to keep her part of the note as income to help raise her young daughter Madeleine.

Rita—the note broker—warned me that Eileen wanted to sell but had not yet signed a written preliminary agreement. She also told me that Eileen now used her maiden name, McLean, as she had done since her former husband remarried. I told Rita that if we got the deal her commission was assured, and my firm sent Eileen McLean one of our preliminary agreement forms to sign.

However, Eileen didn't sign it. I called her on the phone and asked why. She frankly told me she was shopping the contract and wasn't able to make up her mind. I tolerated this for nearly three weeks and one day told her flatly that she had to make a decision. She said, okay, I'll go with you. She signed the preliminary agreement and sent it to us.

Then I got to work. My first task was to make arrangements with Tanya Barrett (who was not selling her quarter-interest) on how to handle any forfeiture and repossession if it occurred after I bought the other three-quarters of the contract, and how the property would be managed. We worked out an agreement and she signed the necessary documents.

Next, I ordered an appraisal of the property from G. B. Olivera, a New Mexico real estate agent who was also a licensed appraiser. It wasn't easy finding an appraiser: the property was an hour's drive from almost anything, and two hours' drive from the county seat. But when Olivera finished, the appraisal looked good, the current value substantially higher than the price paid for it.

Then I checked out the payors, Ronnie and Lydia Warnick. I found that they loved the place so much that they had even created a personal website showing photographs of their beautiful desert land. I contacted them by email and on the phone. They were nice but worried about signing an estoppel, and refused to do it. They assured me they would always pay on time and never default.

Then I asked for their Social Security numbers, which they refused to give me. I could understand their reluctance because of concerns over identity theft, but I needed their numbers to run a routine credit check on them. As a note buyer, I was authorized by law to run a credit check on them. But I needed Social Security numbers to do it.

I tried to get their numbers from the servicing agency who was handling the contract, but they also refused to give them. I tried other normal channels for getting the numbers but to no avail.

That left me with only the list of registered voters kept by the County Clerk, who confirmed that the Warnicks were registered voters but wouldn't give their Social Security numbers over the phone. Voting records were a matter of public information and anyone could come in and inspect them in person. These particular voting records displayed Social Security numbers.

I called Mr. Olivera and asked him to get the numbers. He refused because it was a small rural community and he didn't want to irritate the Warnicks—and everybody they might tell about it.

So I paid a lawyer $100 to stop in at the county clerk's office and get the Warnick's Social Security numbers from the voter registration record.

Finally, I could check their credit. It came back perfect. That, along with their perfect three-year payment record convinced me to proceed even without an estoppel—a move I would not recommend in ordinary circumstances. But I figured that if the Warnicks had any claims or offsets, they would certainly have told me by now.

I took the next step and got the title report from Martinez Title, the only title insurance firm in the county. To my dismay, they found some clouds on the title that should have been eliminated when the property sold three years earlier. However, Buford Land Assurance, the company that had insured the title when the Barretts sold to the Warnicks, had gone out of business. All their information had vanished.

In desperation, I contacted Herbert Locke, the attorney who represented the Barrett estate at the death of John Barrett and also at the sale of the property to the Warnicks. Perhaps he could provide information about the clouds on the title.

Herbert Locke had retired and closed his legal practice, but he had the information I needed. However, he told me bluntly that he would do nothing to help me buy this contract because he felt Eileen McLean would give the proceeds to her church, and he felt strongly that such a move was wrong. I suspected that he didn't belong to the same denomination! He refused to tell me a thing.

Stumped!

At my wit's end, I called Martinez Title and talked to its owner, Jimmy Martinez. He did two weeks' research and finally removed the clouds on the title. I had jumped the last of the hurdles—I thought.

Stan Cushman, the lawyer we used on this transaction, prepared all the formal documents necessary to buy the contract. I faxed them to Jimmy Martinez to make sure he approved before we sent them off to the four parties for signature. Jimmy said they looked fine.

Eileen was in a hurry for fast cash. She had pressing personal debts to pay off, and wanted to make that donation to her church. Now that Martinez Title had approved the documents, I told her it shouldn't take more than three days to get everything signed and recorded using Federal Express. I sent the papers out by FedEx with return FedEx envelopes to help speed things up for Eileen.

Eileen was working two jobs, so it was hard for her to find a notary in her off hours, and it took several days for her papers to get back to me.

I was alarmed as several more days went by and John, Jr.'s package didn't arrive. I tried to track it through Federal Express, but they had no record of it. I called John, Jr. and asked if he had returned the papers. He said yes, his friend Alex had dropped the package in the box as soon as he had signed the papers.

Box? What box, I asked.

"The mail box," he replied.

Oh, no! John, Jr. had his friend put the FedEx package in a U.S. Postal Service box with no postage. He'd thought it was like Express Mail.

There was nothing to do but send another set of papers by FedEx, after telling John, Jr. exactly what he had to do.

Once again, I told Eileen she should have her money within three days. John, Jr. successfully returned the signed papers to me and I forwarded them overnight to Martinez Title Company for recording.

As I discovered later, that very day Eileen wrote a check to her church—10 percent of the total amount—figuring it would clear by the time her money arrived.

Now the final blow struck: Jimmy Martinez called me and apologetically said he couldn't record the documents because he needed Eileen to sign them again—she had used her married name, Eileen Barrett, on the documents, thinking it would be less confusing. But three years earlier she had signed the property sale documents "Eileen McLean," and the contract sale documents had to match.

Jimmy Martinez didn't notice that when he checked

the papers earlier and neither did we. So, despite my precautions, we had another delay in getting Eileen's money to her.

Knowing it looked like my fault, I had to call and tell her. She was beside herself with anxiety. She didn't know what to do. She asked me to call her church and explain what had happened—she was too upset to do it herself.

I called the church officials and found they were very understanding. They hadn't realized how much pressure Eileen was under and they contacted parishoners to see if they could find somebody to help.

They found a church volunteer named Joshua Chauncey who owned a computer and agreed to help in any way he could. And did he!

Josh received the documents by e-mail and printed them out. He took them an hour's drive to Eileen's town, found a notary, drove the notary to Eileen's workplace, and got everything signed and notarized.

He then drove two more hours to the county seat with the properly signed documents and personally put them in the hands of Jimmy Martinez. What a hero!

Jimmy recorded the sale of the contract and Eileen's money became immediately available.

Now, how to get our check to Eileen's bank in time? After Eileen gave me written authority, we sent her check by Federal Express to another church volunteer, Ed Wimmer, who drove two hours to her bank and deposited the money in her account.

Thus, when Eileen's donation went to the bank for payment, her account had plenty of money in it.

Whew! That was close! Our whole office was a little frazzled. But Eileen Barrett McLean was the most frazzled of all.

I did the only reasonable thing: I sent her a big bouquet of flowers.

FAST CASH

PART FIVE

Wisdom

FAST CASH

Chapter 13
Taking Pains

"*Due diligence*: Such a measure of prudence, activity, or assiduity, as is properly to be expected from, and ordinarily exercised by, a reasonable and prudent man under the particular circumstances, not measured by any absolute standard, but depending on the relative facts of the special case."

I finished reading the entry in *Black's Law Dictionary* to my Dad.

"Do you think anyone would understand that?" I asked.

"The textbook definition? Sure," he replied. "What you actually have to do in note buying? It doesn't tell you a thing."

"That's the problem. What we really do is so technical I don't know where to begin."

"Begin what? What do you need this for?" asked my father.

"One of the newsletters wants me to write a monthly column. I'm not sure if I want to do it."

"Sure you do. It's an honor. Besides, you always say the industry could use better education."

"It could," I said ruefully. "I just don't want to be the educator."

"Why not? You're perfect for it."

"I'm a note buyer, Dad, not a writer."

"Really? I've never known you to run from a challenge. What do you want to bet that this time next month you'll be a writer too."

Dad won that one. A long time ago. But it didn't solve my problem of trying to explain the technical side of note buying.

Over the years I've given many classes to real estate agents and even lawyers to analyze the problems of notes. The classroom situation is fine for drawing charts and diagrams and lists of things to do, but it's just not suitable for drawing a comprehensive picture of what really happens.

One of my most vexing teaching problems is trying to explain due diligence. The reason is simple: there's just too much that goes into investigating a note.

The only way to learn due diligence properly is to see it for yourself, note by note by note. Like this:

Some time ago my firm got a call from a woman with a note to sell. Her name was Pam Johnson. She gave me the particulars: the security for the note was a large undeveloped acreage in the neighboring state of Oregon. The payor was a doctor named George Wilson, who ran a well-established rural practice and had made all payments on time.

Pam was Dr. Wilson's receptionist, which meant that I would have to make sure the transaction was truly "arm's length," and not a "fake and bake deal" pretending to seller-finance a property for an exorbitantly high price so they can dump a "created" note to raise some fast cash.

The price Dr. Wilson had paid was quite substantial, so that question answered itself. Pam had all the necessary records, and everything was in order.

I'm always a little suspicious of sales between friends or relatives. That extends to the employer/employee relationship here. Because this note required extra caution, I asked Pam and Dr. Wilson for permission to record our preliminary agreement with the county recorder's office. They agreed, I recorded it and I went to work on my due diligence.

Note buyers need to examine everything with great care before jumping onto a transaction, no matter how good it looks at first.

The documents arrived, and I began to sift through the details one by one. I looked first at the seller's closing statement for the sale of the property. This document is prepared by whoever closes the sale of the property, which can be an attorney or any other professional settlement agent, such as an escrow closer or a real estate broker.

The seller's closing statement may not show the down payment, which was the first thing I wanted to examine. The buyer's closing statement almost always shows the down payment, but it can be difficult to obtain, since real estate buyers (note payors) have no motivation to help you buy their note. Fortunately in this case, the down payment showed on the seller's closing statement: Dr. Wilson had paid $50,000 down on this large property, a very satisfactory amount.

I always pay special attention to the down payment on a property, because it tells me a great deal about the quality of the note.

I want to know several things about it:

- I want know that it was really paid.
- I want evidence such as a canceled check or wire transfer to show that the transaction was not faked with a promise, a trade, a side note or any other non-cash trick.
- I want to know whether the buyer had to borrow the money to make the down payment.

Next, I wanted an appraisal of the property to verify the value of the land, so I called a licensed appraiser named Roy Johnson in Ringling, a small town near the property. The appraiser came back with a valuation nearly identical to the price the buyer had paid.

Even so, the price Dr. Wilson had paid for this out-of-the-way acreage seemed a little high to me, so I began to call the owners of neighboring properties.

One was a nice lady named Lola Conrad, who told me she had been trying to sell her land right next to Pam Johnson's for several years with no takers.

I asked her if she thought the price Dr. Wilson had paid was too high. To my surprise, she laughed.

"It's about three times too high."

I protested that I had obtained the valuation from a licensed appraiser in the nearby town.

Lola laughed again. "He's Pam's cousin."

That was alarming. I thanked her and immediately called Pam Johnson. I didn't mention my discovery, but only asked if she would instruct her bank to let me examine her checking account statement to verify that she had received the $50,000 from Dr. Wilson. She gave me written permission to examine that week's transactions.

When I contacted the bank, I found that, sure enough, Pam Johnson had deposited a check from Dr. Wilson in the amount of $50,000 on the day she had said.

Almost as an afterthought, I asked the bank officer, "Did Pam Johnson write a check to Dr. Wilson anytime after that?"

The voice came back, "Yes, the very next day, for $50,000."

I had been set up. The high price, the matching appraised valuation, the big down payment, the perfect payment record, *all illusions just to sell the note*.

And it had cost me probably $5,000 worth of time and expense.

I was furious. I thought about calling the state's attorney general with a fraud complaint, but decided it wasn't worth the effort, so I quietly explained to Pam that I was unable to buy her note and let it go at that.

Several years later I got a call from her. She had taken the property back from Dr. Wilson and was now selling it (at a greatly reduced price, I saw). She discovered that our preliminary agreement, which I had officially recorded with the county recorder, was holding up her sale. She wanted me to release it.

Now her chickens were coming home to roost. I explained that I would be happy to release the agreement if she would compensate me for the wasted effort I had expended on due diligence several years earlier. Without making any accusations, I let Pam know that I understood exactly what had happened back then.

Soon I received a check in a suitable amount to cover my losses—and no argument whatsoever about paying me. I released the agreement and I presume that her sale went through.

That story makes an unmistakable point about doing your due diligence properly. It also shows how tough it would be to prepare a novice note buyer for coping with such a scam.

Phony down payments are rare, but you can see how disastrous they could be if you failed to detect them.

Other problem notes are just as hard to detect and even more difficult to handle—because they depend on acute technical knowledge.

Like this one:

My firm received a call from Richard Weaver asking for a quote. He and his wife Denise had sold some land a few years earlier to another couple, Horace and Rita Anderson, who proved to be excellent payors.

The Weavers explained that the Andersons had since moved a mobile home onto the property and had rented it out, providing them with ample rental income to make the note payments. The Weavers needed to sell the note because they had just started a new business and needed fast cash to make improvements.

They signed a preliminary agreement with us and we proceeded with our due diligence.

We would normally contact the original escrow closer to obtain copies of documents surrounding the creation of the note, but couldn't do so in this case because the Weavers had closed the transaction and prepared the papers themselves.

So we began by verifying the price the Andersons had paid for the property by checking with the county recorder's office.

Then we obtained the payment record from the Weavers and found it to be perfect.

We also ran a credit check on the Andersons and found them to be financially sound. Although a bank serviced the payments each month and showed the balance due, I also personally contacted the Andersons.

I spoke to Rita Anderson, who said that the balance was correct, but complained that the Weavers had not dug the well for the mobile home the Andersons had purchased from them.

I was taken aback. "Excuse me, please," I said. "Are you sure you purchased the mobile home from the Weavers?"

"Sure I'm sure," Rita said. "And our water is still hooked up to the Weavers' pipes next door."

"But I thought you only bought the land from them," I said. "I thought you moved your own mobile home there."

"I don't know what gave you that idea," Rita said. "The mobile home came with the land. The Weavers' son Jimmy used to live in it. They haven't sent us anything about the title to it, either. And they promised, just like they promised us that blasted well. That was three years ago and they haven't started digging yet."

Stunned, I asked Rita, "Did you get anything in writing about the well?"

"Of course we did. Want a copy of it?"

The Andersons then sent me a signed agreement showing that the Weavers were indeed obligated to dig a well—within one year of the date of purchase. That well was seriously late.

You can see how this would affect the note: offsets, just like we saw in Chapter 9.

Now I grew concerned about the different stories I was getting from the Weavers and the Andersons.

I looked into the note in greater detail. It was what's called a "wraparound" in industry jargon, meaning that a bigger note "wrapped around" a smaller note. The smaller note was the first lien on the property, from when the Weavers bought it from Percy Kilbride. The Weavers were still making payments on it. The larger lien that "wrapped around" the smaller Kilbride lien was created when the Weavers sold the property to the Andersons. But the first lien note to Kilbride did not go away just by selling the property. The Weavers still owed the first lien note. The payments from the Andersons on the bigger "wraparound" second lien note provided enough money so the Weavers could pay Kilbride and have some money left over every month. The idea of the "wraparound" is to have a bigger note pay for a smaller note.

The Weavers wanted to sell us the Anderson's wraparound note, not the first lien note to Percy Kilbride. The Weavers agreed to pay off the first lien Kilbride note when we paid them the fast cash for the larger Anderson note. With the Kilbride first lien note paid off, the Anderson note would no longer be a wraparound, it would be the only one left, and thus transformed into the first lien.

I tried to contact Percy Kilbride to get payoff figures,

only to find that he had recently died, and that his estate was being managed by his attorney, William Elliott. A conversation with Mr. Elliott revealed another serious discrepancy in the Weavers' story: although they told us they would pay off the first lien at closing, they had not been making their monthly payments on it as they were supposed to.

The Andersons, on the other hand, had been paying the Weavers on time. The Weavers were keeping the money they were supposed to be paying Mr. Kilbride. They were "milking the wraparound."

Suddenly we had two problems. First, because the first lien was delinquent, the Weavers owed more money than we had thought. The second problem was that the Andersons owed the Weavers less than we had thought because they had offsets!

So I tried to help save the Weavers some money by asking Mr. Elliott if the estate would grant a discount, accepting less money for the first lien. He agreed on behalf of the Kilbride estate.

Now we had solved most of the problems we needed to purchase the Weavers' note.

Then Richard Weaver called. He was livid.

"Ms. Stevens," he said in an agitated voice, "Rita Anderson just came over and told me she's afraid the Kilbrides will foreclose on me. She accused me of not paying them. She said you told her. You have absolutely no business giving such false information to the Andersons."

I waited a moment after he said his piece, then told him, "Mr. Weaver, the Kilbride estate's attorney provided me with documentary proof that your first lien is not current."

"He's just plain wrong. We *are* up to date. Period!" he nearly shouted into the phone.

No point pressing that any further.

"Okay then," I said, "why haven't you given the mobile home title to the Andersons?"

Mr. Weaver gave me the same old story: "That was theirs. We never sold it to them."

"Mr. Weaver, both of the Andersons say otherwise."

"Okay, okay," stammered Richard Weaver. "The title is in our safe deposit box, but we haven't checked it because it's none of the Andersons' business."

"Mr. Weaver, it most certainly *is* their business. Now what about that well you promised to dig?"

Richard Weaver made a surprised sound—he had never mentioned the obligation to us. "Uh..." his voice trailed off.

I told him, "You either have to dig the well and hook up the water or pay for it from the closing money when we buy your note. I've made it as easy for you as I can."

I was getting frustrated trying to help someone who wasn't helpable. I finally said, "The Kilbride estate is willing to grant you a discount, and that'll help you cover the cost of the new well."

That didn't help. Mr. Weaver was totally flustered: "I, uh, hmm, uh, I'll call you back in a few hours."

When he called, he only yelled at me, saying he and his wife didn't want to sell the note.

Puzzling. All the Weavers had to do was produce the mobile home title, dig the well and hook up the water. Why did they back out?

We could only presume that there was some irregularity. Even though we had a legally binding agreement that they would sell us the note, we didn't argue. We long ago set the policy that we would not pursue sellers who back out, and would go on to the next opportunity rather than spend the time and money going to court.

When I notified the Andersons that we wouldn't be buying the note, they were concerned. They had hoped their problems with the well, the water hookup, their mobile home, and the delinquent Kilbride lien would be taken care of.

Horace Anderson asked if we would be pursuing legal

remedies to enforce our agreement, and I explained our "get on with it" policy.

Now the Andersons were really concerned: what if the Weavers tried to sell the note to someone else who was not as careful about contacting the payors?

In order to protect their interests, the Andersons went to their attorney who filed a notice with the county recorder so that the problems would show up any time that a title report was issued. That way, any prospective note buyer would know about the problems, even if they didn't take the care to contact the payors.

The Andersons' attorney also advised them to make payments directly to the Kilbride estate until the first lien was brought current.

We tried one last step to rescue this note deal gone sour. Since we had already negotiated a discount on the first lien, we sent the Weavers a legal notification that if they sold the note by a certain deadline, we would pass the discount along to them. Even with this fair-minded offer, they still didn't want to sell.

The deadline passed.

There was one way left to snatch victory from the jaws of this defeat: we bought the first lien note from the Kilbride estate.

Ha! See how our technical knowledge allowed us not only to buy a good note at a great discount, but also put us in a position to make things come out right for the Andersons?

Sometimes due diligence has to become ultra diligence before it pays off. Like on this note:

One winter not long ago, a note broker named Quincy Sturgis sent us an attractive offer to buy a $200,000 real estate note secured by a first lien. Mr. Sturgis usually buys notes for himself, but this one was too large for him to handle. The package he sent was complete and professional.

The property—an apartment building, a house and a mobile home—was located in Oroville, a small town in Iowa. The payor, Kyle Rathburn, had paid on the note for nearly five years, a good sign, and still owed about 55% of what he paid for the property. The rents were four times the amount of the monthly payment, another good sign—there were ample funds to pay the monthly payments. A preliminary check showed that Mr. Rathburn was creditworthy.

The note sellers, Mitch and Cora Comstock, were a retired couple in their late seventies whose family had owned the property for generations—they had lived on the property right up to the time they sold it to the payor five years earlier. They had moved to a warmer climate and now wanted to simplify their lives and get fast cash.

It looked like a fine transaction, so we began our due diligence. I began by speaking with Mr. Rathburn, who was open and friendly. When I asked why the current payment was late, he explained that his utilities were so high in the winter that it would be another couple of weeks before he sent it, but it would arrive safely. We prepared an estoppel document to verify the balance owing and mailed it for his signature.

Then we spoke to Jared Bloom, the real estate agent who sold the property five years earlier. Mr. Bloom's office also collected the payments, and he sent us a copy of the good payment record, along with the closing documents from the sale to Mr. Rathburn. We noticed that the mobile home was still in the Comstocks' name, and hadn't been documented properly, but that would be easy to remedy at closing.

Mr. Bloom was also a licensed appraiser, and we ordered an appraisal, which came in at over what Mr. Rathburn paid for the property. Mr. Bloom hadn't been able to inspect the inside because he couldn't get together with Mr. Rathburn to let him in, so we only got a "windshield" or "exterior" appraisal. But it still looked good enough for us to hire an Oroville lawyer, Omar Gibson, to help us with the transaction.

The title insurance report we ordered arrived, and it too looked good. Not only did it show the deed of trust we wanted to buy, but it also showed that Cornhuskers Commodity Bank had recently loaned Mr. Rathburn a large sum of money on this and several other of his properties. We liked the fact that the bank had a second lien on the property, because that meant they had an incentive to see that we got paid in order to protect their inferior position. We also liked the fact that Mr. Rathburn owned several other properties, since that suggested financial strength.

We were impressed. This note looked excellent.

Then a small problem appeared: When we checked with the county's tax department, we found that Mr. Rathburn had not paid his real estate taxes for five years. The county treasurer had already posted notices to sell tax certificates on the property, which would yield 14% interest. That could be an ominous development.

I asked Mr. Rathburn to bring the taxes current, but he said he wouldn't be able to for several months. He was concerned about a $25,000 balloon payment due on the note. I said that if he would pay the taxes now, we would amend the note and waive the $25,000 balloon payment. Mr. Rathburn said he didn't have the money.

The small problem now looked larger. I urged him to pay the taxes immediately. I telephoned, faxed and e-mailed him repeatedly. No response. And he didn't send us the estoppel, either.

A few more days went by and I contacted Mr. Bloom, who was collecting the payments. Mr. Rathburn still had not paid the current payment and another was due soon. The problem was growing.

We reported it to both Quincy Sturgis, the note broker, and the Comstocks. The Comstocks expressed surprise and offered to take less money for the note. They were old, they said, and just wanted to relax and enjoy the remainder of their lives. They suggested that Mr. Rathburn might be angry because he didn't want them to sell the note—they had offered him a discount previously, but he never took advantage of it. They thought he might be trying to delay or frustrate our purchase to buy time so he could pay off the note at a discount.

We now contacted Cornhuskers Commodity Bank. We asked if they would pay the taxes and the delinquent payment to protect their second lien position, or, in the alternative, loan the money for it to Mr. Rathburn.

Trent Ford, the Cornhuskers accounts manager, flatly refused, saying he would simply let the property go if trouble arose. He was emphatically not interested in lending more money to Rathburn since he was late paying them too!

Big problem. As if that weren't enough, Omar Gibson, our Oroville attorney, said he had discovered several electrical and housing code violations on the Rathburn property. The documents were almost a year old and the violations had not been corrected.

Gibson also said the local scuttlebutt was that Rathburn was planning to sneak the mobile home across state lines and sell it if we didn't buy the note. Everyone except us seemed to know he was in deep financial trouble.

Now it was all clear to me. The Comstocks were trying to dump the note on us to avoid legal entanglements with Rathburn.

I called them and politely said we would not be buying their note, and gave them all the reasons why. They sounded totally surprised. I suggested they get a lawyer and foreclose before things got any worse. Mitch and Cora Comstock thanked me for bringing these unexpected problems to their attention (yeah, right).

I stewed for several hours over the hundreds of dollars and all the time I'd put into this lousy note. I don't like to lose.

I went over the documents again and, behold! There *was* a way to outwit fate on this one: we bought the county's tax certificates on the Rathburn property and made 14% interest.

See? It's one of those technicalities that makes the difference between failure and success.

Some time ago I gave a bid by telephone on a land sale contract for the DreamOn Motel with bar and restaurant in Milwaukee, Wisconsin. A land sale contract is an agreement similar to a note and lien on real estate.

I recognized the contract from several previous inquiries, which told me that Willis Burbank, the note broker, was having a hard time finding a buyer for it.

What was so risky about this property that the contract was being shopped all over the country?

There was only one way to know, so my husband Manfred and I decided to go to Milwaukee to inspect the property in person.

We made a few advance arrangements with Mr. Burbank, first for a meeting with the seller (a man named Joseph Fulton), and then with Milton Freewater, a Milwaukee attorney we could hire to look over the contract.

When we landed at the airport in Milwaukee, Manfred suggested that we not use our reservations at the DreamOn, but instead just walk in off the street and ask for a room. We would get a more realistic impression of the place if they didn't know who we were.

When we checked in, the clerk gave us an ordinary room on the second of three floors, and the first thing I noticed about it was the mirror on the ceiling above the bed. DreamOn indeed! I reserved judgment and looked around. The furnishings were all a little shopworn, but not inadequate.

We had decided upon dinner our first night in Milwaukee

at The Landgraf, a German restaurant where the chef was a friend of Manfred's from the old days in Europe. The hostess seated us and Manfred asked to see the distinguished Mr. Karl Appelmann. Delighted, the chef invited us into the kitchen where the two men chatted over old times for quite a while.

Manfred asked Karl if he knew anything about the DreamOn Motel. Karl cocked his head and squinted at Manfred.

"Well, my old friend," he began, "nothing much, except that they had a shootout over drugs about six months ago. The gunman took a hostage, but he let him go. Is that what you wanted to know?

Manfred remained silent and just nodded his head.

Karl added, "Oh, but that was before the new owner took over."

"Did things get better then?" asked Manfred.

"Not that I know of," said Karl.

Manfred and I exchanged glances, and we said our goodbyes and went back to our table.

It was a quiet dinner.

That night at the motel we got little sleep because of the constant noise. An endless string of cars stopped just below our room, noisy people piled out, went to the room above us and five minutes later drove away in a squeal of tires. The traffic went on and on. Finally, at 5:00 a.m., Manfred observed a lone man leaving the room above and driving away in an expensive car. A floating drug operation, no doubt about it.

The next morning after breakfast in the DreamOn restaurant, we strolled around to see what the neighborhood was like. A residential area lay immediately behind the motel and commercial strip. The houses were pleasant but run-down. We found a real estate office almost across the street from the motel—with heavy bars in front of the windows—where some nice people assured us this was a good neighborhood. We didn't ask why a real estate office needed window bars in a good neighborhood.

Then we went to see Milton Freewater in his law offices. He spent the rest of the day with us going over all the
details of the contract. We had a dinner meeting scheduled
with Burbank the note broker and Fuller the seller at the
Lakeshore Grill, a noted Milwaukee restaurant, and wanted
to be completely prepared.

We returned to the DreamOn to freshen up before our
dinner appointment, and Manfred went outside to take the
usual photographs of the property. While taking shots from
all angles, he noticed a large man hanging around the motel's
restaurant. After going around the corner for a side shot,
Manfred came back toward the front and saw an elderly couple
on their knees pleading with the man, who was holding them
at gunpoint. It was a robbery! The man took their money and
ran.

The police quickly appeared and interviewed Manfred,
the only eyewitness. By the time they finished with him we
were late for our dinner appointment.

Manfred and I arrived at the table and joined Burbank
and Fuller. We introduced ourselves and ordered dinner.
Burbank was a real estate agent, all smiles and good will, while
Fuller was a crusty businessman who had bought and sold
motel properties for many years.

We apologized for the delay, explaining pointedly that
an armed robbery on the motel property had kept us.

Mr. Fuller looked at us and said, "That's surprising. I
owned the place for twenty years with no problem."

"Oh, really?" I asked. "And what about the hostage-
taking?"

"Oh, that," he replied, unabashed. "It was nothing."

Burbank went ashen.

I looked straight at Mr. Fuller and said, "I'm not sure
I want to buy your contract, Mr. Fuller. If I do decide to, I'll
lower my bid substantially. I found out some things I didn't

know. But let me think about it."

Upon our return to Seattle I contacted the payor, Mr. Atul Prakash, an East Indian businessman living in Chicago who had bought and refurbished several motels, and was buying more. Milton Freewater knew Mr. Prakash's attorney, and assured us that Mr. Prakash himself was a person of impeccable character.

I called Mr. Prakash on the phone. He had owned the DreamOn Motel for only about 6 months, but had cleaned the property up, was doing a lot of remodeling and bringing the income up. He assured me he would see that security was tightened and there would be no illegal activity there in the future.

Six months passed. Mr. Freewater sent a letter confirming that the illegal activities on the property had ceased and were no longer a problem. I then submitted a new and very low bid. Mr. Fuller accepted it and we closed the contract negotiations.

Mr. Prakash has lived up to his reputation. His payments have been timely and accurate.

Teaching note buyers to personally visit the property securing the note is probably my toughest problem. It costs a lot up front, that's true. It saves a lot more in the long run. That's even more true.

FAST CASH

Chapter 14
Divorce Liens

I've never been divorced, but I sure know a lot of people who have.

Wall Street Brokers handles a large volume of notes from divorced couples.

These notes are called "divorce liens."

We get so many that we even put up a website called DivorceLiens.com.

Designing it gave me a problem: what do you say?

How do you talk about money to someone undergoing the trauma of a divorce?

What do you say to them so it doesn't sound crass and commercialized?

How do you get through their suffering to offer both parties financial hope?

I thought and thought. I talked to many friends, single, married, divorced, remarried, redivorced—everything.

Here's what I came up with for the website:

Divorce is tough. For both of you. A Divorce Lien can ease
the stress. You can arrange a Divorce Lien so:

She:
- Keeps the house
- Avoids relocation costs
- Has time to pay for his share of the house
- Retains a fair share of the home equity
- Has the same familiar environment for her-
  self and children

He:
- Gets a lien on the house
- Can sell the lien for cash
- Gets money for new living quarters
- Has cash to pay attorney fees

Or—he gets the house and she gets the cash.
How do you get the cash? You sell the lien to us.

We've helped people with Divorce Liens for over
25 years. We're a family business. We're Wall
Street Brokers, Inc. We can help.

It's more than just a sales pitch, we really try to live up
to it. As in all note transactions, it's not easy.

Sometimes it's just as tough to cope with a divorce
lien as it is a divorce.

Even the names for it get weird. Sometimes they're
called "marital liens" and in some instances they're known by
the obscure legal term, "owelty liens."

"Owelty" refers to the equal splitting of assets.

So you see how technicalities even enter into the very
commonplace world of divorce and divorce liens.

To give you an idea how technical even an ordinary
divorce lien can get, consider the story of Joan Helms:

Our firm received a call from a woman named Joan Helms, who wanted to sell a divorce lien. She explained that she was having difficulty finding a note buyer.

"I tried to sell my note a month ago," Joan told me, "but the note buyer I dealt with gave me one excuse after another. Then he unexpectedly withdrew his offer! I can't tell you how outraged I was."

She told how she'd stormed off to the city library and used their computers to look through the *Divorce Magazine* website. There she found one of our articles, and surfed around and saw our name in a number of professional newsletter webites.

"I want to deal with a reputable business," she said. "And you seem to know what you're doing. Can you help me?"

I told her we always do our best, but that everything depends on the details. I asked her for some preliminary facts about her situation.

Joan Helms explained that she had been in a long-term marriage which eventually went sour and ended in divorce about a year earlier. Her ex-husband George was awarded the family home—a brick, 4 bedroom, 3-1/2 bath residence with a swimming pool. Joan got her share in the form of a $36,000 note secured by second lien documents against the home.

George Helms was making monthly payments to Joan on the lien, which was unusual. I told Joan that most divorce liens do not have monthly payments, but only a large balloon payment due at some agreed-upon date. I surmised that monthly payments indicated a probable financially sound note, so this was a good one. I made a preliminary agreement to buy Joan's note, subject to what we found during our due diligence.

We got busy and obtained copies of the complex real estate documents and the divorce papers. Thankfully, they were in order.

One task done.

We then ordered a preliminary title report from Central Title Company. The title insurance company told us it would take a week before we'd get the report. Joan was anxious to get fast cash and asked if we could speed things up, so four days later we checked with Central Title. To our shock, we found that their researcher had abandoned our folder on his desk, so the title search hadn't even begun. Central Title put a rush on it to make amends.

We then sent a certified letter to the payor, ex-husband George Helms. The letter explained that we were in the process of due diligence about buying the note and lien from his ex-wife. We wanted to be sure he agreed with the balance due, and that he had no claims against it. It seems that George wasn't home when the certified letter arrived, and he still hadn't gone to the post office to pick it up. I checked with Joan, and she suggested that I call him 15 minutes before his favorite evening television program, when she knew he'd be home.

So, at 7:45 that evening, I called and he answered, just as she said. I explained who I was and what I wanted. He was very polite and gave no indication of any problem. He said he hadn't received any certified letter asking for a balance verification, but I could e-mail it to him. He said he'd look at it and if everything was in order, he'd sign it and get it back to me.

So I sent him the e-mail. I phoned him the next day and he said things looked fine. He said he'd sign it and send it back. But I didn't receive anything in writing as he'd promised.

While waiting for the return of the verification, we ordered an appraisal on the house, wanting to be sure it was worth what it stated in the divorce papers.

The next day Joan called us, weeping uncontrollably. Between sobs she told me that since they'd divorced, they still had dinner together often, and went on family outings with their 13 year old daughter.

"I was at the house last, last night," she stuttered. "George and I had dinner."

I waited as she caught her breath. "Yes?" I said.

"He told me not to sell the lien!" she wailed. "He's going to Mexico tomorrow for a week's vacation. When he gets back he wants to buy the lien himself. It'll take me three months to get my money by the time he gets around to refinancing!" She broke down into wracking sobs.

She knew she'd get her money from us in a week. She needed it badly.

"And there's the other thing," she said, recovering. "I don't like him trying to control me like that. That's one of the reasons I divorced him in the first place." An edge of hardness tinged her voice now.

"Is your offer to buy my note still good?" she asked.

I emphatically said, "Yes!"

"Then I've decided. I'm going to do it my way. I'm going to sell the note to you. Do we have time to finish before George gets back?"

"A week? If we really push we can do it," I assured her.

"It's ironic," she said. "Just a few months ago I offered to sell him the note and he ignored me. But now that I have a real buyer, he's up to his old tricks, trying to frustrate everything I do."

I told Joan that she was facing the most common problem in the note business—once the payor finds out the note holder is selling the note, the payor interferes and wants to buy it, thereby eliminating the transaction altogether.

Now we had to work fast. The transaction had to be closed in one week. We knew we'd have to take a chance and buy the note without George's written verification of the balance. Risky, but it was one less hurdle.

We finally got the title report—and found it was full of problems.

George Helms is a common name, so we had to identify the right George Helms to eliminate liens against others
with the same name.

Once we got that sorted out, we found five documents
recorded from Joan's divorce itself, not to mention the first
lien to the bank. We had to verify all information on the first
lien.

Assignments of all 5 divorce/real estate documents had
to be drawn, as well as 5 release documents in anticipation of
when the note would be paid off. The title company had to
approve all documents.

The appraisal came in at the last minute, very close to
what it had been appraised for during the divorce. We FedExed
the papers to Joan, who took a day off work so she could sign
them, get them notarized, and get them back to us before
George came back from Mexico!

We did it! We got the papers, recorded them, and dis-
bursed the funds to Joan. She was elated. She bubbled her
appreciation for our help and said she'd be talking to us again.

A few days later she called, sounding triumphant. "I
paid all my bills," she said. "And George knows I sold the
note."

"How did he react?" I asked.

"He was furious for a moment, but I think he knew
there was nothing he could do about it. When he stopped sput-
tering, he only asked if his payment might be considered late
because it's due tomorrow."

Joan told him we'd probably give him a day's grace
considering the circumstances. We did.

Since then, George has paid regularly, and everything
is going just fine.

That wasn't very technical at all, but you see how a
note buyer also has to be alert for human foibles. Speaking of
human foibles, here are some more:

Richard Terfel, a father who had been divorced for two years contacted us about a note he wanted to sell. The equity in the family dwelling had been divided equally in the property settlement, with his ex-wife Linda given ownership of the home and the obligation to pay the first lien lender.

Richard received a note signed by Linda in payment for his half of the equity. The note was secured by a second lien on the home, and was due in one lump sum five years from the date of divorce, or six months after Linda remarried, or upon the sale or refinancing of the home.

Richard and Tiffany, his "significant other," wanted to buy a new home, and needed to sell the note for cash. Buying a new home was especially urgent for Mr. Terfel because a custody change involving the oldest of his three children meant he would probably have his daughter, Heather, living with him soon. He also wanted to pay off Malcolm Walstone, his divorce lawyer.

We were familiar with Broadmont, the upscale area where Linda lived. Her equity in the house had been good at the time of her divorce, but the market had skyrocketed, increasing the home's value tremendously. We knew that Richard's second lien was more than ample security for his note.

Linda had landed a good-paying job and rented the basement for extra income. Reports showed us that Linda was creditworthy. The note was outstanding.

Until we read it again carefully. A glaring fault practically jumped off the page at us. The note was not payable at a definite time! The terms stated that it could be paid off in five years *or* six months after Linda remarried *or* when she sold or re-financed the house. Therefore, if Linda didn't meet any of the conditions—if she didn't pay the note in five years or remarry or sell or refinance—she could argue that she would never be required to pay off the note! In practical terms, *this note might never pay off!*

[handwritten: NON-NEGOTIABLE notes]

That made the note "non-negotiable." As we saw in Chapter 5, there are legal requirements for a note to be "negotiable" and one of them is that it must be payable **at a definite time**.

Because this note was "non-negotiable," we could not be a "holder in due course," the legal protection against many possible claims that you'll recall from Chapters 8 and 9.

In divorces, there's always a risk of the payor making claims. We would not be protected from claims without the "holder in due course" status, and that status was made impossible by the uncertain language in the note.

We explained our concern to Richard, and asked him if Linda would agree to amend the note to make it "negotiable" by putting in a definite date of 5 years and eliminating the other verbiage.

Richard explained that he and Linda were not on the best of terms, and that she would most likely refuse to amend the note.

The problem surprised him: he had paid stiff legal fees to Malcolm Walstone and expected everything to be taken care of. However, we frequently run into this problem because divorce lawyers are not always familiar with the law of negotiable instruments. It's a specialty in law, just like there are specialties in medicine.

Richard claimed the intention of the settlement was that Linda would pay him on or before 5 years. But that was not what the note said in its present condition, so we offered him two prices: a low price for the note in its current non-negotiable condition and a high price for the note if Linda would amend it to be negotiable.

Circumstances came to his aid: Linda was having difficulties with Heather and wanted Richard to take custody, which gave him leverage to persuade her to amend the note.

A court hearing on the matter was scheduled in a few weeks. After Richard and our firm consulted with our respective lawyers, I agreed to buy the note immediately for the low price. I gave Richard two months to have Linda amend it, at which time we would pay him the high price less what we'd already paid him. If she did not amend the note within the deadline, Richard would not be entitled to any more money— a fair arrangement.

In the meantime, Linda provided us with a signed estoppel document verifying the note balance and its present terms. On a little piece of yellow paper attached to the estoppel, she wrote, "I hope my pending bankruptcy does not affect your transaction, along with the three other liens."

Our long experience with divorce liens told us immediately what this was: a fictional "poison pill" intended to sour the deal to spite her ex-husband. We had thoroughly investigated Linda's financial condition and knew there was no bankruptcy and there were no other liens. We disregarded it entirely.

When we discussed the message with Richard and Tiffany, they said there was no way Linda would ever let herself go into bankruptcy—money was too important to her and she always managed to get it—and that yes, they believed we came to the proper conclusion. Had we been less experienced, this warning from the ex-wife would have scared us away from the deal.

We closed the transaction and paid Richard Terfel the low price. He had two months to get Linda to amend the note to make it negotiable and deliver the original note to us or receive no more money. We had placed the original note in the hands of Malcolm Wallstone, who passed it on to Linda's lawyer so he could obtain the proper amendment and return it. Everyone involved knew about the two month deadline.

The time passed. On the day of the deadline, at close of business, we received a copy of the amended note, with a copy of Linda's signature. We did not receive the original. Richard called, asking for the rest of his money, ready to come into our office to pick up his check. We told him that the original note had not been delivered to us by the deadline, which dashed his hopes.

We thought it was odd to get a copy at the last minute instead of the original. We were suspicious of another spite fight from the ex-wife, and the next day called her lawyer. He told us his client simply hadn't had time to come into his office and sign and amend the original, so she had faxed a copy. She would be stopping by this very day to amend the original. We realized that Linda had deliberately delayed the process.

Later that day we received the original amended note, now negotiable. We didn't think it was fair to punish Richard for Linda's spiteful act, so we paid him the rest of his money anyway, even though we were legally not obligated to do so.

A week later, we discovered that one of Linda's parents had passed away, and she would be inheriting a substantial amount of cash. She would have ample funds to pay the negotiable note payable at a definite time.

So you see, knowing the technicalities of non-negotiability and holder in due course status makes all the difference in divorce liens, just as it does in other notes.

Divorce liens have a unique problem because of the emotional upheaval of divorce. Note sellers and their ex-spouses can get pretty nasty:

The intercom speaker on my desk blared, "Jimmy Lee Johnson from Florida on line one."

I picked up the phone and asked, "May I help you?"

"I understand you buy liens?" the smooth voice began.

"Yes, we do. What kind of lien do you want to sell?"

"It's like your website says, a divorce lien," Jimmy Lee said. "Isn't that what it said on that divorceliens.com thing?" he asked someone while covering his phone mouthpiece.

I could barely hear a woman's voice answering him. But I clearly heard him say to her, "Of course we got to sell it." How she responded to that was lost in muffled sounds. Then Jimmy Lee said to me, "Well, it's not my divorce lien, it belongs to my girlfriend Shirley Joan."

"Shirley Jones?" I asked.

"No, her name is Shirley Joan Granum. Shirley Joan is just her first name."

Well, Shirley Joan was *two* of her first names, but it was clear that she didn't want to do the talking and that Jimmy Lee was a little too insistent about getting her to sell her divorce lien. That's a red flag, so I listened intently as the tale of Jimmy Lee Johnson and Shirley Joan Granum unfolded.

Jimmy Lee and Shirley Joan had moved to Florida only a week earlier, and they needed fast cash to get settled into their new life. They had come from the little town of Rickersville in south Texas to put as many miles as they could between themselves and Shirley Joan's ex-husband, Billy Bob Granum.

Shirley Joan had divorced Billy Bob nearly a year earlier, but Billy Bob just wouldn't give up, and kept sending her one love letter after another. When Shirley Joan first moved from Rickersville to Austin and Billy Bob couldn't find her, he sent his love letters through her mother in Corpus Christi. That annoyed Jimmy Lee no end, since he was supposed to be the love interest in Shirley Joan's life now. That's why he was so insistent about making her sell the divorce lien—to break the last link between the two.

Billy Bob had gotten the house out of the divorce, and Shirley Joan had received her share in the form of a divorce lien, or—as the legalese goes in Texas—an owelty lien, which is an ancient term for splitting things equally. Shirley Joan's owelty lien was in the amount of $30,000, and Billy Bob was paying her $400 a month on the note.

Shirley Joan finally took the phone and talked to me

herself. She *did* want to sell the lien—it wasn't all Jimmy Lee's idea. She was getting her payments from Billy Bob through her mother, just like the love letters. But she emphatically didn't want him to know her whereabouts. She needed the cash, alright, but she, too, wanted to sever all connections with Billy Bob.

I promised to keep her whereabouts confidential.

We agreed on a price, and a few days later Shirley Joan signed a preliminary agreement to sell her note. The agreement was subject to our due diligence in checking out the details of the note. Shirley Joan furnished me a complete set of divorce papers and the note and lien documents. They were in good order.

I then called Billy Bob and introduced myself. I told him I was intending to buy the note.

You'd have thought I hit him with a hot iron.

"Ah don't know hoo yew arr," he snarled at me in his thick Texas drawl, "but you listen to me, now, you hear? If you buy that note, I'll never pay you a dime on it. And you know how I'll get out of it? I'll go bankrupt, that's what. And if that Shirley Joan sells her note to anybody, why, I'll up and put her daddy right in jail, yessir, that's what I'll do. Caught him trespassing on my yard, got him dead to rights. And she knows I can do it, too. You just tell her that, you hear? Now you go talk to my lawyer. I'm not talking to you any more."

I understood. I get this a lot when investigating a divorce lien situation. Emotions get in the way of common sense and common courtesy!

I got the name of Billy Bob's attorney, Duane Lazarus, and left a message with his receptionist. He never returned my call.

A few days later Billy Bob called me with a chip on his shoulder.

"Are you going to check on my credit?" he challenged.

"I'd like to, Mr. Granum," I said.

"I don't care what you'd like. I don't want you checking my credit. I don't want you buying the lien, and I don't want you involved with my ex-wife Shirley Joan!" he screamed.

I let it roll off my back. "Look," I said in a kindly voice, "I know it's been tough for you, Billy Bob. The divorce was stressful and I'm here to listen. I understand. Have you felt this way for long?"

"You don't know nuthin'," he said. He didn't budge.

"Billy Bob, wouldn't you feel better if I bought the note? Then it would be strictly business and that might be easier to deal with. I'd really like to be friends with you."

"You ain't my friend."

He stayed defiant. But I didn't antagonize him—I just listened to him rave. His cell phone went dead and that ended that—for the time being.

Well! I've learned over the years that divorce lien notes involve fragile emotions. I don't take the antagonism personally, I know it's coming. And I have a lot of empathy for both spouses.

A week passed and Billy Bob called me again.

This time he was all smiles.

"Hey, I got to thinking," he began in his best sweet-talk voice. It was strange how his Texas drawl smoothed out when he seemed to want something. "I'm real sorry I was so rude like that. It's just the divorce got to me, you know?"

"I know, Billy Bob. I'm glad you're feeling better about the whole thing."

"I am. And, you know, if you bought Shirley Joan's note, I'd owe it to you, right?" I could hear the smile-and-pat-'em-on-the-cheek tone growing.

"Yes, that's right, Billy Bob." I said, waiting for the punch line.

"Since I'd owe you some already, could you loan me some more then? I'm short on cash 'til I get money from my lawsuit."

So that was it. Well, that's better than spinning his emotional wheels.

I said, "Unfortunately, I can't make you an additional loan—I'm not in the loan business—but if you need to lower your payments I'd be willing to negotiate."

"You would? Well, that would help."

And so we got down to a long personal chat and finally became okay with each other. When we were through, Billy Bob faxed me a letter saying it was okay for me to order a credit report on him.

As the days went on prior to closing, Billy Bob called me several times. On his sixth call, he was bubbling over. He had just won the lawsuit that gave him a large settlement.

"You know, Miz Stevens," he said, "once I get that cash money in my pocket, I'm just gonna pick up and sell this house and leave Texas. For good. I'm goin' to move to California. I'm goin' somewhere up in them Sierra Nevadas. Find some peace and quiet. I've a mind to be one of them mountain men, I do. And I tell you what."

"What?" I asked, genuinely curious.

"I might even come up where you are and take your whole office out for some fried chicken or something."

"That's sweet of you," I said, smiling.

He went on and on, telling me his hopes for the future. He apologized many times for being rude before. He vowed that he never had any intention of filing bankruptcy.

What a change. The antagonistic redneck Billy Bob Granum was really a good-hearted teddy bear. He now wanted some tranquility in life.

I did one last pre-closing interview with Shirley Joan and told her of the change in Billy Bob.

"Oh, he's always been that way," she said. "He can act gruff, but he's really just a very nice guy. Remember that business about calling the cops on my daddy for trespassing? It was right after I moved out of the house, and daddy went to pick up my stuff. But it was just bluff. He never called the cops. And he'll pay you right on time. Never miss a penny. He's compulsive about it. Always has been."

I knew that was a fact from Billy Bob's stellar credit report.

I said, "I know it's none of my business, but why did you break up, then?"

"It wasn't the money. He got too friendly with one of the neighbor ladies, you know what I mean?"

"Oh."

We closed the deal and gave Shirley Joan her fast cash. I hope she and Jimmy Lee have a good life together.

As for Billy Bob, he decided he didn't want to lower his payments. He didn't need to with that big settlement he got. He just said, "Let's just get this over and done." And then he talked about those mountains again.

And one day he called and gave me his new address up in the Sierra Nevada. He really did it.

Soon afterwards he sold the house and paid us off.

Divorce liens also face the problem that some payors want to buy back their note for the same discount that you get. Some get downright snotty about it:

But one note in particular drove that point about snotty payors a lot farther than usual, so it's worth telling.

The transaction started like most divorce liens: a man named Daniel Baker contacted us several times trying to decide if he wanted to sell his lien. He had divorced his wife, Wendy, who got the house, while he got a lien on the property.

Mr. Baker's note was due in one payment of $18,000 five years from the date of the divorce. We offered $8,500 cash. That didn't seem like a lot to Daniel, but it was as much as we were willing to risk. He called again in a few days, but made no decision.

Daniel Baker had remarried—to Gail, the woman he left Wendy for—and his need for fast cash won out over his indecision. After half a dozen calls to us, he decided to take our offer.

While making the final arrangements, I telephoned his ex-wife Wendy, but as soon as I mentioned her former husband she hung up on me.

We hired Samuel Duncan, a lawyer in Oklahoma, where the property was located, and he closed the transaction for us.

A week after we bought the lien, we got a payoff request from the title insurance company. We didn't know the details—maybe Wendy was selling the house. But we were excited at the prospect of getting that $18,000 payment so soon after putting our money at risk. That's rare speed in divorce liens, which are sometimes hard to collect.

The next thing we heard was flabbergasting: Wendy had filed a lawsuit against us! Daniel, it seems, had told Wendy the amount we paid for the lien. Her lawsuit claimed that because we only paid $8,500 for the lien, she owed us only $8,500, and not the $18,000 outstanding on the lien.

That, of course, was nonsense, but we had to get a judge to say so.

We hired Samuel Duncan again, and the case went to trial. Wendy lost, as we knew she would. The judge ruled that since Wendy owed $18,000 to her ex-husband on the lien in the first place, it didn't matter now who owned the lien. She owed us $18,000, period. The court awarded us a judgment for the full amount.

Immediately we got a notice that Wendy had instructed her insurance agent to remove us as fire/hazard insurance beneficiaries. It seemed a petty thing to do, but it would not affect the payoff amount.

Wendy's court appeal deadline came and went with no further legal action. Just a few days later we got a short handwritten letter from her. She told us she had to take care of some important things that would affect the selling price of the house, including a new roof and bathroom floor. She asked, "Will you please consider taking $15,000 for this settlement?"

I couldn't believe the gall of this woman!

First she hung up on me when I tried to talk to her about the lien. Then she sued us and lost. Then she took us off the fire/hazard insurance. Finally, she asked us to accept $3,000 less than the court *ordered*.

I wrote back as politely as I could, noting all these facts and asking for an explanation of why we should do her any favors.

Her reply read like the script of a three-hankie movie:

- Wendy originally thought that Daniel was going to make a deal allowing her to pay off the lien at a great discount.
- Then she found that her ex-husband was signing a deal with us, ending her hopes of a reduced pay-off.
- "I'm sure that was all in his plans to hurt me and the children again."

First hankie.

As for hanging up on me, Wendy was a little apologetic, but stressed that:

- she was still distraught that Daniel had walked out on her.
- She emphatically did not want the divorce.
- "As soon as I heard you say his name over the phone, my blood pressure went up, my anxiety level went up, and I hung up on you."

Second hankie.

Wendy waffled around the last issues:

- She didn't try to explain removing me from the fire/hazard insurance.
- She readily admitted she lost the court case.
- Without skipping a beat, she then pleaded, "I am asking for help with things that would affect the selling price of the house."

Third hankie.

I actually considered giving in to Wendy's plea—to a degree. I thought about offering her a compromise, accepting $1,500 less than we were entitled to—half of the aid she sought. As usual, I submitted the idea to the others in our firm.

They were not sympathetic. To be fair to all sides, I decided to check with the title insurance company to see if Wendy's claims about the selling price were true. It turned out that Wendy was refinancing the house, with no intention of selling it. She was just looking for a free ride.

I sent her a final, short note: "Request denied. We expect the full payment in accordance with the terms of the judgment."

She paid in full two weeks later.

Sometimes you have to be hardnosed. Like with Wendy.

Sometimes you have to be a softie. Like with Clara, who I'm going to tell you about next.

One day our firm received a call from a woman with a lien to sell. Clara Youngblood said she was divorced and her ex-husband Ed had been given the house and custody of their three children, while she received a lien on the home. She now needed fast cash more than the lien, and wanted desperately to sell it quickly.

As she described her lien, I could see it was a fairly typical divorce lien put together during the legal proceedings with no regard to its cash value.

It had no monthly payments and one lump-sum payment of $30,000 in ten years. It also had a huge first lien ahead of it, which is also typical. All these features were bad for the cash value of the lien.

I explained to Clara that her lien had no payment history, so I couldn't judge its quality, and that there was no security for me, because the first lien holder would have first claim on the property in event of a foreclosure, leaving me with nothing.

I could only pay her $10,000 for the $30,000 due in ten years, I told her. To my surprise, Clara said that sounded great. That was a little strange, but I told her to bring in the papers and we would start the process.

When Clara came into my office, I found her to be a nice woman in a tough spot. She needed money to solve some financial problems, and seemed nervous and a little scattered. I calmed her down and we looked through her papers together.

Immediately, more problems emerged. Clara's ex-husband Ed was supposed to have signed a note and second lien on the property according to the divorce decree, but hadn't done it. We couldn't do anything without a valid note and lien.

So I told Clara to go to her attorney and have him get the papers signed so she could record the lien. She said that although she was usually on good terms with her ex-husband, they were having a dispute at the moment and he might not cooperate, but she would try.

As she departed, I watched her scurry down the hall. She was a sweet woman, perhaps pathetic, but something struck me as being a little off. I thought she might just drop the idea of selling the lien, which didn't bother me because it was of such low quality.

Time passed. I nearly forgot Clara and her divorce lien. Then one day she called again and told me she got the lien signed and recorded. We made an appointment for her to come in so we could look over the papers again.

I ordered a title report on the property and another glaring problem emerged. There was not only a first lien, but *Ed had also obtained a second lien on the property in the amount of $35,000*! Thus, Clara's divorce lien was a *third lien*. That's the bottom of the food chain in the note buying business. Most note buyers won't even look at them.

Clara tried to come in to talk about the lien, but she called much later and said she couldn't find my office and re-scheduled her appointment. There was definitely something amiss with Clara.

When she came in, she explained her situation fully. Clara and Ed had been married for fifteen years. Then Clara was seriously injured in a car accident and laid up in the hospital for several months. While she was going through a long rehabilitation, Ed found another woman and divorced Clara. Ed got custody of the children because she was not available to care for them.

Ed was living in the mortgaged home with the kids and lady-love Magda. They were not married. Clara had kept a good relationship with Ed, and she got along with Magda. Clara saw that Ed needed Magda's income to help him pay the mortgages. Ed was struggling, but he was trying his best to support his family.

Then Clara explained the problem that had come up with Ed. She was upset because he had demanded that she only have visitation with their children under supervision.

I asked, "Why is that?" She replied, "Ed thinks I can't handle the kids by myself because of my injuries."

Although she had received an insurance settlement that allowed her to live modestly, the lawyer was costing her a lot of money, and she needed cash. She still wanted to sell her divorce lien for $10,000.

I really felt bad. I told her that because of the second line of credit, her note had no value at all, and I couldn't buy it. She put her face in her hands and cried, then suddenly sat up bright and cheery. She departed saying she would see me again soon.

Now I was really worried. I called Clara's lawyer Nolan Tracy and asked if she was mentally competent.

He said, "Legally, yes."

The unspoken thought was, "Practically, no."

The lawyer had deliberately made the divorce lien unattractive so nobody would buy it and the full $30,000 would be there for her in ten years. He had advised Clara not to sell the lien.

To my further surprise, Clara came into my office the next day. She just wanted to chat about this and about that. She began coming into my office nearly every other day. I became more and more involved in her life, being as solicitous as I could.

One day I just felt I was in over my head and flat out told her that Mr. Tracy didn't want her to sell the divorce lien. She said she didn't care what her lawyer wanted, it was her money and she wanted it now.

That was perfectly clear. So I told her there was another way out. I said, "Why don't we see if we can get Ed to buy the lien from you?"

I had previously figured out that by paying $10,000 for the lien, I would make about 11% interest compounded monthly, a fair profit. I got on the phone with Ed and said, "I'm a note buyer, and Clara is sitting here at my desk. She's told me enough about your family that I can see quite a bit of financial pressure on both of you. If you buy the divorce lien from Clara, you would save a lot of money. She's willing to sell."

Ed was stunned. "You mean I can buy the lien for $10,000 and that's all I'll ever have to pay?" he asked.

"Yes," I said. "Then Clara will be off your title. All you'll have to worry about besides the first mortgage then is that second line of credit."

Ed, it seems, had not used the entire $35,000 credit line, but only $15,000 to pay his lawyer for the visitation battle. He could take the $10,000 from that credit line now and pay it back in installments. It was clear to me that the only ones profiting from this visitation fight were the lawyers.

I got Ed to sign an agreement that he would pay Clara

$10,000. She signed. He felt great relief, and Clara was really happy.

Clara then signed all the release documents, Ed brought the check into my office, she got her money, and everybody was happy.

I was merely the go-between in all this. I didn't make a dime. In fact, it cost me a great deal of time, money and trouble. But there are times in any business, even in note buying, that you have to act for the needy without charge.

It's an old tradition, so old that the Romans did it. Their term for it was, "Pro Bono Publico"—for the public good.

Chapter 15
Buying Hope

Sometimes you just have to ignore the technicalities.

A note may check out so bad that nobody in their right mind would buy it.

You buy it anyway, because your gut tells you it's right.

And then it pays off. You make your handsome profit. You beat the odds. And you end up getting fast cash to someone that really needs it.

It feels great.

But there's a catch.

As you no doubt have figured out by now, this only works if you've been in the note buying business a long time.

Long enough to develop that gut feel.

Long enough to see good deals go bad and bad deals go good.

Long enough to smell it coming, even if you can't explain why.

So I'm going to devote this chapter to the worst, messiest, most wonderful notes I can recall.

I am not advising anyone to take the kind of risk described in these stories, even if the idea of bucking the odds seems irresistible.

I'm telling you about it because it happened. And in an imperfect world, you need a few perfect things for inspiration now and then.

But like they say in those sky-diving commercials on television, don't try this at home.

Not without a *very* golden parachute, anyway.

I recently got a call from a dear friend I once helped to buy a note. I've known Jana Pender since high school and the note was for her son's college. I recalled working with her attorney after her grandfather left her some money, and how, with a diligent search, I found a good place to put her inheritance.

She called to say that her note had just paid off and she was ecstatic. She practically cried for joy into the telephone, "I can't thank you enough! I haven't forgotten that you did all that work for free! And it was so much more money than we expected!"

"I'm glad I was able to help," I replied cheerfully.

Then it sunk in. What was that about the note paying more than she expected? Notes aren't like stocks—they yield interest, not capital appreciation. She should have received exactly what she expected.

I asked Jana about that.

"I was going to ask you," she said, surprised. "I don't understand either."

"How much was it?" I asked.

"Over $30,000 more than we thought."

"Well, I'm very happy for you, but something's wrong here."

I told her to send me copies of all her payment records, so I could figure it out.

A few days later her package arrived I retrieved my own file on the note, and sat down to unravel the story.

Opening my folder I saw that the note itself was unremarkable. It had a creditworthy payor named Brace Westerman and five acres of good real estate as security, along with a colorful and successful roadside restaurant called Utah Jack's. The land alone would cover the note, not even considering the restaurant.

The balance owing when I found the note for Jana five years earlier was $133,000. It had payments of $1,600 per month at 9 percent interest. The note had been scheduled to pay off in five years (which it did), leaving a balance of about $87,500, to be paid in a lump sum. I double-checked the arithmetic and there were no mistakes.

However, the records showed that Jana had received not only the regular monthly payments, but at payoff also received a check in the amount of $124,500!

Jana did indeed get more than she expected—$37,000 more!

Going back to the payment records, I quickly saw the reason why: it had been a delinquent note waiting to happen, and I hadn't foreseen it! (Well, there wasn't really any way I could have.)

Here's what happened. Soon after Jana bought the note, Mr. Westerman skipped a payment. Several months of late payments went by, but he then brought the note current. However, it became a pattern: late payment, late payment, bring it current, then late payment, late payment, and on and on. Going over the whole five years, I found that *nearly all the payments were late!*

Late, but regular, so Jana never made a fuss about it.

But I was still puzzled. Why would that result in a $37,000 difference?

Simple. By re-reading the note carefully, I found it contained a clause that said:

IF PAYMENTS ARE AT LEAST 30 DAYS PAST DUE, THE PRINCI-
PAL BALANCE SHALL BEAR INTEREST AT A DEFAULT RATE OF 14 PER
CENT PER ANNUM. SAID 14% DEFAULT RATE SHALL BEGIN ON THE
31ST DAY FOLLOWING THE DUE DATE OF THE PAYMENT UNTIL THE
PAYMENT(S) ARE BROUGHT CURRENT.

Each late payment triggered the default interest rate—
and the payor evidently never noticed. How could that happen?

Emerald City Title Company had been servicing the
payments for the note before Jana bought it, and I left them
with the job after arranging for her to buy it. That explained a
lot.

Knowing a little about the note, it's my guess that Brace
Westerman just figured it was a continuation of his old situation: send his usual $1,600 payment to the title insurance
company, get his receipts back, put them in his file, and wait
to make the next payment.

I'm certain Jana did the same on the receiving end—
never read a single receipt. She's very talented and artistic,
but if it involves finances—well, she called me to help with
this note for a good reason.

I'd also bet that the payments were made by Eddie
Conrad, Utah Jack's manager, not by Brace Westerman, the
owner. Eddie probably never bothered to read the receipts.
Why should he? The payments remained $1,600.

But for every month Eddie made a late payment, less
of that $1,600 went to pay the principal down, and more went
to pay the higher default interest rate. After five years of mostly
late payments, that added up to a much higher ending balance
for Utah Jack's—$37,000 higher.

If Eddie or Brace had either one noticed that late payments were costing them money, it's hard to imagine they'd
be so broke they couldn't find some way to boost their payments a month in advance and keep them there.

It's also hard to imagine they wouldn't have realized what a huge liability they'd rack up with a 5 per cent per month penalty over a period of five years.

No, it must have been simple oversight. I'm sure that nobody read the receipts from the title insurance company. I can imagine the shock Brace and Eddie got when the lump sum payment turned out to be $37,000 more than they expected.

On reflection, it couldn't have been too much of a shock, because they paid it without complaint.

Fine with me. Now Jana has some college money for her son—when he's ready in a few years.

> That wasn't really a bad note gone good, it was just a delinquent note that gave everybody a surprise.
> Now we're going to see a really bad note:

Not long ago a note broker contacted my firm with an unusual offer. I knew this broker—his name was Richard Atkinson—as a person of high professionalism, so I wasn't surprised when he started the conversation with a warning.

"I want to be straight with you, Lorelei. I have a note here that's not very desirable, but you've always been willing to take a risk, so I thought I'd pass it by you—just in case," he said.

I told him that I appreciated his honesty.

"Go ahead," I said. "Tell me about this not-very-desirable note."

The sellers, said Mr. Atkinson, were an elderly couple named Taylor who were living in a nursing home in Colorado. The Taylors had run out of money and had no place to turn to other than state government assistance. However, the state could not assist them as long as they held this note as an asset.

"They have to sell this note for a decent cash price as fast as possible," said Mr. Atkinson, "so the nursing home can be paid and the State of Colorado can complete its paperwork on their assistance application."

Mr. Atkinson added that the Taylors' children were attempting to sell the note for them.

"What security do they have for this note," I asked.

Mr. Atkinson replied, "This is the undesirable part: the security for this note is a mobile home out by North Bend, right here in Washington."

"North Bend is a nice place," I said. "A mobile and the real estate under it?"

"No, just the mobile home, no land."

"No land?" I asked uncomfortably.

"No land," Mr. Atkinson confirmed. "It's a double-wide, 3 bedroom home with 2 carports and a patio. You'll want to take a close look at it."

"No kidding," I said.

Well, crazy or not, I sent Katy, our staff lawyer, the thirty miles to North Bend where she was to inspect the property—if you could call a used double-wide "property." She found it was badly in need of repairs. It clearly never had much "tender loving care." Katy reported that light sockets were hanging out of the wall, the outside was half painted, and it was generally in shabby condition.

I talked to the manager of the mobile home park— who was also the real estate agent in the area—and he explained that the unit would likely stay on the market for a long time if we had to repossess it. Even if it did re-sell, he said, it would probably bring only a small down payment and long term note.

The payor, a married woman named Betty Garfield, was a bright spot in this otherwise dismal picture. She had lived in the mobile home for six years and had a good job with a major corporation for 15 years. She had kept up a good payment record all that time, along with a commendable credit rating.

When I talked to Betty about the note, she mentioned that she'd just bought a house and would be moving into it in only two weeks, leaving the mobile home vacant until she could sell it.

She assured me that she would continue to make the payments promptly, whether or not she lived there. I believed her, feeling the determination and honesty in her voice.

Next I checked the documents. To my alarm, I found that the Taylors had done their own paperwork when they sold the mobile home six years earlier—and that meant most of it was missing and what there was had been done wrong.

The Taylors had given it their best effort and thought they'd done it correctly, but the paperwork was a mess. First I found that the mobile home title did not have the proper names on it. Then I found that the taxes had not been paid. The Taylors couldn't help me fix the problems, because Charles Taylor, their oldest son, was now signing all papers for them, which just added another layer of complication. I could see that straightening out the errors and omissions would be a horrendous task.

But I decided to buy the note anyway.

Perhaps I did it more to help the Taylors get fast cash for their nursing home expenses than to make any money on the deal. I thought the time it would take to set everything right would eat up what little profit the note offered.

There was always the chance that Betty would never sell the mobile home and it would sit there vacant for a long time—the mobile home market in the area was not good. It would be awful if we had to foreclose and take the place back.

But somehow I had a gut feeling that Betty would live up to her word and pay. It was not a large note, so the small amount of cash involved lowered the risk.

Thus, after many hours of detail work and some expert assistance from the note broker, my firm closed the transaction by paying about 75 cents on the dollar.

Betty sent the first two payments on time.

Then, to our great surprise, she sent us a payoff check for the entire amount. She had sold the mobile home—for cash.

Go figure. Some notes just won't go wrong no matter how bad they seem.

Every now and then you get into a note that you really want to buy, but the details are just horrible. You have a bad feeling about how it'll turn out, but you hope the future will prove you wrong.

And you jump right in, like I did with this one:

We got a call one day from a note seller named Mary James. She said one of our competitors had referred her to us. I wanted to know more about that!

It seems she had a note secured by both real estate and a business situated on the real estate. Our competitor only dealt with real estate notes. Since we were known in the industry as a versatile note buyer interested in both real estate and business notes, we got the referral.

That's the kind of competition we don't mind at all.

Now for the note: Mary James had run Pristine Lake Manor, an adult care home in River Bend, Oregon, for several years. It was well-established in the Glenmoor community, an upscale residential neighborhood near a golf course and a university campus. Its attractive location made it desirable for family and friends to visit.

The grounds themselves were so well-groomed that the place looked more like a palatial home than an elderly care facility. Its manicured lawns and perfectly maintained buildings made it blend in seamlessly with the adjacent golf course fairway. Members of the local community liked the home so much they came into the facility to sing and keep company with the residents and help out in many ways.

Pristine Lake Manor had earned an impeccable reputation for catering to elderly people with significant mental problems requiring continuing care. The staff was renowned for its compassionate care for residents suffering from such conditions as Alzheimer's disease, various types of dementia and even elderly persons with Down syndrome.

The care facility was so well-run that numbers of its employees had worked there for more than a decade. The home's safe location, excellent facilities, and its caring staff gave it a reputation second to none. And Mary was a successful business manager who kept the home solvent and thriving.

Two years earlier, Mary encountered personal problems that led her to sell Pristine Lake Manor. She sold the business and the real estate to Donald and Edna Gundelfinger for $450,000. The Gundelfingers had made a $75,000 cash down payment on the business and real estate, borrowed $250,000 from a bank on a first lien on the real estate, and signed a note in favor of Mary James for $125,000 on a second lien for the rest of the real estate.

We did some preliminary checking on the creditworthiness of the Gundelfingers. The credit report was good, and the two year payment history showed they had made every payment on time.

We inspected the property and found it in tip-top condition, a credit to its community. In fact, I was so impressed that I went to an old friend from university days whose mother was slipping into the early stages of Alzheimer's disease. I told her that Pristine Lake Manor was the ideal place for her mother. My friend contacted the facility and found it was full and put her mother on a waiting list.

We gave Mary a preliminary bid, but we emphasized the bid was subject to an appraisal of the real estate before we could make a definite commitment. Mary looked at our offering price, then said she'd consider our bid and get back to us.

A couple of months later, she called us again, saying

she was still thinking about it. However, we didn't hear from her for a long time.

One day, a note broker faxed us an inquiry asking us to bid on a note. We immediately recognized the note as Mary James', and realized she was still shopping it. The James note was the note broker's first transaction, and his hopes were dashed when we told him that we already had the transaction in our pending files.

Finally, Mary James came to us some time later and wanted to accept our offer, if we still wanted to buy it after getting an appraisal on the real estate.

We immediately started doing a thorough due diligence.

First, we verified that Oregon-Columbia Trust Bank held the first lien on Pristine Lake Manor, meaning Mary's was a second lien note.

Then, the appraisal came back showing that the value of the property was $225,000, which was less than the amount owing on the first lien. There was no equity in the property to secure Mary's second lien.

Basically, although a second lien was recorded, we were looking at an unsecured note, as a practical matter.

It was such a large note, and no security!

Mary really needed some money. Though her note was not secure, my gut told me "it's a good deal." I had investigated the situation enough to understand all the pitfalls. In spite of all the negatives, I learned a long time ago that a good note is one that pays, and this one was paying.

I bought the note—but not with company money, and not with my savings, but with money in a special high risk account set aside just for deals like this.

As it worked out, the Gundelfingers paid us off just a year later. We made a nice profit.

And best of all, my friend's mother got her place at Pristine Lake Manor.

I know this is beginning to sound like *Goody Two-*

Shoes Meets Pollyanna, but bear with me. There's only one more story of a bad note that couldn't go wrong.

Our firm occasionally uses direct mail postcards to search for notes to buy. Although long experience has taught us that the returns will be few, we devote some time each year to searching public records for names and addresses for our mailing list. Of the few responses we do get, most involve delinquent notes. Such was the case when Ellsworth Hubbard responded to our postcard.

Ellsworth explained that a few years before, he'd sold his dinnerware distribution business to a man named Sam Brackenridge. Mr. Brackenridge had made a substantial down payment but still owed Ellsworth about $20,000 for the business. To secure the note debt, Mr. Brackenridge had given Ellsworth a second lien on his residence in Spokane.

Ellsworth initially spent a lot of time training Sam how to run the business. Sam and Ellsworth became almost inseparable while Sam was in training. However, as the months went by, Sam and Ellsworth got into one disagreement after another about the business, a common problem when a small business changes hands.

The disputes boiled down to one major complaint: Sam claimed the business could not make the income Ellsworth had represented. The decisive factor had been the loss of three major accounts within the first few months, lowering Sam's income significantly. Ellsworth and Sam couldn't resolve their differences so they ended up in arbitration. The outcome was a downward adjustment of the sale price, and the note balance was lowered to $12,000.

But that wasn't the end of the problem. Even after arbitration, Sam still had trouble making the payments. Ellsworth was on the fence about what to do to get his money. He had few options. He could do nothing, wait and hope for the best. Or he could sell his note and get out of the picture.

He dreaded getting into another legal tangle with Sam. So he called us.

Most note buyers would avoid this transaction, but it piqued my interest because it was an intriguing challenge. The money involved was small compared to our average note transaction, but the risk was high. It would be a complex and engaging problem that I could work on almost like a hobby.

I did some research and found that Ellsworth's note was really a *sixth* lien, instead of a second. You don't see many of those.

A little more research revealed that one of the liens had been paid off years earlier, and after a diligent search, I finally found the people to sign a release. That bumped it up to a fifth lien.

That's still too weird. I examined the title to see how so much could happen to one piece of real estate.

It was one of the messiest titles I've ever seen. The house appraised at $180,000. The first lien was $75,000. Then there were three liens from the State of Washington totaling $15,000. That put Ellsworth Hubbard's lien fifth in line. A total of $90,000 was ahead of Ellsworth's fifth lien.

Then I found several more liens and judgments that had subsequently attached the property, but were inferior to Ellsworth's lien. Most liens in Washington State are ranked in priority by the recording date, so in the event of a foreclosure, Ellsworth's lien would be paid before theirs. Despite this disorderly situation, the $12,000 balance owing to Ellsworth was well secured.

Though Wall Street Brokers rarely buys delinquent notes, this one looked desirable. I offered Ellsworth Hubbard $6,000 for the $12,000 balance and he accepted. This was a small amount to risk, and the rewards would be good if we ended up getting paid off. We took an educated gamble.

We didn't know exactly what we wanted to do about the delinquency so I called the payor, Sam Brackenridge. His voice told me he was deeply worried about our firm buying his note. He sounded a little too anxious as he explained his bad luck with the business. He stammered a little as he told me that he had a plan to increase his income. He calmed down a little and furnished proof he'd been chipping away at paying off his liens with the State of Washington bit by bit—a piece of information we'd found while investigating the transaction.

Mr. Brackenridge wanted to start a payment plan. He asked if it would be agreeable for him to pay $260 per month. He was almost pleading. He and his wife had lived in their home for 32 years and didn't want to lose it.

We talked it over in our firm and decided to accept his proposal. Though we knew we could get our money via foreclosure, we would rather receive payments than get involved in a time-consuming legal proceeding.

When I told Sam Brackenridge we'd agree to his plan, he thanked me profusely for giving him a chance. I was embarrassed that he felt at our mercy. While we never threatened him, he just assumed that the normal course of a professional note buyer would be to get a lawyer and foreclose.

I had no intention whatsoever of taking the Brackenridges' home of thirty-two years away from them. He kept up his payments just as he promised.

Sam still has a way to go before payoff, but if he gets into trouble again, I have another plan: we can do some bartering. He has dinnerware in his business inventory and I've always loved *Rosenthal*. Perhaps he could satisfy the note debt with dishes.

FAST CASH

Chapter 16
Endings

One day I asked our company's founder—my dad, Larry L. Stevens—and my executive assistant, Gloria, "In the note business, what's the difference between taking an acceptable risk and gambling?"

They both smiled and thought I was setting them up for a note joke.

"No," I said, "it's a serious question. I have to write about it for one of my columns."

Gloria thought the question was inappropriate. "Business is work and gambling is play. They're just two different things."

Dad also thought it was inappropriate, but for a different reason. "Acceptable risk? Gambling?" he said. "That's like asking a pilot the difference between smooth flying and turbulence—they're just two sides of the same thing: air. Well, business has two sides, too: opportunity and risk. You can't have opportunity without risk any more than you can fly without air."

Gloria mused a moment and said, "But, it's true, you *can* make a fortune buying notes. It's not just gambling."

I injected, "But it's just as true that you can *lose* a fortune buying notes. Isn't that gambling?"

"Whew!" Dad said, thinking back over the years. "We've had our share of both, haven't we? But we survived. Isn't that acceptable risk?"

Gloria said, "That's your talent, Larry. You can pick the good ones most of the time and cope with the bad ones when you have to."

Dad said, "I don't know about talent, Gloria, but I know it takes skill, if you're lucky enough to pick some up along the way."

"Lucky enough..." I repeated, then brightened up. "That's right, Dad. Don't forget about dumb, blind luck."

"Okay," said Gloria, "it's all three, talent, skill and luck."

"Alright," agreed Dad, "it's all three. You use your talent and skill to make every note deal an acceptable risk, but sometimes you push it too far. Then luck steps in and it becomes a gamble. The outcome all depends on how you handle it."

I laughed. "Then it boils down to this: If you win it was an acceptable risk. If you lose it was a gamble!"

We all laughed.

So here's what I concluded: The note business is like all of life: a mix of opportunity and risk.

What you make of your life is part talent, part skill, part luck. Talent is what you're born with—it can't be taught. Skill is what you do with what you're born with—it's taught best by study and doing, not just one or the other. Luck is what you run into or what runs into you—then it's up to your talent and skill to make it work.

What can a good note buyer do to strike a balance between acceptable risk and gambling? Two things:

First, get the best legal advice you can. Successful note buying depends on knowing note law in detail. I always make sure I have a good attorney, preferably one experienced with notes, and that's harder to find than you might think.

Second, be sure you can afford to lose all your money and still smile.

It's the second thing that's hard.

Now, about attorneys:

Many years ago, I was diligently working on a complicated note. It was secured by property in Georgia, a state far from my office in Seattle.

The note seller, Maurice Hardcastle, couldn't find the note. We both checked all the usual places and couldn't find it. Mr. Hardcastle finally contacted the payor, Joan Fredling, and asked if she'd be willing to sign a replacement note. Joan was a cooperative person, but wanted to run it by her attorney, Trevor Jonas.

In the meantime, I'd received a title report on the property showing many liens. It was one of the most complex title reports I'd ever seen. There were unresolved bankruptcy, divorce and estate issues clouding the title.

At first, I didn't know whether so many problems could be solved. But I plugged along with my investigation, getting tidbits of information here and there. It took me a good three weeks to gather this hard-to-get information, analyze it, and figure out how it all fit together.

Then I received a call from Trevor Jonas, politely explaining he was the attorney for the payor, Joan Fredling. He was concerned about her signing a replacement note. What might happen if the real note showed up? His client might have to pay both notes. Could Mr. Hardcastle put up a bond to ensure that Joan would not suffer consequences?

Good lawyer, I thought. *He's really protecting his client.*

Trevor hadn't represented Joan when she purchased the property and wanted to know if I had a current title report he could review. He explained he wanted to familiarize himself with the transaction before he could advise his client what to do. I immediately furnished him a copy.

As Trevor and I got to discussing the intricacies of the transaction, I began to notice that he seemed very familiar not only with real estate, but also the details of note buying. In my many years of experience with lawyers, I hadn't run into anyone quite like Trevor.

He possessed insight you couldn't expect from the average lawyer: he'd ask me a question—I had the right answer; I'd ask him a question—he had the right answer.

We spent a month on the transaction, talking nearly every day, trying to solve the missing note and complicated title problems. Though we were working from different viewpoints, we both wanted to solve the entire picture, which would make things run smoothly for my purchase of the note from Maurice Hardcastle, and leave Joan Fredling with good clean title and no exposure about a missing note.

Trevor asked Joan to look in her property file, to see if she might accidentally have been furnished the original note from the escrow company. Sure enough, that was exactly what had happened!

Joan now had the original note, which she furnished to Trevor—no need for a replacement note now!

After we got all the paperwork in order, I finally bought the note.

Admirable. This lawyer had enough smarts to find a missing note and solve a lot of other technical problems. Buying notes isn't really esoteric, but does take practical experience to learn the nuts and bolts. Most lawyers simply don't have deep experience with note buying.

As the days went on, I began to ask myself, "Why was Trevor Jonas so knowledgeable about notes?"

My curiosity finally got the best of me, so, I gave him a call.

"Trevor," I said, "I know this might sound odd, but how do you know so much about note buying? Most lawyers don't."

Trevor chuckled. "I wondered how long it would take you to ask. I got involved in note buying practically right out of law school, and that's about twenty years now. Negotiable instruments was one of those subjects we merely touched on in class and I could tell there was a lot more to it. I think I'm part detective because I just kept nosing around until I found out there was a note market and a note industry. Notes looked like a good thing to buy for my personal portfolio and my pension plan, so I guess I've bought fifty or more over the years."

So Trevor was an experienced note buyer! No wonder he knew so much—he had practical experience as well as legal knowledge, an ideal combination. I was so impressed that I retained him to work on a very complicated note deal. It's been an excellent business relationship ever since.

> Could you turn this story into a general principle? Well, would real estate agents use lawyers that didn't even own a house? Probably not. So the best bet for note buyers would be to use lawyers who buy notes with their own money.

Now let's turn to a gamble that every note buyer dreads:

One day a phone call came in from a man in Houston, Texas, wanting to sell my firm a note. His name was Clevis Butler, and he said his note was secured by vacant land in the north end of Seattle, not ten miles from where I was sitting.

Mr. Butler sent the papers by mail and everything was in order. Our attorney Albert Ross prepared the documents, which we mailed for Mr. Butler's signature. He returned the notarized documents with the original note.

He requested that we wire him the money to Houston, which we did on the day of closing. The transaction went into our files and we went on to other business. The payments came in regularly from the payor, a Mr. Walter Opel, a Boeing engineer with a good credit rating. It was the most ordinary of transactions.

About a year later I got a call from Mr. Opel saying he would make no more payments on the note. I asked why and he refused to answer, saying only that he wanted to consult his lawyer before saying anything more.

Consternation!

First thing the next morning, two private investigators came in to ask a few questions. They looked like characters answering a Hollywood B-movie casting call for gumshoes.

What did I know about Mr. Butler, they wanted to know.

They had been hired by Emerald City Title Company, which had been victimized by this man using a highly unusual scam:

Mr. Butler located vacant properties belonging to out-of-state owners, forged a deed to himself, then listed the property for sale with local real estate agents. He sold the property on a seller-financed note, kept the down payment and then sold the note for fast cash. He had sold many properties following this pattern, including the one in North Seattle.

The real owner, a widow named Claudine Penfield, discovered that someone had illicitly sold her property out from under her. She notified Mr. Opel, who was shocked and gave us that mysterious call saying he would be making no more payments. Then Mr. Opel submitted a claim to Emerald City Title, which covers forgery and fraud of this type in its policies.

We too put in a claim to our title insurance company, Western Pacific Title. Unfortunately, even though we had title insurance for the full amount owing on the note—$30,000— they paid us only $20,000, saying that we were not entitled to the benefit of the $30,000 bargain, but just what we paid for the note, minus all payments we received, plus a reasonable rate of interest.

Lesson? It's not perfect, but title insurance is a must on every real estate note transaction.

Mr. Butler turned an apparently acceptable risk into a real gamble and our title insurance company turned it back into an acceptable risk.

As a footnote, citizens will be pleased to know that the FBI also investigated this fraud. Not long after we received our compensation from Western Pacific, an FBI agent came to our office asking if we had ever purchased notes from a seller using any of some fifteen names.

The agent said each name on their list was actually another alias of "Clevis Butler," the man who had sold us the fraudulent note. "Butler," too, was evidently just another alias, and the FBI couldn't say what the suspect's real name was. Luckily, none of those other aliases appeared in our files. The agent speculated that the suspect must have had experience working for a title insurance company.

As another footnote, citizens will not be pleased to know that we never heard of any suspect being caught.

Now, on to another acceptable risk:

One morning our office got a call from a sweet young woman who introduced herself as Sherry Gladstone.

She got right to the point: "I live in Tennessee and I saw your website. It says you pay fast cash for notes. Well, I have a note and I need fast cash."

"Okay," I replied, "tell me a little about the note."

"I sold 45 acres out in Hollow Tree three years ago. I got $130,000 for it from Dave Boone. He owes me $60,000 on a note."

"Is it a first lien note?" I asked.

"Yes, it is. I need that fast cash your website talks about. How much will you pay me for my note?"

"Can you fax me the documents?" I prompted. "Then I can give you a preliminary quote."

Sherry faxed me the documents and then called back.

"Look, Ms. Stevens, I need to tell you something. Don't get me wrong, but I don't know you, and that worries me. I need some money fast and I've had bad luck getting it."

"What kind of bad luck?"

"I tried to re-finance my house two months ago and the mortgage broker told me several times that my loan would go quickly. He kept stalling me and stalling me. I really need the money. Then he finally said he couldn't make me the loan."

"I see," I said.

"Now I'm in a predicament. I don't want it to happen again—being promised fast cash, me relying on the promise, and then I don't get the money. I'm leery of strangers."

"I can understand that," I said. "Your documents just came in on the fax. Let me look them over a minute, and I'll tell you what we can do.

The documents were clear and professional. I offered her $55,000 and said, "We can move quickly and we should close within a week of receiving the title report."

"How long will it take to get the title report?"

"Let me call them and see," I said.

So I called Heritage Territorial Title Company in Tennessee. Gina Harlow, the title officer, told me it usually takes two days. I reported back to Sherry and she happily signed the preliminary agreement to sell the note.

I ordered the title report the same day. Heritage Territorial told me they would send a search to the abstract company, which they would receive the next day and they could then provide me with the title report.

I also ordered the appraisal the same day. Since the property was vacant land, it had no address. I furnished the appraiser, George Boots, with the long two-page legal description. George figured he could email the appraisal to me within a couple of days.

I told Sherry I would call her every day until the note sale closed. Close communication with the note seller is comforting, both to the seller who is "kept in the loop" and to the note buyer so the seller doesn't disappear or back out.

I began the due diligence for our firm. One thing we always do is check with the county assessor to see how much the property is worth in the assessor's eyes. This gives us a preliminary view of the value, prior to receiving the final appraisal.

But the assessor could not find the Hollow Tree property described on the legal description. There were over 640 acres in the area which had been originally owned by the locally prominent Barlow family. They had sold off pieces here and there, and the assessor could not figure out which tax parcel went with our two page legal description.

Two days passed and we did not receive the title report. I called Gina and she didn't know what happened. She said it was just taking a little longer, but not to worry. It was likely that it was extra work because of how much acreage was involved. She told me that Martin Abstract Company had to send her their report before she could furnish the title report.

The next week I called her every day and got the same story. Gina Harlow's failure to get me the title report was reflecting badly on our company's ability to act quickly. Professional colleagues who don't do their part competently can bring an undeserved stain on your reputation.

I spoke to Sherry several times that week. She sounded tired. The title company's delay left her frustrated and frantic. She burst into tears and blurted, "Oh no, this can't be happening again. I really need the money fast! This is so awful!"

I assured her I would push the title report through. I decided to bypass Gina, and called Martin Land Abstract Company. I spoke to Joe Martin, the owner, who said no one had ever ordered a report from him. More than a week had gone by and Heritage Territorial had done nothing!

I immediately ordered the report and contacted Heritage Territorial's competitor, Bitter Springs Land and Title Company. We got the report in two days.

But all that time had gone by, and for nothing!

I called Sherry and told her what happened. She didn't blame our firm. She was simply exasperated. No matter whose fault it was, our offer to buy her note had stalled.

Then she told me what was behind her need for fast cash: she was 8 ½ months pregnant! She'd suffered expensive complications. She'd had to quit her job months earlier than anticipated and needed the cash to live on until she could go back to work after the baby was born. The hospital required a deposit before they would deliver the baby! Time was running out!

No wonder the poor woman was so distraught!

The appraiser, George Boots, reported he was having difficulty locating exactly which property was included in the description, the same problem the tax assessor had. Now that the title report was in our hands, we had the tax assessor's parcel number, which we furnished to Mr. Boots.

Now it was a simple matter to identify the parcel, and the tax assessor reported the fair market value of the property was $125,000.

We sent Sherry her final papers and proceeded to closing.

But we still didn't have the appraisal. Instead, we had a dilemma: should we hold up the closing until Mr. Boots finally got it done? If we did, Sherry would be even more distressed. If we didn't, we were betting $55,000 that the tax assessor's $125,000 valuation was right.

To me, the proper decision was clear. We closed without the appraisal, so Sherry Gladstone got her fast cash, which wasn't so fast.

George Boots' appraisal arrived two days later at $125,000.

Early the next week, Sherry's husband Elton called: their family had a new member, Melinda, a healthy little girl, 6 pounds, 2 ounces. And their bills were all paid.

Then there are the really unexpected problems:

When John Midlee and Terry Morgan were married, they found their combined life savings enlarged with a generous wedding gift from Terry's father Tom. It enabled them to realize their long-time dream of owning and operating their own restaurant.

They had met in a Seattle hotel where John was a mid-level hospitality executive during one of Terry's layovers as an airline flight attendant. He had helped her out of a mixup in her room reservation and invited her to dinner to smooth her ruffled feathers—and keep the airline's good will.

At dinner in the hotel restaurant, they discovered their shared ambition to enter the food service industry. She'd always wanted to manage a restaurant and he'd always wanted to run day-to-day operations in a restaurant. After numerous flight layovers and dinners together and long talks about their mutual interests, their relationship deepened into love. It wasn't long before their wedding day brought Tom Morgan's generous gift.

Now to make their dream come true. After an exhaustive search for just the right business, the newlywed Midlees found The Surge, a popular seafood restaurant and lounge in a good downtown location. It had been a great success for years under owner Bob Moore, who felt it was time to retire and enjoy life far from the scurry and stress of a busy kitchen.

The Midlees took their time investigating The Surge and getting to know Bob Moore, but once they made up their mind, they swiftly made a hefty down payment and purchased the building along with the restaurant and lounge business. The Midlees agreed to pay monthly payments to Moore on a secured note for the remainder of the money.

When the transaction closed, John took over the restaurant and lounge operation while Terry kept her job with the airline to provide extra income for future expansion of The Surge.

Bob Moore was more than pleased getting the note payments on time as the Midlees prospered in their new business. Then, only a few months later, the IRS knocked on his door with an audit of his finances for the past five years. To his dismay, the IRS auditor found numerous small discrepancies in his accounts that, put together, made one whopping tax debt he owed to the government.

In desperation, Moore contacted us for a quote on his note. We made him a good offer and he quickly sold the note to our firm. He was then able to pay the IRS obligation and from that time on we received the Midlees' payments on the note with no problem.

The Surge brought John Midlee into daily contact with "the regulars" who made his lounge, The Whisper Room, a thriving profit center while the restaurant ran along with a modest but reliable profit. It was one of these Whisper Room regulars named Marcy Silsbee who changed everything: John's daily contact with her over the months, while his wife was away for days at a time, developed into an intimate relationship.

The other lounge regulars were not blind, and word soon got back to Terry that her husband was deeply involved with a barfly. The young bride was devastated. In the horrendous divorce case that followed, she was awarded the restaurant business and all associated property.

Terry Midlee's dream was shattered. She no longer had any interest in The Surge. She quickly sold the property to a daring restaurateur named Jim Kinney, who had started several theme restaurants with new ideas only to see them fold as the fad wore off. He wanted something solid now, and saw The Surge as a permanent home.

Terry carried a large secured second lien note—a wraparound like the one we saw in Chapter 13. From the monthly payments she received from Jim Kinney, she continued her payments to us on our first lien note. Her big note from Jim Kinney gave her the money to pay us our smaller note payments. Terry immersed herself in her flight attendant job.

Things at Jim Kinney's Surge appeared to be going smoothly for three years. Then one December night The Surge burned to the ground—a total loss. The cause of the fire was unclear to the fire marshal, but an arson investigation turned up no suspects. Jim Kinney was ruined.

It was a shock, but we were not worried about payment. After all, we had the first lien and we were named as first lien holder on the fire insurance policy. Fire / hazard insurance is another must for note transactions.

The insurance company did not act swiftly, and Terry Midlee missed several payments to us. We contacted her to continue payments and found that she was not only young, but also quite naïve about finances. She told us she didn't have money to pay our note because she was no longer receiving any money from Jim Kinney. We explained to her that, even though The Surge burned down and Jim Kinney quit paying on her wraparound note, she was still legally obligated to pay us. Terry was horrified.

She asked her father, Tom Morgan, to help. He was strong in defense of his daughter, and firmly told us there was no money. We explained the obligation to him as well. He was appalled. But, because of the circumstances, we agreed to hold off on any legal action, expecting to be paid soon from the insurance proceeds.

We waited. And waited. With our patience growing thin, we asked Tom Morgan for an explanation, and he told us that Jim Kinney was fighting it out with the insurance company—he would not agree to the small sum they were offering him to settle his claim. It dragged on and on and on.

Finally, after more than a year, Tom Morgan called to tell us the insurance company had reached an agreement with Jim Kinney, and soon the insurance draft would arrive. It was about time!

A couple of weeks passed. We heard nothing. I called Tom Morgan and he had no news. I decided to check with the insurance company and they told me the insurance draft had been paid two weeks prior. The draft was written to Jim Kinney, our firm, and Terry Midlee. We knew Jim Kinney could not use the insurance draft without our signature and that of Terry Midlee, so we expected Jim to show up any day. He didn't.

Tom Morgan looked into the situation and found that Jim Kinney had signed his own name on the back of the insurance draft and deposited all the money into his personal account. For some reason, the bank hadn't noticed that other signatures were required. Jim Kinney then cleaned out his bank account and disappeared.

Now what to do? We knew that Terry had more to lose than we did, and we knew her father wanted justice for his daughter. We really felt for Terry. First betrayed by her husband, and now by her buyer!

Tom Morgan came forward to pursue the matter, and we agreed to sit back and wait.

Morgan hired a private detective who soon located Jim Kinney. Morgan then hired a lawyer who made legal claims against Mr. Kinney and the insurance company. Law enforcement authorities also got involved and launched a criminal investigation into Jim Kinney's actions. Kinney was later convicted of bank fraud.

During this turmoil Tom called us every week to keep us updated. After several more months, he appeared in our office with good news.

He handed us a payoff check from the insurance company and said, "There, for my daughter. Justice is served."

I said, "You know, Tom Morgan, you're a nice dad."

I saved the next story for last, not because it's the best, but because, like many of my stories, it goes to the heart of the human condition. And in this case, that "human condition" is mine:

At Wall Street Brokers, we're always asking questions. How can we find more notes to buy? How can we minimize the time and effort of chasing down those notes? How can we make a handsome profit? In a tight market, is there an alternative way to find notes?

It's obvious that if you own a house, sell it, and finance it yourself, you create a note. We have bought nearly a dozen fixer-upper houses over the years and resold them by carrying a note. In a tight market where notes were harder and harder to find, that didn't seem like a bad idea.

So, our family decided to buy a house, fix it up, and re-sell it by carrying a note. We would be able to make a profit comparable to getting a big discount on an existing note, even if we charged the buyer an ordinary interest rate. The profit plus the ordinary interest would make us good money.

Perhaps this would be easier than endlessly searching for scarce notes—and give us a greater profit for our time and money.

My husband Manfred and I knew that we had to find just the right kind of house: one that wasn't good enough to sell without work, but wasn't so run-down it couldn't be refurbished at reasonable cost.

Then one Sunday afternoon while we strolled on the beach of an island getaway, a "For Sale" sign caught our eye. It stood in front of a vacant and sadly neglected cottage in an idyllic setting at the foot of a wooded hill. Despite its run-down condition, it was still solid and it commanded a stunning saltwater view. This was the perfect place.

A curious neighbor who introduced himself as Del Weese had seen us stop short at the "For Sale" sign and cheerfully told us that the property had already sold. I'm sure I detected a smile of pleasure at our disappointment.

We called the real estate agent, Ellen Damm, who confirmed Mr. Weese's claim. We told her to let us know if the sale fell through—we might be interested.

A few days later, Ms. Damm called and told us that the other buyer was having trouble getting money, so if we made a fast offer, she could probably get it accepted.

We asked her for the key to the house so we could inspect it, but Ms. Damm had lost hers. There would be no chance to look inside the house in advance, but we felt this property was the one. We figured that no matter what, we could not lose.

We made an all-cash offer, subject to inspection of the property. Within a few days Ellen managed to get a key and we began our inspection.

The house was old but sturdy, having been reinforced over the years by former owners who must have been master craftsmen. The layout was cozy, with a fantastic view of the water and mountains through the all-glass front which led to an expansive deck. The waves of high tide lapped against a gravel beach below the solid bulkhead. Families of ducks crowded the beach, begging for a handout, with seagulls and ravens hovering warily while eyeing likely contributors. The sea animals on the beach were plentiful—sand dollars, clams, geoducks, and barnacles galore.

The inside was dark and badly in need of repair. The failed buyer, we discovered, had already come in and started his own remodeling work, tearing out a wall that we would have to put back to suit our needs.

The seller immediately approved our offer and we bought the property.

We didn't know it at the time, but Mr. Weese had liked

the failed buyer and we created a surly neighbor by beating his favored one out of the deal.

With the property paid for, we now faced another cash outlay—the costs of fixing up the property to make it salable. Based on our experience fixing up nearly a dozen houses, we knew to double our estimate of the cost and time required— but we hoped it wouldn't come to that.

Then the work began. First we enlarged the parking area on the hill behind the house and we fixed the electric hillclimber, which eliminated a walk up 90 wooden stairs from the house to the parking area.

We cleared an old nature trail down the steep embankment and built a new retaining wall behind the house to prevent the hill from sliding. With those basics taken care of, we added a gazebo for aesthetics and completely landscaped the yard.

The shallow well that served the house for years had to go—it was so inadequate that the previous owners asked neighbors if they could use their bathrooms to shower. We certainly didn't want anyone buying this house from us to suffer such humiliation. So we quickly drilled another well at the top of the hill.

Finally we had to deal with the septic system, which had never worked well, according to the snide Mr. Weese. We hired a company to pump the septic tank, but their unenthusiastic crew insisted that our septic system had failed. We were dismayed, but contacted another firm with a more attentive crew, which found the problem was just a broken pipe. The septic tank and drainfield were fine. So we got the tank pumped and everything worked just great.

Inside, we completely re-wired the house, plumbed and painted it, installed new carpeting throughout, and replaced the hot water heater, bringing everything up to present code. Then we swept the chimney clean and installed new cabinets in the kitchen.

Finally the fixing was done. The place looked gorgeous. New skylights and light paint brightened up the interior. The yard was perfect. Everything was ready for a new buyer.

It was just in time for the summer market. This is the kind of island waterfront—not far from a big city—that people love. It was time to snag a city slicker in need of a second home, or a die-hard professional who liked the relaxing daily routine of a ferry ride to and from the city.

We advertised the property heavily and held an open house every Sunday for the entire summer. Not a bite.

The Lookie-Loo population loved the place, but no one made an offer. Summer was over and nothing. We glumly stopped advertising and decided to take down all the "For Sale" signs.

Suddenly, out of the blue, we got a call. John and Beverly Marshall had been driving around the island and saw a flyer about the house. They wanted to look. We arranged for a neighbor to let them in to see it. Two hours later, they called and said they definitely wanted the house, and made an appointment.

The two eager beavers showed up with a small child— half an hour late. John Marshall was a successful professional with a huge salary; Beverly had closed down her personal business a year earlier. Both had suffered devastating divorces in the not-too-distant past. They didn't have much down, but could afford large payments for the first two years to make up for it. They provided information about the stability and amount of John's income. It looked good. We were relieved we'd found a buyer!

The Marshalls warned us their credit might be blotted because of past problems. We checked and found that their joint credit didn't look too good. But our gut feel about these buyers was good, and we accepted their offer.

They asked us to do minor but time-consuming repairs to the house, which we gladly did. We tested the well water and made sure it was safe for drinking. We hired a soil

scientist to prepare a report on the probability of the hill sliding, which showed a good safety margin.

To our shock and surprise, several neighbors complained to us about drilling the well without a permit. We
showed each neighbor a copy of the permit. Although no one
said so, we suspected Mr. Weese of spreading the rumor. Our
diligent effort to protect our reputation paid off: when we got
things straightened out with the neighbors, Mr. Weese was so
impressed with us that he even asked our firm to handle the
sale of his house!

Yes, we are receiving a nice cash flow on the note.
Yes, we made a decent yield on our cash money. But we also
tied up quite a bit of cash. It took us ten months from the day
we bought the property to the day we sold it. We sunk a lot of
time and effort into administration, paperwork, and coordi-
nating the physical jobs on the property. And all just for one
note.

This fixer-upper turned out to be like all the others
we've done: it took about twice as much time and money as
our original estimate.

So we've come to an unalterable conclusion: For the
same amount of time, effort, and money risked, paying fast
cash for a note where someone else has already done the buying, fixing, and selling is just as profitable and requires much
less work—if you can find the notes.

FAST CASH

Epilogue

That's how to make a fortune buying notes. It's a life's work, a career, a human enterprise, almost a mission, if making a fortune can be considered a mission.

As I promised in the Preface, you now have a reasonably accurate picture of what it's really like being a note buyer.

No hype.

No hoopla.

Just what it's really like.

You can see why I didn't try to write a step-by-step, follow-the-yellow-brick-road type of workbook with checksheets and maps to massive wealth: it would be either sheer make-believe or totally technical gobbledygook.

Note buying is not a simple field and there's no simple way to explain it. There's no list of fifty nifty ways to find notes. There's no week-long course that sets you up in business. There's no magic formula that turns imagination into money. You learn note by note by note.

That's why I decided to tell you how to make a fortune buying notes by sharing my *experience* buying notes. That's how I learn. That's how you learn.

275

What you learn most is that it's really about the human condition. Every note is a human interest story. You run into the best and the worst and a lot of in-between.

How big a fortune can you make buying notes? I'm not a fortune teller. It depends on your gifts—talent, skill and luck.

But I can tell you this: with any luck at all, you won't be homeless even if you don't become Bill Gates. With skill and luck, you may own more than one home. With talent and skill and luck, you may want for nothing.

Personally, I've found that the real fortune is *being* a note buyer. The money makes it possible, but it's such an interesting life that I'm constantly thankful just to be living it.

Read the book again and you'll see what I mean.

I wish you luck.

And skill.

And talent.

Bibliography
and
Index

FAST CASH

Bibliography

Books

John D. Behle, *The Paper Game: How to Profit Through Buying, Selling, Trading, Creating and Improving Real Estate Paper*, self published, Salt Lake City, 1991.

Dyches Boddiford, *The Investor's Guide to Discount Notes & Mortgages and other Cash Flow Streams,* self published, Atlanta, 2000.

Bill Broadbent and George Rosenberg, *Owner Will Carry: How to Take Back a Note or Mortgage Without Being Taken,* Third Edition, Creative Solutions, Inc., San Luis Obispo, California, 1998.

William Bronchick, *Financing Secrets of a Millionaire Real Estate Investor,* Dearborn Trade Publishing, Chicago, 2003.

George Coats, Smart Trust Deed Investment in California, Second Edition, Barr-Randol Publishing Company, Covina, California, 1990.

Peter Conti and David Finkel, *Making Big Money Investing in Real Estate: Without Tenants, Banks, or Rehab Projects,* Dearborn Trade Publishing, Chicago, 2002.

Sanford W. Hornwood and I. Lucretia Hollingsworth, The Number One Real Estate Investment No One Talks About, Prentice-Hall, Inc. Englewood Cliffs, New Jersey, 1987.

Jim Napier, *Invest in Debt: The "How To" Book on "Buying Paper" for Cash Flow,* Jim Napier, Inc., Estero, Florida, 1983.

Laurence J. Pino, *Cash In on Cash Flow: How to Make Full Time Income With Part Time Effort in America's Hottest New Business*, Simon & Schuster, New York City, 1998.

John Stefanchik, *The Stefanchik Method: Earn $10,000 a Month for the Rest of Your Life-In Your Spare Time,* William Morrow, New York, 2000.

W. Eddie Speed, *Streetwise Seller Financing: Sell Your Property up to 70% Faster*, Colonial Funding Group, Southlake, Texas, 2003.

Lorelei Stevens, *Lorelei's Legal Lessons: The Essential Guide for Successful Note Buyers*, NoteWorthy Investments Inc., San Francisco, California, 1994.

Lorelei Stevens, *Make Money: Buy Notes Wisely*, Wall Street Brokers, Inc., Seattle, Washington, 2002.

Lorelei Stevens, *Seller-Financing*, Fifth Edition, Wall Street Brokers, Inc., Seattle, Washington, 2002.

Online Bookstores

The Paper Source: www.PaperSourceOnline.com.

NoteWorthy: www.noteworthyusa.com.

FAST CASH

Index

finding notes *(continued)*
  locating lost notes, 13.
fire insurance, 34, 40, 109, 117-
  18, 171.
fire and hazard insurance, 7, 32-
  33, 44, 58, 66, 101, 234-35.
first lien *(see lien)*
foreclosure, 2-3, 24-26, 82,
  103*ff*, 135, 177, 208, 213,
  237, 252-53.
  non-judicial, 25.
  notice, 38.
forfeiture, 193.
forgery, 18, 20, 260.
fractions, 174-75.
fraud, 205, 268.

G
guarantee, 104, 137-38.
gurantor, 76.

H
holder in due course, 117, 127-
  130.
  defined, 66.
  prevented, 134-36, 226.
house (home), 3, 134, 221, 225.

I
institutional buyer, 40, 55.
interest, 94.
  compound, 95.
  rate, 5, 94, 97, 104.
insurance, *see type: fire, fire and
  hazard, title*
Internal Revenue Service (IRS),
  70, 167-68, 188, 266.

J
junior lien, 105-06.
judgment (court), 175, 236.

L
land sale contract, 214-17.
land value, 33-34.
late payments, 243-44.
lawsuits, 71, 76, 83, 128, 137-
  38, 175, 231, 234.
  discrimination, 133-34.
lawyer *(see attorney)*
legal description, 66, 263.
liability, personal, 139-40, 166-
  67, 188.
lien,
  defined, 3.
  first lien, 3-4, 57-58, 134-
    37, 156, 174, 210, 234,
    236, 249-50.
  first lien note, 80, 104, 154,
    156, 207, 262.
  second lien, 3-5, 80-82, 134-
    37, 155, 174, 212-13,
    225, 236-37.
  second lien note, 3-4, 107,
    221, 237, 250, 267.
  third lien, 164, 238-39.
loan vs. note, 139, 231.
lost notes, 13, 29, 130, 257-58.
  where to look, 131.

M
marital liens, *see divorce liens*
mental competency, 85-86, 89,
  238.
mobile home, 206, 209, 246.
  title, 208-09, 211.
monthly payments, 3, 5, 45, 75-
  76, 94-95, 108, 130, 136,
  189, 208, 211, 221, 266.
mortgage *(see lien)*

N
negative amortization, 94-95,
  97.

Don't you know someone who
would enjoy

FAST CASH
?

Just mail in our simple-to-use form
here to order a copy for them!
-or-
Call (425) 454-7009!

DISCOUNT SCHEDULE

2 copies	$38	25 copies	$375
5 copies	$90	50 copies	$700
10 copies	$160	100 copies	$1,300

Order from: Merril Press P.O. Box 1682 Bellevue, WA 98009

Please send me_____copies of **FAST CASH**.

Enclosed is my check or money order made to Merril Press in the
amount of $_____.

Please charge my: ☐ Visa ☐ Mastercard ☐ AMEX ☐ Discover

Number:_____ Expires:_____

Signature:_____

Print Name:_____

Street: _____

City:_____State:____ ZIP Code_____

Phone:(____)_____E-mail_____